Advance praise for

MY BROTHER, MY LAND

"A breathtaking display of literary prowess that tells the story of an entire homeland through the frame of one woman's life. Sami Hermez expertly weaves together different perspectives and narratives, all the while handling the delicate gift of the Sawalha family story with precision and care."

—HALA ALYAN, author of *Salt Houses*

"A powerful, gripping, disturbing account of the struggle for dignity and freedom. Through a single family in a West Bank village, the entire tragic dispossession of Palestine unfolds: Israel's brutal military occupation; militant Islamic resistance; a litany of funerals where few are spared; a family scattered, with the *sumud*, or steadfastness, to maintain their dream of liberation."

—SANDY TOLAN, author of *The Lemon Tree*

"*My Brother, My Land* does more than simply humanize the Palestinian people, their struggle, and the difficult choices they often undergo to survive and resist the Israeli military occupation. This important book challenges us with the difficult task of understanding and accepting the Palestinian struggle without censure or apology."

—RAMZY BAROUD, author of *My Father Was a Freedom Fighter*

"In *My Brother, My Land*, we are brought into a close relationship with Sireen, an eager narrator of a remarkable, yet emblematic story of one Palestinian family, and Sami Hermez, a dedicated witness, committed to Palestinian freedom. A work of intergenerational truth-telling, this book encapsulates in written form the tradition of Palestinian steadfastness."

—NOURA ERAKAT, author of *Justice for Some*

"*My Brother, My Land* challenges anyone who wishes to see Palestinians as mere victims without agency. Telling an individual history of Palestine since the Nakba, it sheds light on how inhuman dispossession and oppression have been met with solidarity, kindness, and above all love. A heartbreaking story, but also one that leaves hope for a continued, just struggle until full liberation comes."

—ILAN PAPPÉ, author of *Ten Myths About Israel*

"This beautifully written book is both a deeply personal story and a textured social history, weaving intricate and intimate details of a Palestinian family's life with the collective Palestinian narrative. Sami Hermez's combined use of his voice and Sireen's demonstrates a collaborative, ethical, and engaged way in which to record oral testimonies."

—YARA HAWARI, author of *The Stone House*

"A masterful story about one West Bank Palestinian family, *My Brother, My Land* uncovers how colonial rule helps shape ruthless violence, resistance, and betrayal, but also devotion and love, intimacy and loss. Reading this book, I laughed and cried, felt unsettled, disturbed, and inspired—I could not put it down."

—NEVE GORDON, author of *Israel's Occupation*

MY BROTHER, MY LAND

MY BROTHER,
MY LAND

A Story from Palestine

Sami Hermez

with Sireen Sawalha

REDWOOD PRESS
Stanford, California

Redwood Press
Stanford, California

Printed in the United States of America on acid-free, archival-quality paper

Library of Congress Cataloging-in-Publication Data
Names: Hermez, Sami Samir, 1977– author. | Sawalha, Sireen, 1966– author.
Title: My brother, my land : a story from Palestine / Sami Hermez, with Sireen Sawalha.
Other titles: Story from Palestine
Description: Stanford, California : Redwood Press, 2024. | Includes bibliographical references.
Identifiers: LCCN 2023029788 (print) | LCCN 2023029789 (ebook) | ISBN 9781503628397 (cloth) | ISBN 9781503637061 (ebook)
Subjects: LCSH: Sawalha, Sireen, 1966–— Family. | Palestinian Arabs—West Bank—Biography. | Arab-Israeli conflict—Personal narratives, Palestinian. | Arab-Israeli conflict—Occupied territories—History.
Classification: LCC CT1919.P375 S29 2024 (print) | LCC CT1919.P375 (ebook) | DDC 956.04092—dc23/eng/20230729
LC record available at https://lccn.loc.gov/2023029788
LC ebook record available at https://lccn.loc.gov/2023029789

Cover design: Derek Thornton / Notch Design
Cover illustration: Nour Ziada @ Nour_archive
Text design: Elliott Beard
Typeset by Elliott Beard in Freight Text/Freight Sans

For Diala, Alia, and Samir
and
Bassel, Zeid, and Salma

"Love is our motive, not hatred . . . that's why we shall win."

—Anonymous Palestinian revolutionary,
Off Frame: AKA Revolution until Victory

CONTENTS

AUTHOR'S NOTE

This is a true story. When I first started working on it, when I first met Sireen and she began telling me stories, I was a young and nervous student at Princeton University. Along the way, I got distracted. I finished my PhD, wrote a different book, and started a family. Although the time I gave to this project waxed and waned, my commitment never wavered. Throughout the years, Sireen continued recounting stories from Palestine. Initially, she was motivated by a desire to show how her family was intimately connected to and impacted by the political events of the Second Intifada, the period during which we first met. But there was always a tension between this motivation and conveying the story of her life, her family's life, her brother's resistance activities, and the general Palestinian condition. This is a tension I tried to preserve when writing this story.

I struggled with the process of stitching together an account that spanned decades. I was weighed down by a perhaps-unhealthy obsession with accuracy and with making sure the narrative I was assembling was the one Sireen wanted out in the world.

Sireen made the process easier. Her stories, her words, and her unflinching determination and passion to tell the story of Palestine through the trials of her family provided me with the inspiration to write. Through the process of storytelling, and as the digital tape turned and captured our voices, I found my feelings intersecting with Sireen's life, her past woven with my present as I spent more and more time with her—recording conversations, meeting her friends and family, meeting for coffees in various cities, and watching her children grow. We encountered each other too many times to count, had many dozens of meetings and social outings over the years, and logged hundreds of phone calls. The story that came together through this process is about Sireen's family life through her eyes and at times in her words, but more often than not in mine. What you read has been reviewed and approved by Sireen at multiple stages of the process, from early drafts to the final proofs. Her words, as they appear, are as true to her spoken words as possible, excluding any liberties I took in translating and minor edits I made for readability. She gave me permission to narrate around her memories in the hope of submerging the reader in the family's experiences while providing an accurate narrative that retains the voice of her actual oral storytelling. To preserve Sireen's voice, I alternate between her voice and the narrator's in two different fonts.

Narrating allowed me to write speculatively about instances where neither of us was present and thus did not know exactly how things unfolded—namely, instances involving prison experiences, secret operations, and clandestine moments. In all cases, speculation was informed by research and carried out with an eye toward accuracy and truth. It is for all these reasons that we decided to sign this book with both of our names. As you'll see, in this book you are accompanying me as I curate, recreate, and narrate the larger story of Palestine *with* Sireen.

As I collected Sireen's story, as we went back and forth with drafts to ensure that my narration honored her wishes, and as we met just to catch up and simply be in each other's company, we grew to be friends, and later, to be like family. "You're like a son," she would say to me on several occasions, while I would come to see her as an older sister. And as our relationship developed, this book became more than a collaboration; it became an intertwined life—a collective story that settler colonialism upturned by fracturing our communities and delineating where our stories begin and end.

In this process of entwining lay multiple layers of love. Or perhaps love is that which allows for intertwining—love for Sireen, for her family, for Palestine, for the world around me, for a humanity that can embrace all life. And yet, when one tries to write from love, ethics weighs immensely like a boot on one's neck. How does one write? How does one do justice to love?

Love. And a million second-guesses.

We Arabs and Palestinians exist within a history of being second-guessed. It can break you if you are not careful. It makes a subject out of you, this second-guessing. It subjugates the way you think and what you prioritize. It took me a long time to overcome it. It took years of writing and revising to refuse such thinking in producing this story—to refuse, as much as possible, to let the second-guess control my writing.

Research for the book helped with this. I undertook years of research that involved numerous conversations with almost all living members of Sireen's family; meetings with friends, neighbors, and other members of the village community; observations during several visits to Palestine; and archival research at the Center for Palestine Studies in Beirut, Lebanon. This story also relies on a variety of primary and secondary texts and videos. I have included notes for readers who wish to understand more about where some of the details (and sometimes, direct quotes) come from and to read further if they question my accuracy or the truth. Of course, in matters of life and death, in matters of settler colonialism and occupation, truth is a tail we can chase forever. This, mind you, is what the occupiers intend. And there is that second-guess rearing its head again!

Two final notes. The first concerns the Arabic script for place names used throughout the text. This Arabic script is an important reminder of the history of these places in the face of the deliberate erasure of Palestine. Second, the question of how to handle naming people was of much concern to me, as there is no way to anonymize and detach certain people from Sireen. While most names remain unchanged, I have changed the names of Palestinians suspected of collaborating with the Israeli military because this book is neither trial nor verdict. There is no conclusive evidence that can be defended in a court of law that these presumed collaborators were indeed collaborators. I am not here to judge or expose based on hearsay.

SAMI HERMEZ
November 2022

It has been seventeen years since we began this project, Sami and I. There were times when I thought this book would never see the light of day. Times when I felt this Palestinian story would be lost, like Palestine. Times when I thought the odds were slim that my voice, a Palestinian voice, would be heard. Now, as this book goes to production, I feel I can breathe a little.

When I was born, my mother named me Sireen, and my father thought it would bring the family good luck and prosperity. He even named a business after me that operated for some time. When you read this book, you may ask yourself, Where is this prosperity, and where is this good life? But indeed, compared to my siblings, I have had a good life. Compared to what my brother experienced, I have lived well. Compared to many other Palestinian daughters, sisters, and mothers, I have been lucky. Out of gratitude and a sense of duty, I wanted to write the story of my family and my people for the sake of the memory of those who passed and the benefit of those who are still here and are still to come.

It has been seventeen difficult years, unkind years at the end of which this book feels like a blessing. During these years, at the school where I taught, a student accused me of being a terrorist, and after a battle with the administration that stripped me of my dignity, I was let go from my job. I sued, but due to poor representation in court, I lost the case. And I lost hope. Then, two years ago, I was diagnosed with an aggressive breast cancer, and I lost strength and will. This book kept me going. I never stopped dreaming of the day people would read it. I held on tightly to the dream, pushing Sami to continue with the project. While sitting in radiation, unsure of my future, the only thought in my mind was, I need this book to see the light of day soon! The belief that it would bring me justice kept me going. I hope in reading it you will see it as an invitation to learn more, to talk to me, to us, and to hear our stories. While this is a personal story, it is also a Palestinian story, my people's story, of the suffering we endure. Yet many other Palestinians have stories perhaps even more vivid and complex, the collective of which, written and unwritten, is the Palestinian story. This is my family's chapter.

SIREEN SAWALHA
November 2022

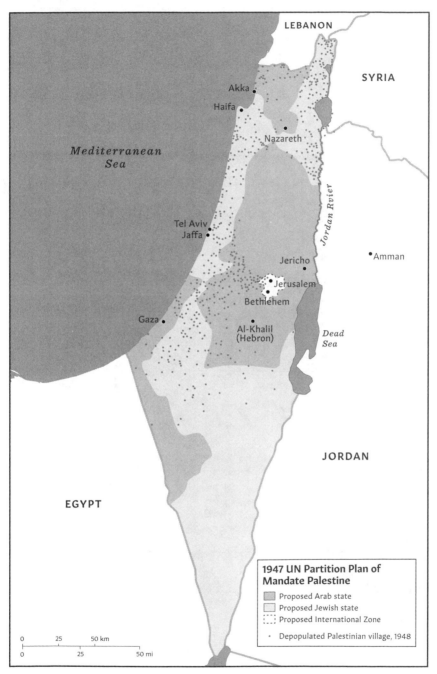

1947 UN Partition Plan of Mandate Palestine

- Proposed Arab state
- Proposed Jewish state
- Proposed International Zone
- Depopulated Palestinian village, 1948

1947 UN Partition Plan of Mandate Palestine

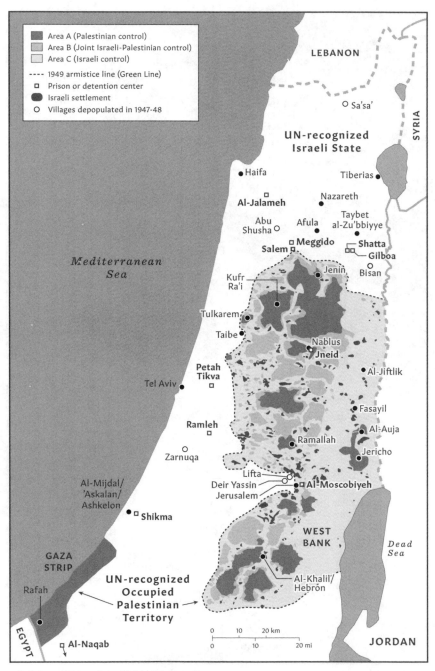

Division of Mandate Palestine, 1948–2010

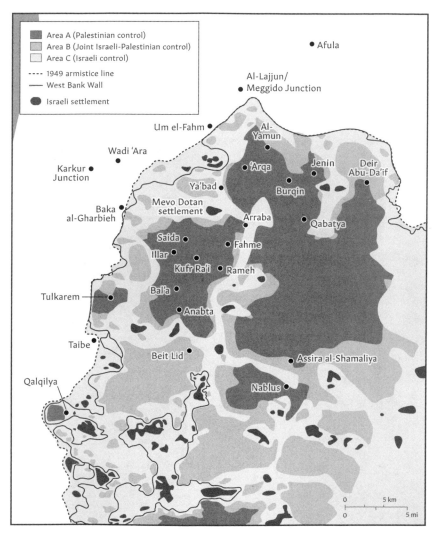

Afula

Al-Lajjun/
Meggido Junction

Um el-Fahm

Al-
Yamun

Wadi 'Ara

'Arqa

Jenin

Deir
Abu-Da'if

Karkur
Junction

Ya'bad

Burqin

Mevo Dotan
settlement

Baka
al-Gharbieh

Arraba

Qabatya

Saida

Fahme

Illar

Kufr Ra'i

Rameh

Tulkarem —

Bal'a

Anabta

Taibe

Beit Lid

Assira al-Shamaliya

Qalqilya

Nablus

0   5 km
0   5 mi

Northern West Bank, Jenin-Nablus-Tulkarem Area

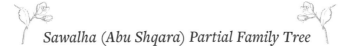

Sawalha (Abu Shqara) Partial Family Tree

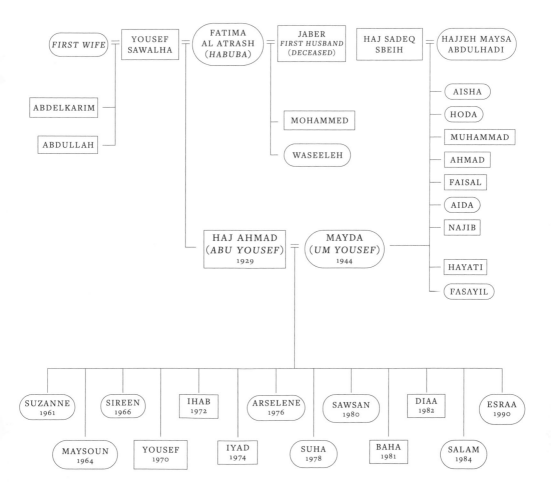

FIRST WIFE ═ YOUSEF SAWALHA ═ FATIMA AL ATRASH (HABUBA) ═ JABER FIRST HUSBAND (DECEASED) — HAJ SADEQ SBEIH ═ HAJJEH MAYSA ABDULHADI

ABDELKARIM

ABDULLAH

MOHAMMED

WASEELEH

AISHA
HODA
MUHAMMAD
AHMAD
FAISAL
AIDA
NAJIB
HAYATI
FASAYIL

HAJ AHMAD (ABU YOUSEF) 1929 ═ MAYDA (UM YOUSEF) 1944

SUZANNE 1961

MAYSOUN 1964

SIREEN 1966

YOUSEF 1970

IHAB 1972

IYAD 1974

ARSELENE 1976

SUHA 1978

SAWSAN 1980

BAHA 1981

DIAA 1982

SALAM 1984

ESRAA 1990

MY BROTHER, MY LAND

PROLOGUE

Visitor's Room, an Israeli Prison, 1999

Returning to the prison consumed all of Um Yousef's energy. Afterward, she remained in bed all day. But like the full moon, she had to return. She had to see her son. For in his absence, her chest was tight, her breaths suffocating.

"*Habibi, ya 'eni*, how are you?" she asked him excitedly.

"I'm good. God makes things easy," Iyad responded, his face lit up with joy. Then he paused and glanced around. "Where is the Haj?" he asked his mother.

"*Abuk kan ta'ban.* Your father was tired the past two days. He didn't think we would be able to see you," replied Um Yousef. Iyad met his mother's words with a slight frown and lowered eyebrows. He nodded. His father had been dealing with diabetes for over ten years.

Sireen examined her younger brother as he exchanged words with their mother. She could see him panning the room, as if still expecting their father to emerge from the shadows. His broad shoulders shrugged at the news. She saw her eyes in him—earthy, with a blend of green and brown, now shimmering against his short, dark beard.

It was hard to imagine, despite all the years that had gone by with him in prison, that my brother had been involved in resistance activities. That my brother was a prisoner of war.

She thought back to the last time she saw him free, a time before she had left for the US. The two of them were brother and sister, this was true. But they might as well have been strangers leading separate lives. Strangers who left indelible marks on each other.

1

Sireen had been around in Iyad's early years. She had spent many hours telling him stories and taking him on imaginary adventures. But it had been a decade and a half since they had lived under the same roof. A decade and a half since their paths began to diverge.

There is one story I always remember. The story of Shater Hasan, the brave, smart, hardworking Hasan. In my version, Hasan falls in love with the king's daughter. The king agrees to let them marry on condition that Hasan is able to retrieve a stolen jewel on the peak of a mountain. Seven hills, each guarded by a hyena that Hasan has to outwit, stands between him and the peak. It is a near-impossible task. Sometimes the story took me two nights to complete, and Iyad listened to every word. Shater Hasan is ultimately able to outmaneuver the hyenas, free the jewel, and live happily ever after with the king's daughter.

"Sireen, I miss your stories," Iyad blurted out.

Sireen smiled. It was as if the two of them were little again.

He wanted her to talk about her life, but the prison walls did not inspire her. She glanced at her mother. Although she knew there was tenderness underneath, their relationship had always been rocky. She did not want to discuss her problems in the US around her. And Iyad would likely not understand or might take their mother's side anyway. She decided the less they knew, the better, so she stuck with generalities.

Mother and sister sat with Iyad for over an hour that day. His face was bright and alive, the two women were all smiles, they all laughed together, and he felt rejuvenated. But there were moments when they avoided eye contact and fidgeted, studied their hands, repeated questions they had already asked about Iyad's health and whether he had enough food. When they felt the sting of the place and were reminded of the walls around them. Walls within the walls of occupation within which each of their lives was framed.

Before they left, Iyad pleaded with Sireen to help him. "Sireen, you have to get me out. Use your contacts in the US. Don't leave me here."

Princeton, NJ, 2005

Sireen is standing in her kitchen across from me. It is nine in the morning on a Monday, and her three children are at school. She is patiently watching, waiting for a stained kettle to come to a boil. When it whistles, she turns off the stove, adds two tea bags and half a handful of dried *miramiya*, and stands over the simmering tea, staring into space as steam rises. A moment later, she glances at me with a twinkle in her hazel green eyes. Around her cheeks, deep dimples fold like waves excited to caress the shore.

Do you smell that? That's the scent of Kufr Raʿi, كفر راعي!

The sweet scent of sage fills the kitchen air, but I don't know her village and certainly can't smell it. I smile.

To Sireen, Kufr Raʿi is more than a land, more than a village, more than its people and its structures; it is a life. Her life back in Palestine. And for a moment, she feels home—home in the presence of the jasmine tree that has always hung over a green steel gate. Home in a suspended future.

She places the kettle on a wooden tray and carries it into the living room. She sits down, pours two cups of tea, and looks out at the snow in her garden that stretches out toward a vast meadow, horses galloping in the distance. Princeton University is only three miles away, across Carnegie Lake. The weather is freezing and unforgiving this February.

I sit beside Sireen, separated by a small side table, stroking my three-day stubble, watching her hard and weathered yet still-gentle hands as she raises her cup of tea to her lips. Her fingernails are short; it's easier this way to do the gardening. She's applied an orange-red polish to them, a color that stands out well against her olive skin.

Behind me, a desk with a monitor and piles of paper, her children's homework layered between unpaid bills. On the floor, two wireless joysticks and scattered toys in front of a box TV—no matter how much she tidies up, there is always the mess of a house well lived in. Soft sunrays refract through two large windows, delivering a lightness to our morning encounter.

On the side table between us, she has placed a tray with toasted Jersey-made pita bread and three small bowls, one with zaʿatar, another with oil—both brought from Palestine during her father's latest visit—and a third with homemade *labneh*. She dips into it but tells me this spread is otherwise for me, as she has already eaten.

We begin with chitchat about our previous encounters and the people we know in common at Princeton University.

The two of us have only met twice before today. The first time was through her close friend Rima, who introduced me to Sireen a few months earlier, some time between Yassir Arafat's death and Mahmoud Abbas's election—or ascension—to the presidency of the Palestinian Authority. Arafat had done so much for the Palestinian cause, but he may have also ruined it, buried it, and all but delivered the capitulation of his people. He left Abbas, his right-hand man, a stooge-like figure, to effectively inherit his rule. However great Arafat was—and I'll leave that judgment to others—he was certainly a poor judge of character. In any case, those events mean less to me now as I write this story, and I have to search my notes to recall the coincidence. What I still remember from that time is Rima—and Sireen.

I had met Rima a few months earlier, while conducting a mini-ethnographic project as a graduate student in a class at Princeton University. As a new member of the Princeton Committee for Palestine, I hoped this re-search would help build community connections. Rima, a real estate broker, encouraged me to meet her friend.

So Sireen and I met that first time at Small World Coffee. It was loud and busy with the hustle of people getting their coffee and trying to find a seat. Sireen had a youthful, fashionable appearance; she wore a red dress under a black jacket, and black stockings and boots. Her hair was permed, neck length, brown with highlights, with a slight part on the left side. Around her neck was a colorful beaded necklace. Her wrists were adorned with a number of silver bracelets with little gems—ruby, emerald, sapphire—and her fingers were wrapped with silver rings with stones of matching colors that brought out the glow in her eyes.

We sat down in a far corner with our coffees. She was full of energy, shoulders back and chin high as she spoke, smiling and speaking with her hands as much as her lips. Despite her energetic outward appearance, it did not take long for her to express that she was fatigued, and I could hear sad-ness and worry in her voice when she talked about her family in Palestine. She shared snippets of her home and her life growing up in Kufr Ra'i and of her brother Iyad and his adventures resisting the Israelis.

In some ways, that moment was not unlike others that would come to pass between us. Sireen was often rushing to tell me her story—the story of her family, of her life in the village, but most of all, the story of Iyad. Sireen took every chance to tell her stories, even in our casual encounters, and I always enjoyed listening. She would tell and retell the events of her family's life as if it were her last chance, as if she needed someone to make sense of it, as if she might lose the memory of it all if she didn't retell it. And the storytelling was not for my ears alone. She would take any opportunity she could when we sat together with mutual friends.

The next time the two of us met was at a gathering in the home of Rima and her husband, who was a successful doctor. They were both Palestinian refugees who had immigrated to the US decades earlier with their parents. On that cold and snowy December evening, I arrived with two other students, forty minutes late, and got teased for perpetuating a stereotype about "Arab time." Sireen was already there.

At dinner, the conversation veered quickly to Palestine as Sireen captivated us with her storytelling in a heavy Palestinian-accented English peppered with Arabic words. We all listened, with interest and some discomfort, as she recounted fragments of her difficult life in Palestine. Her arms orchestrated the words through the space around her and together with her voice, with its highs when she spoke about resistance and its lows when she told of loss, brought defiant and melancholy images to life. Yet the seriousness of her story was softened by her laughter, which kept the night alive.

Today, in our third encounter, I've come to her house to begin collecting her story in earnest. No longer motivated by my college class research, I am driven by something deeper—wanting to fight empire, chase its tentacles (and troops) out of the lands I call home, follow the path of Che Guevara, have my life's work somehow connect to the struggle for the liberation of Palestine. Romantic thoughts of struggling against injustice. Yes! But then, there is no resistance without romance.

The story of Sireen's younger brother Iyad fascinates me: his rise as a resistance fighter against Israeli occupation forces, his years in prison and his perseverance under torture, his involvement with the Islamic Jihad. In time, I will discover that it is Sireen's entire life that is worth retelling, and, indeed, it is this larger story, not simply Iyad's, that I will recount in these pages.

Sireen is dressed in black. She is mourning the death of her father. Her father, who was mostly absent in her life but somehow remained her pillar of comfort, her foothold in this upside-down world. Her father, who should have still been alive.

I give her my condolences. The moment feels awkward. It is why I have already delayed this meeting by a few weeks. I don't know how to continue with life in the presence of someone's grief.

Sireen and I continue to make small talk. My tape recorder is still off, and I am stalling—perhaps unconsciously nervous of the commitment involved in receiving a life story. Instead, I listen to her complain of pain in her back and knees, and I continue to sip my tea and dip my bread into *labneh*. She expresses how exhausted she is even as the day has barely begun. Already she has been up for several hours preparing a packed lunch for her husband and breakfast for her kids before dropping them off at school. When the children return, she will have to feed them before rushing her two older ones to soccer practice and dance class and whatever else they are enrolled in. These few hours in the morning, when her youngest is not yet back from kindergarten, are her only precious moments of peace. Yet she is unable to keep still. In the summer, if there is no work at home, she often spends her mornings gardening. So when the winter months arrive, they are especially harsh on her otherwise active body, and in these long, cold months she comes to treasure morning visits to and from friends.

When there is finally a pause in our small talk, I take it as a sign to begin. I can't delay the inevitable any longer. I turn on the recorder and ask her to tell her story.

Well, first things first. My name is Sireen Ahmad Yousef Sawalha. This is the way it is written on my identity card issued by the Israeli military administration. In my Jordanian passport, my name is Sireen Ahmad Yousef Abdallah, but both are inaccurate, since my family name is actually Nimer.

Part I

"MOTHER IS GOING TO GIVE BIRTH"

1

1966–1967

I was born on June 27, 1966, almost one year before the war of '67, in Kufr Ra'i, a small village in the Jenin District, قضاء جنين, approximately twenty-five km southwest of the city of Jenin, جنين, in the northern part of the West Bank. June 27 is the official date my grandfather wrote in the registry, but my mother kept her own family records on the inside of a closet door. There, she registered my birth as June 22.

In May 1967, Sireen's mother, Mayda, took Sireen and her two sisters to Jordan to be closer to their father, Haj Ahmad, who was working in Abu Dhabi at the time. In those days, Mayda wore her dark-brown hair shoulder length and half up. She arrived in Amman sporting a light-yellow blouse, a skirt of a different yellow shade falling below the knee, and low heels that made her walk awkwardly. She was twenty-three, and although her skin was smooth, her always-serious look showed more years on her and perhaps also showed the responsibility that came with having three children. Her husband was a man in his late thirties who almost always wore tailor-made light-colored dress shirts and black or brown suit pants. He had a big smile that brought out the energy in people. His hands had seen hard labor, and, looking at the few early wrinkles on his face, one could suspect he was no stranger to loss.

In the years before the 1967 war, travel to Amman was easier. Sireen's family carried Jordanian passports, and there was no official border crossing that distinguished the two banks of the Jordan River. In Amman, the family rented an apartment for eight Jordanian dinars while Haj Ahmad worked on the family's Abu Dhabi residency permits.

However, their permits were taking an unusually long time to process.

*

They were still waiting for their papers in Amman when, on June 5, 1967, Israeli forces attacked Egypt, setting off a six-day war that involved the armies
of Syria, Jordan, and Iraq. The Israeli government claimed this was a pre-
emptive and necessary war because the Egyptian army was planning to wipe
them out. Yet there is little proof of this, and the maneuvers of the Egyptian
army in the Sinai showed no indication that the Egyptian president, Gamal
Abdel Nasser, was preparing to attack.

The Arab armies were defeated and, in the process, lost the territories
in Palestine that since 1948 have been referred to as the West Bank and the
Gaza Strip. They also lost the Syrian Golan Heights and the Egyptian Sinai.
This is how Zionist forces came to occupy all of Historic Palestine.

The defeat of four Arab armies struck at the heart of Arab identity and
crushed the promises of Arab nationalism. For some, the moment served
as the beginning of a new age of popular revolution as people began to lose
hope in Arab states achieving Palestinian liberation and took matters into
their own hands. The moment was also the beginning of the age of cynicism
toward the future of the Arab world—a cynicism that would be compounded
with every successive defeat trying to liberate a land that had first been occupied in 1948.

Loss. Loss compounded by deception. All compounded by a realization
that the world would not return to the way it had been.

How lost without direction people must have felt in those days as they
walked the streets of Beirut, Damascus, and Cairo—and newly occupied al-
Quds, القدس, Jerusalem. How bottomless their appetites must have been as
they devoured the news broadcasting from radios in neighborhoods across
the region. After the shock, it likely took the events of subsequent decades—
the continuation of defeat, the submission—for the feelings of loss to inten-
sify. Yet still, this moment is one many Arabs feel defined by and continue to
return to as they dig through the archaeology of loss.

Mayda was restless in bed all through the first night of the war. She knew
something was not right. She was rarely the optimist and often stubbornly
held on to unpopular positions. She was not swept away by the euphoria on
the streets and news reports suggesting that the Arabs were going to win the
war. She thought hard about the possibilities. Arab governments, she felt,

were not the key to their liberation, as much as she might repeat this rhetoric in her waking hours. Palestinians had to take matters into their own hands.

She yearned for her home in Kufr Ra'i and for the three hundred dunams of land Haj Ahmad had bought that was rich with apricot, olive, plum, and cherry trees, among other kinds of fruit trees. She finally sat up in bed fearing that all this would be lost—expropriated—if she was not there to claim it.

On the morning of the second day of the war, Mayda had made up her mind. She was going to return with her children. Her short, slim legs stiffened at this thought. Stay! her body seemed to scream. Running in the direction of war was terrifying—but losing her home was a worse fate.

Mayda was young and the decision was not easy, but she knew how to make decisions and stick to them. She was also brave, a trait she would pass on to several of her children. So, when her mind finally settled, she became determined to walk into the fire, and no one, not even her husband, would be able to stop her. She couldn't fathom having her life in Palestine, and the larger purpose it held, robbed from her if she remained in exile. And she was undeterred by the reports of war on the radio.

My mother decided to take the three of us girls back to Palestine. Suzanne, born in 1961, and Maysoun, born in 1964, could both walk, but I was still a baby and had to be carried. Mother carried me in a sling on her back and began the walk home. She took nothing with her. We took a car from Jabal Hussein in Amman to a village in the Jordan Valley. There, my mother paid someone to help with my sisters as we crossed the narrow stream of the Jordan River on foot. It was dark. I think my mother intended it to be this way so we would not be spotted. She walked with us through the river. No bus, no car, no pushcart. Me on her back and my sisters alongside us. She was intent on keeping her land.

Mayda had witnessed the ethnic cleansing of Palestine that began in 1947 and extended through 1948, when 750,000 Palestinians were displaced. Although she was a child then, around four years old, she internalized the experience of her parents hearing the news of the UN vote to partition Palestine in November 1947. And she was scarred by the stories of massacres that began to reach her as the Zionist paramilitary organization, Haganah, began implementing ethnic cleansing operations against Palestinians a month later. She heard of the massacres and depopulation in Lifta, لفتا, and Sa'sa', سعسع; in Abu Shusha, أبو شوشا, Deir Yassin, دير ياسين; and beyond, all in the months before the declaration of the Israeli state at 11:59 p.m. on May 14,

1948, when the British officially left Palestine. She also heard about the depopulation of Zarnuqa, زرنوقة, whose village leader tried to surrender to the Zionists and one of whose most powerful families proposed to give up their arms and put themselves under the protection of the Haganah. Only a few weeks later, the Haganah expelled them, under threats of death and rape, and followed the expulsion with demolishing their homes.

Mayda saw the Jordanian and Iraqi troops in the months after the Israeli declaration of independence as they tried to defend against the expulsion of her people. The Syrian, Lebanese, and Egyptian armies fought in that war too, but all the Arab states were newly independent themselves, with soldiers hardly equipped for battle, severely outnumbered even when combined, and barely operating as a united front. On top of this, King Abdullah of Jordan had made a pact with the Zionists whereby he was not to fire into land that the 1947 partition plan designated as part of the future Jewish state. In exchange for this guarantee, the king would gain control over central Palestine. His troops did not engage to the fullest. They did not advance into Western Jerusalem or beyond, as the Palestinians in those areas had hoped and expected.

By January 1949, the Arab governments were forced to declare a ceasefire and sign armistice agreements with the new Israeli government. The armistice produced a demarcation line known as the Green Line—the line that divided the Gaza Strip and the West Bank, including Jerusalem, from the rest of Historic Palestine. The Green Line became the new state's nonpermanent border and comprised much more land than promised in the 1947 UN partition plan. Everything inside the Green Line became the UN-recognized Israeli state, what Palestinians call "the inside" or '48 Palestine.

Mayda was young, but she remembered it all vividly. It was hard to forget the year that marked the beginning of the Nakba, the catastrophe, for her and her people, when over four hundred villages and towns were ethnically cleansed in less than a year to make room for the founding of the Zionist state. She felt it personally as she became cut off from villages and cities she used to visit. She was prevented from visiting the Mediterranean Sea throughout her youth. She came to learn of how people walked to Jordan, Syria, Lebanon, and Egypt, and she didn't want to be another statistic, nineteen years later, as she stood on the cusp of her people's second expulsion.

One could hardly keep track of how scattered the Palestinians became. Even among those who stayed in Mandate Palestine, conditions varied. Some settled in refugee camps over the Green Line in what became the

Jordanian-administered West Bank and the Egyptian-administered Gaza Strip—nineteen such refugee camps were established in the West Bank and the Gaza Strip after 1948. Others who had relatives or sufficient means took up residence in villages in the West Bank or the Gaza Strip rather than in camps. Still others remained and continue to remain within the Green Line, in '48 Palestine.

The Zionists recognized those internally displaced people only if they gave up claims to their original villages. Of the displaced, most were herded by the Zionists into nearby Palestinian villages that were not depopulated and took refuge with family or coreligionists. In rare instances, the Zionists allowed some families to set up a new village near their original land but never allowed the families to return to their land itself. In a few cases, Palestinians were allowed to return to their former towns, like Haifa, حيفا, but were still prevented from returning to their former homes or lands there. And all Palestinians who remained in the new state lived under military rule for the first eighteen years, in contrast to Jewish Israelis, who enjoyed all the rights and privileges of citizenship. Still, Mayda preferred to take her chances under military occupation than to live with the psyche of displacement. It was enough to know the story of her husband, Haj Ahmad, who could not return to his family home near Nazareth, الناصرة. She had also witnessed some of the refugees in the West Bank living in makeshift homes outside the old city of Jenin, heard how the first Jenin refugee camp had been destroyed in a snowstorm, and seen the conditions in which they lived after a new camp was established on the outskirts of the city in 1953. She knew this was unbearable.

As we crossed the Jordan River, Suzanne lost her shoe. She began to cry. The Israeli soldiers were nearby. They would open fire if they heard her, although I think my mother was more afraid that they would turn us back than she was of them shooting us on the spot. My mother immediately threw her hand over Suzanne's mouth to muffle her cries. We went undetected, but we had to stop to search for the shoe before continuing.

My mother told me that on our journey, all we ate was a shared loaf of bread and homemade tomato paste. That's it. Whenever we got hungry, she gave us some to eat. Suzanne still likes to eat this.

What I remember most from what my mother told me, though, is how people were walking in the other direction screaming at us to turn around. We were walking into the war zone while so many people were fleeing the West Bank. With blank faces and lowered eyes. With dignity tucked in the lining of their luggage on their backs. That's how I imagine it. Some left in fear for their lives. Others who came from villages close to the Green Line were forcibly expelled. Many people went to Jordan, and they left everything behind, except the few belongings they could carry.

To stay and face the unknowns of war or to leave for safety not knowing if one would return—these are impossible choices.

As Mayda and her children crossed into Palestine, defeat was everywhere. One could see corpses along the roads, military equipment abandoned on the roadside, and ill-equipped Iraqi and Jordanian soldiers, downtrodden and discombobulated, wearing expressions of defeat.

Once they reached the other side of the Jordan River, the family took shelter in an empty mosque, then found a ride to Nablus, نابلس, and from there, to their village. All in all, the journey took around eighteen hours.

When we arrived at our *balad*, our village, we found it vacated. Later, we learned that people were hiding in a field of fig trees, afraid the Zionists would bomb their homes with planes from overhead. They remained there till the end of the war before returning.

By the end of the war, the Zionist forces had expelled one-fifth of the Palestinian population of the West Bank. To keep Palestinians out, a day after Mayda's return, the military administration passed its first order deeming any return as infiltration. This was one of over two hundred such military orders that, between 1967 and 1970, not only prevented people from returning but also stripped them of their homes and any material belongings to return to. These same orders have been continually renewed over time, which, in turn, has continually renewed Palestinian displacement.

Despite these obstacles, Mayda returned to raise her children in Palestine. In her narration of the events, little details sometimes differentiate her memory from Sireen's. In Mayda's story, Haj Ahmad had returned with them. He spent several weeks or so in Kufr Raʿi before leaving again for Abu Dhabi to return to work. He stayed long enough for the Israeli census count but then had to leave before a permit identification system for the newly occupied was developed. Neither of the older sisters remembers it this way. Like Sireen, they do not recall their father in their story of return, nor do they recall that he had taken turns carrying them. In the girls' memory, their father was already in Abu Dhabi, as he would be throughout their childhood.

If he returned with us, he would not have been absent for several years and would not have needed my mother to file for family reunification. And if he did return, there was no way the Israelis could have conducted a census during the first weeks after the war, with all the chaos.

In the grand scheme of their lives, it is all the same, whether he returned with them or not. What connects their stories is the emotional truth and material reality of two years of family separation because their father did not have a permit to enter his village in the West Bank. Mayda spent those two years working to gain family reunification, building their house, and raising her three daughters, mostly alone but with some support from her parents.

In the census, only Palestinians (and their offspring) who were registered were considered by the occupying authority to be legal residents of the Gaza Strip and the West Bank. A document, a mere registry of people, dispossessed ninety thousand West Bank Palestinians, a third of whom resided in Jerusalem. Ninety thousand people disappeared from the registry and thus were deprived of their ability to return.

We returned to our two-room house, with no kitchen and an outhouse for a bathroom. My mother spent almost four decades sweating over our house and building other rooms as the family grew.

The Sawalha house, nestled among four other homes near the top of a hill, would become the focal point of their lives growing up. Its walls cradled them in the winter as they huddled together around a coal furnace. Its large, green steel gate, never separated from the jasmine tree, always welcomed Sireen after school. And its courtyard, in spring, was vibrant with flowers and the laughter of children. It was a house with strong foundations from which a fierce resistance fighter would one day be born.

Sireen fondly remembers the energy of her parents and siblings contained within their house. And she recalls the brightness of the smooth white interior walls decorated with red, yellow, and green pastel strokes.

On the outside, our house was so colorful. Dark green with red-framed windows. My mother repainted inside and out often. The house was all we owned, and it was kept alive by my mother, who was always working on it and repairing it after every Israeli military incursion into our home. In fact, thirty-five years after our return, she repainted the living room, not knowing that it would be the last time before tragedy struck us all.

2

1969

Two years had passed since Sireen trekked home from Jordan with her mother and sisters. Two years since she had seen her father—her father, who was like the moon on a cloudy night, like an imaginary friend, the great absent presence in her life.

I was three when my father was finally able to return to Palestine under a family reunification agreement. At the time, there was a window of possibility to file for reunification on the basis that one's spouse and children lived in the West Bank. My father did not stay long that year. He never did during my childhood. He came home every summer, spent his first few weeks going from tea to coffee, surrounded by family and villagers welcoming him back. Then, a month or two later, with sadness written on his face, he would return to Abu Dhabi, where he first worked as a plumbing contractor managing a small workforce. Later, he opened an electrical appliance store.

Haj Ahmad was born in 1929, at the end of a season of Arab upheaval against the British Mandate and Zionist intentions to rule Palestine. He was born in the north of Palestine, near Nazareth, in the village of Taybet al-Zuʻbbiyye, طيبة الزعبية, or Taybeh, as most people call it.

My father's father, Yousef, married two women. His first wife was from the house of al-Zuʻbi, the largest family in Taybeh. He had two children with her, Abdelkarim and Abdullah.

My grandfather's first wife got sick and was partially paralyzed, so his family encouraged him to marry a second woman. This second woman was from Kufr Raʿi. Her husband had died while she was still very young, and he left her with a son, Mohammed, and a daughter, Waseeleh. So she remarried and would become my grandmother. Her name was Fatma, though I never knew this growing up because we always called her Habuba, the loved one.

Haj Ahmad's father passed away in the latter half of the 1940s, when he was about sixteen years old. His father's passing was the first sign that life was going to be harsh. But he did not let death crack his heart and remained tender with his mother and, later, with his wife and children. The loss of his father made him reliant on his half brothers, whom he sought as anchors. Shortly after his father's passing, his mother returned to Kufr Raʿi to be near her family and to be close to lands that her husband had purchased in the village. Kufr Raʿi was about an hour's drive from Taybeh. Haj Ahmad moved with her, though he spent much of his time in Haifa and Nazareth, working as a wage laborer alongside his half brothers.

Then, in 1948, when the towns and villages of Palestine were separated, cut off from each other by the new Zionist state, Haj Ahmad found himself a refugee. He was deprived of his work in towns that had become part of the new state and separated from his father's village and his half brothers, who remained in Taybeh. He was forced to make the Jordanian-administered West Bank village of Kufr Raʿi his permanent home.

It was his second grand loss. As if life were a scaffold of loss under his feet, rising as tragedy piled upon itself. A scaffold that would continue to grow into the sunset of his life.

The intense pain from the loss of his community softened his heart. Loss strengthened his connection to Taybeh. And it was the pain that Haj Ahmad lived with that was the reason Mayda returned to the West Bank in 1967.

For over twenty years, Haj Ahmad did not see his brothers. For over twenty years, he did not see his village. And while Kufr Raʿi was a physical home that he could trace through his mother's bloodline, he never felt at home there. Sireen felt he was always trying to escape it.

While Haj Ahmad did not return to Taybeh for over two decades, some people did try to smuggle themselves across the Green Line. The Israelis killed many of them. It was only in the early 1970s, after the Israelis had oc-cupied the West Bank and removed barriers to crossing the Green Line, that

Haj Ahmad returned to Taybeh, and then only for a day trip with his young daughter Sireen.

He was fortunate that his village was not among the over four hundred depopulated ones. It survived erasure. His house was also not destroyed or overtaken by Jewish Israelis. But that day of the visit, he experienced burning in his heart. He felt like a stranger in his land, unable to walk freely among his family. Sireen saw her father descend into silence when they arrived at his house. She recalled his shoulders slumping, his head drooping, and, for a moment, it was as if a mountain had collapsed.

This visit, which should have been a permanent return, would remain in Haj Ahmad's thoughts through the years. He would recall it frequently, especially when he argued with his son Iyad about being involved in the resistance. Or each time construction began on a new Israeli settlement being built on stolen Palestinian land. Or when he learned that Iyad had been captured by Israeli soldiers.

Haj Ahmad's migration to the Arab Gulf came around 1953. The oil boom was starting to produce unparalleled wealth for Gulf Arab states, and people in those countries viewed Palestinians as an educated, skilled class. Palestinians could find work as laborers in various trades or as professionals, like engineers and teachers, who were needed to satisfy the growth of Gulf countries. This was a time when Palestinians were viewed more as refugees than as revolutionaries, before Arab rulers saw Palestinian revolutionary spirit as a threat to their rule and began to treat Palestinians with suspicion. It was a time of great sympathy and solidarity. Haj Ahmad was motivated to leave Palestine with promises of prosperity that he could not find in Kufr Ra'i.

But his need to escape another fate also propelled his departure. In the early 1950s, while the Israeli state was cementing its institutions and continuing its attacks on Palestinians in the Gaza Strip and the West Bank, including in Jerusalem—territories still not under its control—and while Palestinians were trying to infiltrate the new border and wage resistance attacks at Israeli targets as they struggled for return, Haj Ahmad was embroiled in a battle of his own. His mother had decided he would marry the sister of his stepbrother's wife. He was no match for his strong mother. His protests were unsuccessful, and he eventually agreed to get engaged. He left for Kuwait shortly after in a final attempt to escape marriage.

It was a long journey that took him to Amman on the Hejaz Railway. From there, land smugglers using various trucks and tankers took Haj Ahmad through northern Syria to Basra, the southern tip of Iraq. From Basra, he walked to Kuwait through the desert on a journey in which many perished.

He worked in Kuwait for three years and finally, in 1956, returned to Palestine when he learned that he would not have to face marriage, as his fiancée had broken off the engagement and married another man. His mother, Habuba, missed him, but she was overcome with shame and disappointment as her son's prospects for marriage collapsed. He did not stay with his mother for long. But the next time he left, instead of relying on smugglers, he embarked on a legal travel route with visa in hand. He went to Kuwait and then on to Bahrain, working as a plumber in both countries.

It was Sireen's mother, Mayda, who shared these details of Haj Ahmad's failed engagement and early career. Sireen was listening along too, mesmerized by her mother's story, as if it were the first time she was hearing it. Her eyes widened, and she pushed her mother—who constantly needed prodding to indulge the past—to elaborate. Sireen seemed desperate to know more about her father in his youth.

The day Mayda met Haj Ahmad, she had been walking to the site of the village mosque, still under construction, to give *zakat*, or alms. Haj Ahmad caught a glimpse of her. She had dark-brown hair tied in a ponytail with a few loose bangs. Her skin looked baby smooth and glistened under the sun, but despite being at the tender age of fourteen, born in 1944, and fourteen years his junior, Mayda's face was serious and mature. He found her pretty, but it was her purposeful walk, exuding strength and confidence, that really caught his eye. Mayda saw him too. Haj Ahmad carried his shoulders pulled back and walked with a cool strut and a cigarette dangling between his fingers. He dressed smartly in a full dark-brown suit and a white shirt unbuttoned at the neck. He was a tall, burly man with honey-blond hair, icy blue eyes, and a thick lampshade mustache, and she found him handsome.

Soon after that meeting, Haj Ahmad went to Mayda's father to ask for her hand. Her father resisted. If Haj Ahmad were to marry anyone from their family, her parents preferred it be Mayda's older sister. Her father was also not impressed with Haj Ahmad's more modest background. Mayda's family was one of the wealthier ones in Kufr Ra'i. Her father was the village head, the *mukhtar*, and her mother descended from the well-known Abdulhadi family. But Haj Ahmad wanted Mayda, and with a little persistence, perhaps swayed by the young man's travels and the hope that this might bring prosperity and allow him to support a new family, her father accepted Haj Ahmad's proposal. Theirs was a long engagement because of Haj Ahmad's travels, and they did not marry until 1960, when Mayda was sixteen.

Haj Ahmad returned from Bahrain with money and new ideas. The rituals around the wedding itself were unique. He invited the village with invitation cards, a first, and threw an unusually large celebration. The *mahr*, the marriage payment that he gave his wife, his obligation, was three times what was expected. He adorned her with jewelry himself, against the custom of not seeing the bride until the end of the ceremony. Haj Ahmad and Mayda were also the first in the village to spend their honeymoon in a "big city" like Ramallah, رام الله. He was overjoyed. Mayda gave meaning to his life in the Gulf and reconnected him with Palestine.

After the wedding, Haj Ahmad left for Jeddah, in the western Arabian Peninsula, present-day Saudi Arabia, to work at his brother-in-law's tannery. They treated animal skins and hides and prepared them for shipping. But less than a year later, an incident with improperly treated leather bound for Italy led Haj Ahmad to leave the tannery feeling like he was blamed for someone else's mistake.

My mother's other brother, *Khalo* Ahmad, *Allah yirhamo*, was also in Jeddah at the time and remained there to his last days. He used to give the king's children private lessons in math and was the accountant of one of the princes. He saved up money to open a printing press in Jeddah, which he called the Middle East Printing Press. When my father left the tannery, he went to manage the press.

In those days, business transactions were all made in cash. As the accountant, my father used to tell us that every evening after work, he would take a bag full of money to the bank. The printing press was making a nice profit from printing books and wedding invitation cards.

One day, my uncle confronted my father about improper accounting. My father was the kind of person who had pride. He became resentful at my uncle for what he thought was an accusation and left the business. He was set to return to Palestine when people told him that he should try Abu Dhabi. Back then, people knew very little of the place. They even mispronounced it as "Abu dabe'," the father of a hyena.

My father got on a steamship from Jeddah and headed for Abu Dhabi.

In those days of the early 1960s, what is called the Rubʿi al-Khali, or Empty Quarter, in the southern part of the Arabian Peninsula above Yemen, had no proper highways, so it was common for migrant workers to journey from Jeddah to the coastal city of Abu Dhabi by ship. It would be several years before Abu Dhabi struck it big with oil, but already people in the region were expecting opportunities to open there.

My father was the first from our village to go to Abu Dhabi. They say he installed the plumbing in the palace of Sheikh Shakhbut, the ruler of Abu Dhabi at the time. After that, a lot of people started going. Now, you will find so many people from Kufr Raʿi. My seven cousins live there, and my aunt Waseeleh lived, died, and was buried there.

In Abu Dhabi, which was still under British rule, Haj Ahmad lived in a one-story block home with a zinc roof. The bachelor's life had its advantages, but it was filled for Haj Ahmad with loneliness and longing for his family and home.

My parents used to send each other letters in those days. My father used to look forward to them. My mother expressed a deep desire to be together, and she would include photos of us children taken in a studio in Jenin. In one photo of her and Suzanne, she wrote a note on the back: "My dear, I wish I could give you the cigarette in my hand."

At home, Haj Ahmad cooked on a kerosene stove and washed his clothes with seawater. Fresh drinking water had to be shipped in from Oman. Most of his time was spent between home and work. In the evenings, he came together with other Palestinian men over tea, but the highlight of their week was going to the mosque for the Friday midday service, the *khutba*, which, beyond being a religious duty, was a time of social gathering.

This was his life, save for the summers he spent in Palestine. Over the years, he'd miss attending the birth of most of his children and was the last to learn of deaths in his village. And it remained so till 1988, when diabetes forced him to return to Palestine for good.

In 1969, when he returned for the summer, I was too young to remember it clearly. I'm told that I looked at him carefully and smiled. I understood he was my father because my mother always showed us photos of him and spoke about him often, especially when he sent letters back home and she read to us the parts where he wrote about us. She pushed me to give him a hug, and, apparently, he won me over with a gift. I spent the next few days curious about him, and it amused him. I was his youngest, the one he was intent on spoiling, and at that cute age where I could do no wrong. But we only reunited for a brief time, and he was gone as fast as he appeared.

3

1970

Life in the Sawalha family followed a consistent routine in the days before there were sons who grew up and joined the resistance, sons who brought the family dignity but dragged it through a series of misfortunes.

Mayda woke early each day in a room furnished simply with mattresses on the ground and a beige wardrobe she received as a wedding gift. On the back of one door, she had carved the names and birthdays of her three girls. Her house was an unassuming cement block. The second floor was unfinished when Sireen was born, and the family lived in two rooms on the ground floor, separated by a staircase.

My mother did not move to this house until her second daughter, my sister Maysoun, was born in 1964. At the beginning of her marriage, they lived with my father's family. He was from the *hara al-shmaliyyeh*, the northern neighborhood of the village, and my mother from the *hara al-jnubiyyeh*, the southern neighborhood, only a short walk away. After my father and mother got married, my mother went off to live with her in-laws, as was customary. But problems arose between them, in large part because my mother was not bearing any boys and had come to be called *Um al-Banat*, the mother of girls.

Once, as my mother was getting water from the well, she overheard my father's mother, Habuba, and my uncle's wife whispering that they wanted to push her in so my father could marry someone else. My father was in Abu Dhabi at the time, so my mother told her father. When my grandfather heard, he insisted that he should buy land from his brother-in-law—my maternal grandmother's brother—so my mother could build her own house there. My mother refused at first. She was always mind-

24

ful of social traditions. She had married someone from a different neighborhood and could not move out of it.

Eventually, with her brother's encouragement, my mother acquired a plot of land, around two hundred square meters, from her *khal*, her maternal uncle. It was in the northern neighborhood, and my grandfather gave her the money to build a house.

My mother would often sit cross-legged in the morning staring facedown into a half-empty cup of tea rich with the fragrance of *miramiya*. She would sigh bitterly, *"Ya bayi! Ya bin Habuba, ruhet ou ghalabtni!"* She repeated this call to my absent father, "Oh dear! Oh son of Habuba, you've gone and left me with this burden!" My father, who had gone off to work in Abu Dhabi and left my mother to raise a family.

At twenty-five, my mother alone tilled the land, built the house, and fed the three of us. Her four brothers had left Palestine in search of better lives in France, Spain, and Saudi Arabia. My grandfather and one brother were in the village, but my grandfather wanted her to be independent and make sure my father was the one supporting us.

Mayda found dignity in her land, even if it meant tending to it without anyone by her side, even when she saw the Israelis seize lands to the west, in al-Jiftlik, الجفتلك, Fasayil, فصايل, al-Auja, العوجا, and elsewhere, and thought this expropriation and colonizing of land was a slow kind of death that would catch up with her soon. This was still her life; she had made the decision to return and remain. She lived and accepted it, as we often do, with some bitterness and complaints.

There were just five houses on the hill surrounding Mayda and her girls. In her neighbor's plot, just across the courtyard, Um Farid's rooster would crow as dawn broke through the darkness, prompting Sireen to wake.

When you entered the house, the room on the right was for the girls to sleep in, even when we got older. In the morning, my mother folded all the sponge mattresses in our room, removed the *darj*, a type of hay carpet that separated us from the chilly cement floor at night, tied everything in a bundle, and placed it in a corner so the room was bare. The second room, on the left, was my parents' bedroom. During the day, we left cushions and mattresses on the floor to form an Arabic-style seating area where we ate our meals and spent much of our time. Later, when we had electricity, that room had a TV. In between the two rooms were the stairs, with a small windowless and doorless room underneath that served as a food pantry where we stored food and kept the winter provisions.

There was no kitchen, only a gas stove under the stairs, which we rarely used, and a fire pit outside over which my mother did all her cooking. There was also no bathroom, just an outhouse made of a hole in the floor, surrounded by three cement walls and a curtain. We used to be afraid of going to the toilet at night as kids, so we had a potty placed in our room. If we needed to go, we did it in the room and then threw it out in the morning.

We showered in the same room we slept in. My mother heated water, and we showered in a corner. The water drained out into the front yard, irrigating the pomegranate, lemon, and almond trees my mother grew.

The house remained in this state for at least five years. My mother added to it bit by bit. Soon, she would complete the second floor with help from people in the balad, although she prepared the jableh, the concrete mix, herself.

The layout on the second floor mimicked that of the first—two rooms separated by a hallway. One room upstairs later became a bedroom for my parents.

My mother also installed a modern bathroom with a shower. But she had it locked. She said that when we flushed, we wasted too much water, so we mostly continued to use the outhouse, and we even followed the same old routine at bath time instead of using running water.

Mayda didn't have much time in the morning for Sireen or her sisters. By the time the girls woke up, she was already dressed in a white *mandeel* resting loosely over her hair, a tunic falling below the knees, loose pants underneath, and working boots to weather the mud, thorns, and dust of the fields. Within a few minutes of everyone waking, and before she set off for their fields, Mayda was outside in their small courtyard tending to the tomatoes, chili peppers, and mint, which she grew in the cement basin that lined one edge of the family plot.

In the early half of 1970, Mayda was pregnant and moved slower and more deliberately as she made her way to her land. Her thoughts drifted to what might happen should she deliver another girl.

Her slow movements gave her time to reflect on the changes around her. In the last three years since she had returned, the Israelis had developed a plan for settling and annexing the newly occupied land. They had acquired almost half a century of experience stretching well before 1948, taking over land slowly, thinking of the long game, with time on their side.

A few weeks after the 1967 war, Yigal Allon, minister of agriculture, drafted what came to be known as the Allon Plan, which was motivated by the principle of maximizing Israeli territory while keeping the Palestinian population to a minimum. Mayda did not know about the plan, but she heard of the building of settlements that began almost immediately after the war, forcibly confiscating Palestinian land in the Gaza Strip and the West Bank, especially in and around Jerusalem. The military occupation could not be sustained without the settlement project, and the settlements could not exist without military force. Where there was a settlement, there had to be military presence to ensure its security. While the government did not formally endorse the Allon Plan, it began implementing it in the first decade of occupation. And as early as 1967, Kfar Etzion, the first Jewish settlement, was established in the West Bank, followed by Kiryat Arba in the early 1970s.

In those early years, Mayda also heard of steadily increasing acts of resistance to Israeli occupation. A Palestinian insurrection in the West Bank and the Gaza Strip began targeting Israeli army bases, administrative offices, and military vehicles with bombs, grenades, and other acts of sabotage. In the Gaza Strip, a fierce guerrilla movement emerged, armed with weapons that Egyptian forces left behind during the 1967 war. From its base of operations in Jordan, the Palestine Liberation Organization (PLO), founded in 1964 at an Arab League summit in Cairo, was also able to deal blows to the occupying power. Mayda followed all this closely and felt a deep respect for those fighting and sacrificing their lives. She knew there could be no liberation without sacrifice, and sometimes she imagined what she might have done had she not been pregnant and so busy raising a family.

But by the end of the summer of 1970, King Hussein of Jordan felt his power threatened by the PLO, and he launched a full-scale attack against Palestinian forces in his kingdom. Mayda cringed at this news. She could feel her heart burn. King Hussein's army entered Palestinian refugee camps, which had been set up when Palestinians were expelled from Palestine in 1948 and again in 1967, and rooted out the PLO armed factions, killing thousands.

Amid all the resistance, on a chilly spring day in Kufr Ra'i in 1970, from a house in the *hara al-shmaliyyeh* came heavy moans and harsh shrieks:

Mayda's labor had begun. Suzanne and Maysoun ran for help, one to Um Ali, the midwife, and the other to their maternal grandmother, Hajjeh Maysa. "*Umee rah twaled!* Mother is going to give birth!" they both yelled on their way. Too young to help further, the girls were sent along with Sireen to their grandparents while their mother screamed for God and Um Ali tried unsuccessfully to calm her nerves as she directed her to push every few minutes. It lasted an eternity. She'd scream, "Never again!" swearing throughout that she might meet her creator.

Then came high-pitched undulating sounds that broke the village rhythm: "La-la-la-la-la-la-lee! La-la-la-la-la-la-lee!"

Mayda was no longer *Um al-Banat*.

Yousef was born, and everyone came to know Mayda as Yousef's mother, Um Yousef. The neighbors let out a "La-la-la-la-la-la-lee, la-la-la-la-la-la-lee," again, and again, and again. The eldest son, the pride and joy of the family.

Um Yousef's mother-in-law could not hide her excitement. She offered sweets to the village, and everyone was welcome. They poured in to see the newborn, bringing with them money to put in the baby's wrap, or clothes or jewelry with blue beads for good luck, the *kharzeh zarqa*. Um Yousef's mother made sure her daughter sipped on *shorbet al-waldat*, a type of chicken soup with rice and parsley that was said to keep a woman strong after delivery. She also gave Um Yousef a dish of cinnamon and nuts, believed to help the uterus heal.

Haj Ahmad, who was now also known as Abu Yousef after his son's birth, was not—nor was he expected to be—present on this happy day. He was always, it seemed, in Abu Dhabi. He did not hear of the birth until a few days later through a telegram. When he finally returned from Abu Dhabi, he slaughtered two lambs to feed the village and brought with him velvet clothes for all the elderly women of the family.

4

1972

Um Yousef was home nursing her second son, Ihab. It was summer, and Abu Yousef was back in Palestine. He had just returned from a morning walk and had bought a newspaper. He tossed it on the ground near Um Yousef. She caught the headline: "Explosion in Beirut: Ghassan Kanafani Assassinated along with His Seventeen-Year-Old Niece."

She let out a long sigh. She knew Abu Yousef had once met Kanafani, the great anti-colonial writer, during his time in Kuwait, and she saw the resignation in his eyes as he sat across the room, sipping tea in silence and staring past his feet. Despite the Palestinian revolutionary spirit of recent times, she could feel the blows of the last two years weighing heavily on her and everyone around her. In August 1970, the Israeli forces had pushed hard and launched an offensive to "pacify" Gaza. By December 1971, the Israeli military had killed and captured 742 resistance fighters. Um Yousef received news of how anyone who fed, sheltered, heard about, or saw a resistance fighter was seized by the military. Many of those who ended up in prison were unprepared for interrogation and unable to withstand the torture. The Israelis drew on some of these people to create a network of informants for the military—it was one among many methods for recruiting collaborators to work for the Israeli forces.

News of events coming to her from Jordan were not encouraging either. By spring 1971, the remaining PLO resistance fighters, the *fida'yeen*, who used Jordan as a staging ground for their resistance, were penned up in the Jerash-Ajloun area in North Jordan as the Jordanian forces eliminated their last strongholds. This battle was so brutal that they chose to surrender to the Israeli occupation forces across the Jordan River rather than face exter-mination at the hands of the king's army. No one in the Sawalha family was involved in the resistance yet. But it was nevertheless hard for Um Yousef to shut these events out of her daily life, even if she wanted to. Harder still when Abu Yousef was around, constantly attuned to the news, passionate about seeing Palestine liberated, and rooting for the PLO resistance fighters.

Sireen was not old enough to remember Kanafani's assassination or any of these specific events. She recalls only occasional acts of stone-throwing in an otherwise quiet village and the stories she heard from her mother, older sisters, and neighbors.

I used to hear about this fighting from my neighbor, Um Fareed. Her son, Bashir, went to fight the Israelis in the 1970s and never returned. Every few months, she would save some money and take a trip to Jordan looking for him. She never be-lieved he died fighting, even though the women in the neighborhood identified her as a mother of a martyr, *um al-shaheed*.

Um Yousef tried her best to remain unconcerned with regional politics as she managed her home during Abu Yousef's long absences. She put her kids to work as young as five years old. Not Yousef, though. He was more trouble than help, according to the sisters. Um Yousef disagreed with the criticism of her son. He could do no wrong.

At home, each daughter had a chore, and it was this way until they mar-ried and left their parents' home. Suzanne dusted and wiped the house. May-soun washed dishes after each meal. This was done outside using two tubs filled with water, one for dirty dishes and the other for clean ones. At age five, Sireen was in charge of the laundry.

It was a tiresome task. I would fetch two round, tin tubs from underneath the stairwell that led to our still-unfurnished second floor. I then made my way to the backyard, set the tubs down, and filled each container halfway with water gathered from the well in our garden. I would squat and, for the next hour, using one tub, scrub clothes using soap made from olive oil by my grandmother, Hajjeh Maysa. My only consolation, I still remember well, was the scent of jasmine that filled the yard. After, I would rinse the clothes in the other tub, and once I was done, I hung them on a line that stretched through the backyard.

When I was not doing laundry, I helped Maysoun dry dishes. And when dishes and clothes were dry, I began ironing with a flat iron my mother heated on our kerosene stove, the *babur kaz*. If my sisters and I veered off-script, we were not spared our mother's open palm, a broom, or whatever she could grab to discipline us with. Once, while our mother was out, Suzanne, Maysoun, and I wanted to surprise her by cleaning the entire house, including the walls. As one of my sisters stretched high from a ladder, she tipped the kerosene over, which spilled into my mother's sacks of sugar and flour. It was impossible to hide the damage. Instead of greeting us with smiles, my mother came at us with arms flailing. We got a good beating that day! She then struggled to save what she could of the sugar by drying it in the sun, though this did not stop us from being able to taste kerosene in our sugared tea for months.

The beating may not have been pleasant, but Sireen's memory of the debacle brought her to uncontrollable laughter.

That same year, an abandoned two-story home in Kufr Ra'i was converted into a kindergarten. There were many such abandoned homes scattered around the West Bank as a result of the 1967 war, and the family that owned this particular house was permanently severed from it.

When I was around six years old, the family spoke to relatives in town and asked them to turn the house into a kindergarten and rent it out as such. I remember that I was the only girl among boys. I mean, this wasn't Ramallah, Jerusalem, or even Jenin. We were in Kufr Ra'i, and few people sent their girls to school, especially to kindergarten. It's quite different today, but who in their right mind would do that back then? My mother needed to manage the home, so I guess she found the two hours of kindergarten a good way to keep me out of causing trouble in the house.

It was a fun and playful time, and we would do all kinds of activities. If I recall correctly, I got on stage to sing once. I sang a poem: *"Ya ba-i' at-tufah, ya mun'ash al-arwah"*—Oh seller of apples, oh giver of life to souls.

Akh. I can't remember the rest of it. Wait. Those lines were imprinted in my memory! They'll return.

In kindergarten, Sireen was surrounded by boys. When she was older and began attending the all-girls primary school, her mother did not allow her to mix with boys because she was afraid of reputational damage and the gossip of neighbors. So the paths of Sireen and her kindergarten friends rarely crossed, despite the smallness of the village.

I have not forgotten the faces of those boys. Unlike those lost lines of poetry, their smiles and their *shaghab*, their mischief, are the subjects of my dreams and the content of my tears. I remember playing with them when we were all kids, in the alleyways, in the age of innocence, before my mother forbade me from hanging out with boys.

There was one with us in nursery who was the weakest among us. He had a heart condition and the kids teased him a lot. We were so mean and rude. The boys from the group my age used to play jokes on him. We would bring sandwiches to school, but he was also quite poor and wouldn't come with food, so he would ask us to share some. Once, they took their leftover bread, soaked it in water, and forced him to eat it.

That boy died from his heart condition when he was around twenty. My mother called me up when I was in college in Jordan and told me the news. You can't imagine how sad I was for him, and the guilt I felt for what we had done as children, even though it had been so long ago.

And now, you see these other boys turned men. I can't believe it. They went to prison for years. Now they have kids, and some of their kids are married; they have bellies and graying hair; some are bald. My God, where has the time gone? These are the boys that I played with when I was five years old.

> Oh seller of apples, oh giver of life to souls
> Come in the morning, oh seller of apples
> And sing to our ears with your lovely voice

The school was shut down a year later, and Sireen never learned why. The house remains standing abandoned, its owners fated to die in exile.

As the girls grew and started attending school, their chores increased. They had to first dress their younger siblings, and if their mother was out on the land, they had to also prepare breakfast and pack the mattresses that were laid out the night before. The boys (once there were more boys) had fewer responsibilities, and the elder sisters then had the added chore of cleaning up after them. Only once the sisters were done tending to the boys could they dress, prepare their school bags, and pack their lunches.

Girls from our neighborhood usually passed by us to walk to school together. Often, they waited for ten minutes or so at the bottom of the slope leading to our house, then they feared being late and left without us.

On the days we were late, our teachers lined us up on a wall and gave us a beating. Once, Maysoun and Suzanne turned around and went back home. They just didn't want to face the beating again. They told me to tell the teachers they were sick. I had an exam and had to continue on my own.

My mother also used to hit us with a pomegranate stick, the ʿasayet al-ruman, which was hard and painful. She hit us for the smallest transgressions. She would leave marks. Marks that lasted days. Marks of her fingers across our faces that could even last for weeks. My sisters and I didn't keep each other's secrets. When it came time for the beatings, oh God, we would tell on each other in a heartbeat.

Once, I went to the grocer. His uncle on his father's side was married to my mother's sister, so he was technically family. I was seven years old. He asked me the name of my older sister. I went home later and told Suzanne that he was asking about her, and my sister told my mom. You can't imagine how much of a beating I got that day. My mother was afraid he might write love letters to my sister, which would cause a scandal in the village. She had a saying, *"Itha dihket el-bint wa-ban nabha ilhaqha wa-la tahabha."* If a woman laughs and her teeth show, chase her and don't fear her.

It meant that if a woman smiled at a man, then she desired him. So, she forbade us from that kind of laughter where you start tearing up and your whole face convulses. That wonderful laughter. Now my mother complains that I am not happy, that I am depressed, that I don't laugh. She asked my husband if I drink or take drugs. But she doesn't realize that we used to laugh a lot and joke, but always got hit for it. Afterward, I stopped laughing in her presence. Laughter from the heart was forbidden.

5

1974

On February 12, two years after my mother gave birth to her second son, Ihab, she delivered a third: Iyad. The neighbors were ecstatic. If anyone had doubts about "the mother of girls," they were surely buried now. Our family felt blessed; everyone was happy.

With Iyad, as with Ihab, I remember a lot of debate went into naming him. Someone had suggested Iyad, but my mother had originally been very resistant to this. "He could turn out like Iyad Ismael," she said. "No, he will turn out like Iyad Zaki," a neighbor chimed. Iyad Zaki was the first in his class at the time. Iyad Ismael used to work in a factory in '48 Palestine. One day, he stabbed and killed his employer because the employer cursed and humiliated him. He was sentenced to life in prison. I could see why my mother was worried.

I have no recollection of Iyad's face in those early days. All I recall from the day of his birth is my own pain and trauma.

I fell into a well that day. I don't know how I survived the fall. When they carried me out, I was covered in my own blood. I had lost consciousness, broken a tooth, and cut my lip. All I remember was waking up next to my mother, and Iyad was already in the world.

But I think my fall was written several months before, when I had fallen sick with mumps, and a nurse was called to our house to give me an injection. My mother, Yousef, and Ihab were home when the *tamarji*, Abu Sami, arrived. He came to my bed, sat down next to me, and put his hand on my forehead. I had a high fever.

He pulled out a syringe and inserted it into a vial with a transparent liquid. He pulled it out, pressed into the syringe, and squirted drops of liquid onto my sheets.

I screamed and scrambled to escape with all my fevered strength.

"Hold still, habibti," Abu Sami said in an attempt to calm me.

My mother held me down while he began to insert the syringe in my thigh. I must have been hysterical at this point. Ihab—bless his heart, I think he couldn't stand to see me cry— reached for the *tamarji*'s hand and tried to yank him away from me. But Abu Sami had already inserted the syringe and was releasing the medicine at that very moment.

"No!" he yelled. His voice pierced the air but he was not quick enough. Ihab had already pushed Abu Sami's hand inward. And instead of pulling the syringe out, the needle broke inside my thigh, leaving the top half in his hand. The shock of that motion and seeing the needle separated from the syringe startled me, and silence descended on the room.

"Oh no! No, no, no!" Abu Sami yelled.

Blood started to seep from my thigh. Abu Sami, partially panicked, told my mother to hold my whole leg still. Naturally, I resumed screaming even louder at that point.

There was no time to shout at Ihab; he was too young to understand what he had done. The *tamarji* had to get the needle out of my thigh. To do that, I had to get to a hospital in Jenin. It took about an hour for my mother to find a ride to take us to the city.

First, we went to the Jenin public hospital, but the initial prognosis was that they would have to amputate my leg to prevent the needle from moving through my body and potentially causing life-threatening harm. Not satisfied with that approach, they took me to a private Christian hospital called Mustashfa al-Injeel, which went with the more reasonable option of operating on me to remove the needle.

I remembered the incident painfully for many years and still have a scar. It was a long time after the surgery before I could walk normally. This is why, when I was playing with my friend and was pushed, during that February of Iyad's birth, I think my balance was still unstable and I fell into the well. From that point on, my mom was paranoid, and so was I. There is a saying that *al-talteh sabteh,* meaning the third time will stick, will really be the end, the nail in the coffin.

I've gone through life thinking this. Waiting.

6

Over the years, I made three trips to Kufr Ra'i to meet Sireen's family and experience the village for myself. There, I saw what Iyad saw and learned firsthand what propelled him to resist. I couldn't meet him on these visits. Um Yousef told me how he brought life to the house with his pranks and laughter. Sireen described him as full of energy when he was young. He was strong and active, climbing things and jumping around the house, so much so that his aunt Aida called him Tarzan.

In 2005, my taxi took over two hours traveling north from Ramallah to reach Kufr Ra'i, stopping at three checkpoints along the way. The taxi driver wore his seatbelt when we crossed each checkpoint onto restricted Israeli settler bypass roads. As soon as we were back on Palestinian roads, he removed his seatbelt, as if in rebellion to yet another Israeli rule imposed on him. As we neared our destination, coming from the direction of the village of Rameh الرامة, the road became neglected and bumpy, and instead of pavement, the asphalt was overtaken by sand on the edges until there was barely any asphalt at all, just a dirt path. Our car slowed down as we encountered a farmer herding sheep in the middle of the road. He directed his flock to the side, and we were able to pass. It was summer; the taxi's air conditioning did not work, so the windows were down, and I felt suffocated by the midday heat that mixed with unsettled dust.

Kufr Ra'i lies among a cluster of four villages, set in the northern West Bank between the three major cities of Nablus, نابلس, to the south, Jenin, جنين, to the east, and Tulkarem, طولكرم, to the west. The closest village is Fahme, فحمة, named after coal, they say, after a massive fire struck the village long ago and left behind charred homes. It is more commonly known for a former Jordanian military base outside the village, which became a protected camp for Palestinians who had collaborated with Israelis.

Sireen mentioned this camp in passing once. It had long been disbanded by the time I arrived. The collaborators were shuttled to cities over the Green Line, within the UN-recognized Israeli state, after Fahme was placed under Palestinian control in 1995 as part of the Oslo agreement. Sireen often spoke of who might be suspected of being a collaborator in her town. It came up when she told me about an Israeli ambush on Iyad and when we discussed Palestinian resistance past and present. Collaboration with the enemy—treason—was the ultimate sin, and Sireen was not alone in being tormented with suspicions. It was always on people's minds in Kufr Ra'i, as it was elsewhere in Palestine. And it made sense, for it has always been an Israeli obsession to recruit collaborators, turning Palestinians into the eyes and ears of their settler-colonial project.

The other villages surrounding Kufr Ra'i are the villages of Rameh, الرامة, to the south and Illar, علار, and Saida, صيدا, to the west.

The Israelis hate these villages, including ours. I used to think it was because they were on hills and there was only one main road that went through the village, making them hard to access and control. Now I understand that they have always planted settlements on hills. They must have felt our presence as a thorn since we are deeply proud villages on these hills, and they could not build on them so long as we remained.

In the village, houses are built with some distance between them, but homes get closer together and denser in the center of town—the old city. Where I stayed at the outskirts of the village, the only sounds I heard were those of animals and the occasional breeze, interrupted by a passing car.

On my last trip, I rode in a shared "service" passenger van to Jenin. We passed through Arraba, عرّابة, and Fahme, فحمة, dropping other passengers off along the way before entering Kufr Ra'i. The air this time was far more putrid than it had been on my first visit. A garbage dump had been established at the entrance of the village of Fahme, bordering Kufr Ra'i. The stench was unbearable.

I spent my first morning sitting at the family terrace looking into the distance. They say that one can see Tel Aviv from the highest point in Kufr Ra'i. That day, though, the city had disappeared behind the morning haze. I looked around me, gazing at low, sprawling, rocky hills checkered with various kinds of trees.

My mornings in Kufr Ra'i often left me oscillating between serenity and unease. When a rooster cackles, a nearby dog barks, and the birds chirp through a pleasant summer breeze, one can momentarily lose sight of who is in control of this land. The hills in the distance hum secrets of the morning dew and carry stories of farmers on their way to work. All around, the landscape masks the politics in its midst, and for a moment, one could be excused for forgetting that the horizon is a prison wall and that the land is being settled by strangers. Nature gives people moments like this, perhaps in its attempts to make the rest of the day tolerable.

On my third day, Sireen and I walked into town together. She wore beige trousers and a tank top under a white, light cotton sweater and a lavender shawl patterned with black flowers hanging loosely over her hair. It was not her typical attire. She tended to wear clothes that showed her arms and shoulders, dresses with a lot more color—reds, yellows, and blues—and no head covering.

I feel like I'm the black sheep of the family now. I'm the only one who doesn't wear a hijab, and I'm too independent for my mother. She still thinks she can tell me what to do, what to wear, who to see, how to behave.

I walked alongside Sireen as she looked ahead into the hills of Palestine and talked to me about her past, sometimes wide-eyed like a little girl, pointing fingers at the places where she spent the most time, sometimes with melancholy in her voice when remembering the people that were gone or the places that had changed.

Together, we felt the early morning dew in the sweet but dense air. Smoke from a nearby clay oven, the *taboon*, filled our surroundings with the aroma of rising bread, and the world felt calm but for a few bricklayers in the distance, hammering away at their morning. As we walked and she shared stories, I noticed her eyes soften and stare into the distance, fixating on the unseen, as if she were peering into the Kufr Ra'i of old to help me imagine her village past. She almost lost her balance between these two worlds—living in one, holding onto the other.

I tried to discern through her descriptions what only she could see. What was once a beaten path was now flattened and paved. The steep sandy slope that led from her house to the main village street met the same fate to accommodate more cars.

From Sireen's childhood house, one used to be able to see the tree-scattered land stretch to the village of Saida and spot Burqin, برقين, and Ya'bad, يعبد. But now, there was no stretch of land, only a few dozen new homes built in the last decade. At night, their lights, scattered around the hills, lit up the valley in between. I squinted to imagine the escape routes into the hills between Kufr Ra'i and Saida that I heard Iyad would have used to elude capture from the occupation army. How difficult they would be to take now! One would have to trust each resident along the way not to betray one's whereabouts.

Near where the homes of two families—the Abu Sarhans and Abu Shukris—met the main road, I saw a mosque. But Sireen looked beyond it into a large backyard that only existed in her memory. She heard the muezzin in the far distance. His soothing call to prayer would come from Ya'bad, Sireen recalled, traveling through the air from that nearby town. This was before the backyard was replaced with the village mosque and the five other mosques that followed. Before that, the only mosque was in the northern part of Kufr Ra'i, nestled in the old town, making the mosque in Ya'bad more audible.

The first time I arrived in the village of Kufr Ra'i, it struck me as a poor town. Its heritage was mostly left to wither. There was little remaining of the old village architecture, and my attention was immediately caught by the faces of young men, men whose lives I would come to learn about intimately, men killed by the Israeli occupation forces, their tattered eyes looking down on me from posters that lined the walls of the village. These posters of martyrs were layered atop older faded posters that were plastered upon even older ones.

Construction was haphazard. Most homes were two to three stories high and were generally of two types. The more recent and more affluent homes, usually built with money from places like the Arab Gulf, were massive houses of smoothly cut limestone brick, with annexes, curved stairs, Romanesque pillars, and sometimes sculptures recalling Versailles. These were the minority. Most homes were simpler and made of concrete and were built in installments. Some of these concrete block structures were colorfully painted, but others were not. They stood in raw gray form, or their paint was chipped and shriveled. Some buildings had cobblestone roofs, but the tops of most homes were flat and unfinished, sometimes waiting years for their owners to build second or third floors. Satellite dishes and black water tanks peppered these roofs.

The villages of the Levant have gradually become dense with concrete and people, more towns than villages. And as communal land has given way to private ownership, people have left agriculture and taken up work in cities. New technologies have also changed the way farmers cultivate their land, and new economies have forced families to seek livelihoods in other places and faraway countries. The search for better pay and stable jobs has torn these families apart, and settler colonialism has only compounded this process, constricting their movement, suffocating their freedom, and containing their futures. As new wealth has accumulated from the newfound wage labor, the material life of the Palestinian village has transformed irreversibly. And this transformation is most manifest in construction, with new materials, new techniques, and new spaces and structures that have concentrated life around the nuclear family.

Sireen walked out of the side road that led to the boys' school behind Dar Abu Shukri. It was a two-minute walk from her childhood home. The girls' school was at the other end of the village. It was a long walk—forty-five minutes for a young kid, she told me. I walked it. It was a trek.

My mother would watch my sisters and me from the roof as we hurried off to school. "Don't you dare talk to any boys on the way. *'Ayb!*" she would yell from above. It was her signature way of bidding us farewell every morning.

In those days, from the roof, my mother had a more or less unobstructed view all the way to the corner of my grandfather's house, halfway to school. She was so controlling. She watched us walking back from school, and if we strayed a bit from our path, she might beat us and accuse us of trying to get the attention of boys hanging out in the streets. We were not even allowed to speak to any of our girlfriends who had brothers.

Fraternizing with boys was absolutely shameful. We couldn't even go to a relative's house if there were boys there. So, if I went somewhere and just saw the shoe of a man lying outside the door to a house, I turned around and went home. I didn't take my chances.

Sireen took me into the center of the village that now felt more like a small town. The steady stream of cars disrupted her thoughts and the flow of our conversation in a way that would not have happened in the past. The village baker's store still stood, though somewhat invisible among the many shops that had sprouted over the decades. The baker's role in the village is not as vital as it used to be, as bread now pours in from other places in the West Bank. Sireen and I then turned to look at the original town center on a hill a stone's throw away, where the first homes of Kufr Ra'i were built densely near each other, looking like a mini-casbah. It stood as a ruin, though the mayor was desperately trying to preserve it. I wondered to myself, Does ruin look out at us, this life, and the newer town center, and think it is better off as ruin?

We passed by Mahmoud al-Muttii's shop where Sireen used to buy groceries, then by the shops of Abu Salhiyye, who still sold tobacco, tahini, and other food supplies, and by Ahmad al-Fayeq, the vegetable seller. Sireen looked out at the *hara al-jnubiyyeh*—the southern neighborhood. Her grandfather's house lay atop the highest hill. From almost anywhere in the village, she used to be able to see him as he returned home or see guests as they arrived at his house. Sometimes she would run to see what surprises he brought. Now, it was impossible. Too many new homes obstructed the road leading to the gate, and her grandfather had long passed.

Sireen and I spent our days this way, walking around the village, visiting relatives and her old friends. They welcomed her with warm hugs and kisses and the excitement with which one greets a loved one after a long period of absence. She remained connected to this place, in her element, and confident enough to introduce me to people, who felt enough at ease around her to share their histories with me. Sireen and I grew closer and learned more about each other as well. In the evening, we returned to her house and exchanged thoughts on the day or caught up with her siblings. I wrote down a few notes; she narrated more stories of her life, which I always enjoyed listening to. She never tired of her memories, never tired of sharing with me all the emotions they evoked.

1

1975

Um Yousef was holding one-year-old Iyad in one arm, secured in a sling made from old fabric sheets, and grabbing Sireen by the ear with her other hand, yelling after Suzanne, wanting to get a hold of her as well. The two sisters were going to get a good beating. They had been caught evading work.

Sireen was in third grade, old enough to take on more responsibility on the family land. Abu Khaled, who worked for Um Yousef, came in the spring with his horse to plow the field. But when it came to the groves of various fruit trees—almond, cherry, and plum—the horse couldn't get too close to their trunks, and a large area was always left unplowed. Sireen and Suzanne were each given an ax to remove overgrown weeds around the trees and plow those areas themselves, each sister in charge of a row. Um Yousef ran her fields and her house like a factory. Her second son, Ihab, later remarked that she was the first capitalist he knew, the source from which he learned efficiency, discipline, and the Fordist mode of production, as he put it.

That season, Sireen and Suzanne began to skip trees toward the end of their row, thinking their mother would never check that far, given she was too busy looking after her three young sons. The sisters had been doing this for a few weeks before their mother finally caught on.

Sireen's ear was red for two days, and the two sisters had marks on their calves and upper arms from where Um Yousef's pomegranate stick struck. After their beating, they had to return to work on the trees they had skipped.

I don't think we tried that again! After the plowing came the green almond- and cherry-picking season in April and May. We didn't have a lot of cherry trees.

Not as many as we do today—in the last decades, people throughout the village have planted more and more cherry trees and an even greater number of tobacco plants. Still, my mother sold one or two baskets and made jam with the rest. She spent a week each spring making cherry jam to last us the whole year.

On the other hand, we had around fifty to sixty almond trees—that distant cousin of the plum—and harvesting green almonds, with the kernels still jelly-soft inside, came with strict instructions, as we had to make sure not to mix the different types. I remember Suzanne warning me, "Sireen, *intibhi*, don't you dare mix up the almonds. *El-hajjeh btikhrub baytna!*" Indeed, our mother would definitely bring the roof down on our heads! Fear ensured we rarely mixed them. One was bitter, the other sweet, and each one had its own price and merchants.

Eventually, spring gave way to summer, and cherry-picking came to an end. Yet Um Yousef and her girls had no break from working the land, as suddenly, all around them in Kufr Ra'i, blossoming plum trees painted the fields with glistening hues of red and purple, and the family was once again toiling under an unforgiving sun, picking and packing the fruit. The sweat of the harvest was forgotten when Sireen and her sisters paused for casual breaks to steal bites of freshly picked juicy plums. Sireen recalls the season as days melding beautifully into one another. Then the moment passes, and the days appear torturous and long. Memory becomes unfixed, as the bitter and sweet of her present and past slide into one another.

I didn't always go to the grove to collect plums. My mother went daily for several weeks at a time, but the kids took turns. We would wake up before the light of dawn and head to the fields after the Fajr prayer. I can still smell the scent of morning dew, see my little hands caressing droplets on wild leaves in our path, my childhood feet stepping on soil that appears renewed after the damp air of night.

Reaching the fields early was important. It meant that the plums were still engulfed in their natural morning dewdrops with a fine layer of dust that gave them an extra twinkle. "*Ou'ek*, be careful, don't you ever grab the plum from the bottom," my mother instructed us. We had to handle them with the gentlest touch of our fingerprints, lest the many micro-droplets smear or slide off the plum. If we could pick and pack them as they were, my mother believed the buyers at the market would be more enticed by their freshness. We handled each with care, lay them on crumpled brown paper in their small wooden crates, placed the most perfect ones on top, covered them with a layer of the same paper, and tied them into the crate. Between my sisters and I, we'd pick somewhere around fifty crates' worth in a day. I remember that Suzanne or I would then transport the crates of plums back to the village. My mother put them on the donkey's back fitted with a square metal box atop a set of pillows. We'd place the crates inside it, and then tie them with a rope.

I never rode the donkey myself. I fell once and was afraid ever since. All through the June heat, I went back and forth on foot. It was almost an hour's walk back to the village, walking on cracked, stony, mostly uphill paths.

My mother had an agreement with a truck driver to take the crates to merchants in Jenin or to the Palestinians of '48, who, having better access to the Israeli market, could sell them to Jewish consumers and grocers. Later, some merchants came directly to the house once they knew my mother had good quality produce.

Sireen still remembers when it was easy for Jenin's residents to sell produce to '48 Palestinians. Jenin's economy had traditionally relied on villages and towns to its north, in the lower Galilee, for trade, until being cut off in 1948. The borders reopened in 1967, and trade with the north restarted. So did the supply of menial labor to the Israeli market. Kufr Ra'i, being within Jenin's sphere, witnessed similar economic patterns. It was all part of an Israeli government open-border policy, which was in place because the Israelis relied on Palestinian labor but also because the policy would facilitate colonizing the land. In truth, open borders meant one could close them at will; something given could be taken away.

Our path to *el-wad*, our land in the valley, where the plum trees live, is lined with more houses now than back in the '70s. Back then, once we stepped foot on the land, it was just us, the sun, and the harvest. No one else in sight. No homes. No foundations of homes. Not even the conception of homes.

Sireen recalls going to the land, standing under the sky, the sun at dawn still waking and stretching behind the hills, a soft breeze on her face. But her memory of those trips during the plum season is broken by encounters with snakes. It's not that they only came out during that season, but it's the time that triggers her recollections.

We knew that snakes often curled up around tree branches toward dawn, after they spent their nights roaming the valleys. Dew settled on their scales and provided them with their source of water, and they just lay coiled, asleep, uninterested in our presence so long as we did not stir them. We had to finish before late morning when they woke again to reclaim their branches.

"I'm going to pick the plums from this tree," I yelled over to my mother one day. She continued walking into the middle of the field of plum trees and shrugged, as if to say, do as you like, just get the plums as you've been taught.

I walked up to the tree. I reached out with two fingers to pick the plum but felt something soft and scaly. I jolted back and let out a scream. A snake! It wiggled, hissed, and began to glide down.

Petrified, frozen, I let out another scream.

My mother rushed to me. She knew. My siblings knew. Every Palestinian farmer could recognize that scream.

My mother darted over and grabbed a rock on her way to kill the serpent. But it had unraveled itself onto the ground and, fearing my screams, went into hiding. I never set foot near that tree again, and till this day, I have a terrible fear of snakes.

Sireen and her siblings heard many stories of snakes when they were young, and she had nightmares about them.

When I used to dream of snakes my mom would ask, "Did you beat it, or did it beat you?" The snake in our dreams was always the enemy and represented a traitor. We had to overpower it to undo its hatred. I was often beaten in my dreams.

When farming, Um Yousef and the children took a break midmorning. Yousef and Ihab took turns joining them, and whoever stayed home was left with Maysoun. Iyad was usually brought along. Um Yousef placed him on a large sheet on which the family used to put out a basic breakfast of homemade cheese, cucumbers, tomatoes, olives, and homemade bread baked in a neighbor's *taboon*. The sisters used Iyad as an excuse to take breaks from their labor. Sireen would lie beside him, staring into the clear blue morning sky. She'd tickle him and make funny faces to draw out a smile or a chuckle.

After returning from the land, they began preparations for the midday meal. Soon the house filled with the scent of lunch: mashed lentils; a spinach dish sautéed with onion, salt, and olive oil; a salad, *tabouleh*, of minced parsley and diced tomato; and other vegetarian dishes, mostly from vegetables grown on their land. They had lamb or chicken once a week, sometimes less often. Pigeons and rabbit were a little more frequent because they raised those around the house.

After lunch, the girls played hopscotch, jump rope, or with marbles in the garden. The boys, when they were old enough, played in the alleyways with marbles or toy guns made from the wood of plum crates. On school days, the girls retreated to their room to do homework. By evening, the play and work stopped, and they rarely stayed up late. Sometimes, they sat together with neighbors, as many as twenty people, around the only thirteen-inch TV in the village and watched Arabic shows, the Syrian *Ghawar al-Towshe* being the most popular choice. But they were not connected to the Israeli power grid, which meant they only received intermittent electricity from a private generator. This, of course, had its advantages, because although electric power was weak and not constant, it meant the villagers had more control over their energy, and this was something Israeli authorities could not turn off should the villagers rebel. Indeed, it was one less thing the occupier could dangle as a carrot in what came to be known as the policy "give them something to lose."

There was little difference in the daily management of the land when Sireen's father returned from travels, usually in the summer. Abu Yousef's dawns, though, were slower paced. Maysoun prepared his breakfast. She often stayed behind when her mother went to the field as she was less cut out for working on the land and would cook, clean, and take care of the younger siblings instead. After they woke, the room Um Yousef and Abu Yousef had slept in was converted to a living room and the bed mats turned into a seating area where Abu Yousef ate on the floor. What the girls remember most about his returns to Palestine are the trips to Nablus with him, eating *knafeh*, and being allowed to choose new clothes.

After breakfast, he sat, sometimes upright with legs crossed, other times partially lying down with legs extended, lazily resting on one arm, and alternating between listening to Radio Monte Carlo, or a Jordanian or Arabic Israeli station, and reading the newspaper, *Al-Quds*, which he bought weekly.

My father came home and read the *Al-Quds* newspaper from cover to cover, every word. He read the obituaries, the classifieds with their birth announcements and other congratulatory ads, the economic section, the agricultural section, and, of course, the sections on local, regional, and international politics. And the whole thing was eight pages from front to back. But I swear, we used to read it once, then save it under our pillow, then reread it, again and again, for days on end.

Oh, how we memorized the whole thing! Oh, how precious it was! We held onto it till the next paper came a week later. And we didn't let my mother use it as a dinner spread.

I spoke to Professor Rashid Khalidi when he came to Princeton once, and I told him how right he was when he spoke of the importance of the newspaper in Palestinian life. Oh, how we knew things back then! We came from a small village, from nowhere, but we knew things. My brothers, sisters, and I stood over each other, pushing and shoving, competing to hold the paper and control the flow of the pages. If I finished a page first, I had to wait until the one holding the paper was done before moving to the next one.

How did we learn? How did we become so cultured and knowledgable about the world with only a newspaper? Here, in America, people don't seem to know a thing about the world! The newsstands are filled with newspapers and magazines of all kinds, as much information as you want. It's at your fingertips, at the click of a button on TV, on the radio, or a click away online, but it seems no one wants to know anymore. Information is thrown at people, but they refuse it. Back then, we read that one newspaper like it was telling us a story. And we could retell the news like a *hakawati,* a great storyteller, could narrate legendary adventures.

How do people here claim not to know? Are they evading responsibility? We always knew. Even when we didn't, we pretended we did. Here, people talk about ignorance being bliss. For us, ignorance was a crime. It wasn't an option. Respect and status depended on knowledge.

On the occasions when Abu Yousef followed them to the land, it was only after catching up on the previous day's news. In the summer of 1975, for example, he followed attentively the news of land confiscation for the founding of yet another illegal settlement near Jerusalem called Ma'ale Adumim. Made up of only a few hundred settlers at the time, it would grow into a city of tens of thousands in less than two decades. He was also immersed in the news out of Lebanon and the early clashes that turned into a fifteen-year war. As in Jordan, the PLO would eventually suffer blows there when the Israeli army occupied Lebanon.

When he tired of reading about the world's events, Abu Yousef strolled to the land and took in the scent of the surrounding hills that he missed year-round. He felt estranged at times, however. It was difficult to get into the farming routines and to connect with his children. But they loved having him around, especially because he did not discipline them, and Um Yousef tended to go easier on them in his presence.

When Abu Yousef visited their groves, Um Yousef didn't let him pick fruit. Maybe she didn't trust him to do it correctly, or maybe she didn't want him getting overworked and sick. Whatever the reason, he'd find himself sitting under the shade of a tree and stacking brown paper in crates into which they placed the picked plums.

This was a far cry from Abu Dhabi's construction-filled city life, which he'd recall for his grown children decades later, reminiscing about a country coming to life while witnessing the continuing destruction of another.

8

1976

As Sireen grew up, Israeli patrol vehicles were a constant fixture, but her family's encounters with the military were mostly from a distance—it had not yet invaded the sanctity of their home. With wide eyes, she would catch sight of a patrol vehicle from the roof and watch it snake through town and raise dust in its wake. Often, the soldiers would stop a teenage boy walking along the main road, and one would step out and ask for the boy's ID. In most cases, the boy would pull out his ID, the two would exchange a few words, and the patrol would then continue on its way. In those moments, it seemed like time would freeze, and Sireen could only hear the sounds of her heartbeat. Her mother's stories didn't help allay her fear either.

"Habibti, lazem tnami wi-la byiji el-jesh wa byakhdek." I heard this often from my mother and others when they wanted to discipline us. "If you don't sleep, the soldiers will come to take you," they'd say.

"The soldiers are coming. The Israelis are coming." We heard this a lot. Of course, the Israelis had come many times before, and they would come again. And when I began to see the soldiers up close and hear of youth taken away, I no longer needed to imagine what they would do or have my mother scare me.

As often as the army came through our village, in the '70s it was far more present in the larger cities, like in Jenin. We rarely went to Jenin, but when we did, once or twice a year—if we needed to see the doctor or get our school clothes tailored or buy new shoes—we definitely saw Israeli soldiers. We delighted in going to the cities, but we were also scared because we knew we would see them.

Many people in those days had more contact with Israelis in different capacities. People received treatment or gave birth in Israeli hospitals, and many men from the villages depended on the Israeli market for work. At 4 a.m., after the Fajr prayer, several Egged buses would come through town—Egged is the largest Israeli bus transport company—and the men would line up and get on different buses, each one set for a different destination across the 1967 border. If someone wanted work, they spoke to the supervisor, or *manahel*, which is the Hebrew name we used. The *manahel* was someone from the village—at one point it was my father's half-brother—and he would secure places on the buses. I remember the men would bring back pecans and avocados, which we couldn't find in the West Bank. Later though, in the '80s and '90s, many lost their jobs to newly settled Russian Jews.

We didn't have much hope in the immediate years after 1967. The Jordanians had controlled the West Bank between 1948 and 1967, but now it was under Is-raeli control. Jordan still administered many functions, though, like education and health, until 1988, when King Hussein relinquished Jordanian claims over the terri-tory. We needed the Jordanians, but we blamed them for what happened in 1948 and 1967, because the army failed to fight and lost the land.

Did you know that we had a gravesite for Iraqi martyrs? They were the only ones with a grave because they defended Jenin and were the only ones to fight honorably during the 1948 war. There is a big gravesite that people still take care of and have grown olive trees around. The Jordanians did not receive any such honor.

The fourth girl in the Sawalha family, Arselene, came into the world in 1976. She was named after Arsene Lupin, the fictional gentleman thief and master of disguise created by Maurice Leblanc. Arselene's path growing up was en-tangled with Iyad's, unlike Sireen's life, which diverged from her brother's as they grew.

Once again, at Arselene's birth, Suzanne ran to get Um Ali, the midwife; Maysoun stayed home by her mother's side; and Sireen scurried over to their grandmother, Hajjeh Maysa, yelling repeatedly in a high-pitched voice as she approached her house, "*Umee rah twaled! Umee rah twaled!*"

When the baby girl arrived, Sireen was so excited to finally have a younger sister. In time, and despite the age difference, they would grow close. Arse-lene would confide in her about her thoughts and dreams and, later, about everything she witnessed as tragedy upon tragedy unfolded in the family's life.

Suzanne, Maysoun, and Sireen were now old enough to make the *shorbet el-waldat* for their mother to have after the delivery, and they hosted their neighbors, who came to congratulate Um Yousef. The family spent the next three days receiving guests, but on the third day, the Israeli army entered the village to search it. Sireen was in school when she heard news of this incursion. She had been sitting at her desk in social studies class, looking out of a half-open window, when she began to hear people stirring outside.

As sounds from the commotion started to drift into the classroom, the girls got up from their seats to get a better look at what was happening outside. Boys, most in their late teens but accompanied by a few younger ones, had come to get them out of school. Sireen spotted two she knew rather well and who were her age—Jalal al-Aris, who was her neighbor's son, and Fouad al-Ashgar, who was always around Jalal. The group of boys were planning to burn tires to prevent the army from driving through but wanted to get the girls to the safety of their homes first. Sireen rushed out with her classmates. This was the first demonstration she recalls participating in.

"Go back home," some boys called out. Sireen wasn't sure what to do. To get home, she would have to trek to the other end of the village by the boys' school and would get caught up in the demonstration anyway. So, like some of the other girls, she remained in the street, off to the side, taking cover in the entranceway of one of the buildings.

Some boys laid out tires in two rows on the street at the beginning of the village. Sireen saw Jalal and Fouad trying to help, carrying more than their weight with their small hands. Jalal helped some older boys pour gasoline on the tires, and moments later a few boys lit them up, sending thick and heavy smoke into the sky and forcing the Israeli jeeps to retreat. Sireen didn't really understand why the army didn't push the children back. Later, she figured the military didn't find the confrontation worth escalating, since the villages were otherwise calm and generally compliant.

This demonstration in 1976 was small. Demonstrations usually were in those days. The villages weren't so active, not like cities such as Nablus. When protests erupted in the cities, the Israelis suppressed them and jailed some kids before they had a chance to spread to villages; then in a day or two, they died down. My brother Yousef was only six years old, but he saw me flustered when I came home, and I could see he was afraid of the commotion outside. And although my other brothers Ihab and Iyad were too young to remember this incident, it was their lives that would be most affected by the actions of Jalal and Fouad.

9

1977

If Palestinians did not measure time through migration and the moon, if they had not adopted the Gregorian calendar with Aramaic rhythms, the olive harvest would surely mark the new year. It was, in any case, a festive season.

In the fall harvests of Sireen's youth, children in the village tried to evade farmers so as to steal olives and sell them for pocket money. They ditched school or went to the olive groves immediately after class in small groups. Knowing this, Um Yousef forced her children to head to their land right after school to watch over the few olive trees the family owned.

Unlike the other harvests, when Maysoun usually stayed home, this time my mother chose any two of the three of us eldest girls to go while the third stayed home with our younger siblings. Each day, we were told who was going and who was staying. We took our schoolbooks to the olive grove and waited till sunset. The minute we heard the call to Maghreb prayer, we were allowed to return. We were sent without food, so we went hungry till prayer time. My mother didn't give us any money to buy sandwiches, bread, or cookies from the school canteen either. I remember those days, too hungry to focus on our homework. This was the routine for the latter part of September and sometimes into October.

My father had a plot of land in the valley, *el-wad*, and another on a rocky hill near town where the olive trees grew. This land was called the *hawacheer* for its flat terraces. To get to the *hawacheer* we had to cross through the village and then make our way down to the land from a back road. When it was time to harvest olives, Suzanne, Maysoun, and I went with our mother, who, unlike almost everyone else in the village, never hired anyone outside the family to help with the harvest. When we were older and busier, she finally hired our neighbor, Um Khaled, to help her.

On school days, we would all return home, the boys and girls, change out of our uniforms, and follow our mother to the *hawacheer.* When my brothers were a little older, though, they preferred to spend their time in more exciting ways, with boys in the village planning to resist the Israelis or talking about who in town was collaborating with the enemy and what to do with them.

In the grove, my mother would spread large, thick plastic sheets under an olive tree. One of us would climb up a ladder and pick the olives off their resilient branches, then we would drop them to the ground. Other farmers beat their branches, but my mother banned that type of practice on her trees. She taught us that handpicking olives preserved the younger boughs that produced olives the following year.

Aside from these differences in how to pick the olives, my mother followed the conventional methods of our village for their preparation. Once we returned home, she divided the olives for pickling. She prepared one half by pounding them—the *madqouq*—and the other half by slicing them—the *mshatab.* For the *madqouq*, we took each olive and smacked it with the old wooden garlic beater. For the *mshatab*, we took each one and sliced the top in quarters. It took forever.

My mother then stored them separately. The *madqouq* didn't last as long, she would say. The salt and water would seep in and rot them faster than the *mshatab.*

The olives were too bitter to eat if they didn't undergo a specific preparation. My mother submerged them in salt and water every day for a week. Each day, she switched out the saltwater until the bitterness faded. After that, we put the olives in a container with lemon and hot peppers, sealed them, and waited three weeks before tasting them. The batch we made in October lasted us the whole year.

We sent the remaining olives that weren't pickled to be pressed into olive oil. Back in the '70s, we had two olive presses in our village. People from other villages, and even from cities such as Nablus, Jenin, and Tulkarem, came to Kufr Ra'i to use them to press their olives.

My maternal grandfather, Sidi Haj Sadeq, had one. His son had sent it to him from Germany in the '70s. There was also an older one in the village, made of two large stones on which the olives were placed and then pressed. But Sidi's was new, made of steel and powered by hydraulic pressure. I remember the basin of water used to operate the engines was filled with frogs and terrified us as kids.

When I was young, I often went to Sidi's house, grabbed hot bread from the *taboon,* dipped it in freshly pressed oil, sprinkled salt on it, and ate it. The oil would still be hot and slightly bitter.

Sidi's press still operates today.

I remember his house vividly. It was one of the largest in the area around Jenin. It was built with granite and had a spacious yard. The gate into the grounds had multiple openings—for people, for cars, and even one for a truck. Guests parked in a large space near a guesthouse separate from the main house.

Iyad and I played hide-and-seek in that big house. Iyad was so skilled at locating the best hiding places and squeezing into tiny nooks. Sometimes, I couldn't find him and had to give up.

I remember, one time, I tripped while looking for him, hurt my knee, and cried. Iyad heard me and instantly jumped out of his hiding place, worried about me. I was fine, but he remained concerned and gave me a hug. Iyad worried about us a lot, even when he grew older. The Israelis used this against him.

In the winter, Sidi would sit in one of the rooms that had an Arabic seating arrangement—mattresses and cushions laid out against the walls—and feed us the tastiest chestnuts cooked on a *qanun,* a brass fireplace.

Sidi used to spoil me with things. He once bought me a pink outfit that I still remember because I have pictures of myself wearing it with a boyish haircut that was my style in those years. He'd frequently take me on trips to Jenin, where he'd buy me new clothes, or to Nablus, where he'd get me jewelry from a shop called Shahrazad. And most of all, I remember he'd give me *raha*—Turkish delight—with two biscuits that I ate like a sandwich, something my mother never gave us.

In the fall, my grandparents would lay out twenty to thirty mattresses on the ground of the guesthouse to accommodate the people who came from around the areas of Jenin, Nablus, and Tulkarem to press olives. They arrived on horse and pushcart, and they sometimes had to wait two to three days to have a turn with the olive press before leaving.

My grandmother, Siti, prepared breakfast, lunch, and dinner. She made phyllo dough, kneading it until she produced fine layers that guests ate with sugar or honey. A Druze man we knew well would bring honey from his village near Nazareth in exchange for oil, so they had a lot of honey that the guests loved. Sidi never took money for the use of the press in all those years. He just asked for payment in oil from what users produced.

At Sidi's house, men sat together during the day, sipping on tea, smoking cigarettes, and arguing about politics. They were dressed in their *kumbaz,* a long, loose gown of various colors, but mostly white, blue, black, or brown. Over the *kumbaz,* they wore suit jackets. Sidi almost always wore a men's copper-brown *abaya* over that. On their heads, they wore a plain white kaffiyeh, or a checkered red and white or black-and-white one that is the symbol of Palestinian resistance. They sat on hard, colorful, embroidered cushions, their feet bare, laughing, relaxing, some even taking midday naps. In another corner, close enough for the men and women to hear each other, women also shared cups of tea, talking about the harvest but also debating politics. They wore colorful *abaya*—black robes with green and red *tatreez* embroidery from the outskirts of Nablus, or white robes embroidered with pastel blues or yellows from villages around Jenin. I also remember how the children ran around, lay in their parents' laps, and, on occasion, got into trouble. At night, the air was filled with poetry, with music, and always with stories that visitors brought with them from near and far.

It really was a festive time.

Sidi owned so much land around Kufr Ra'i, much of it planted with olive trees. He would bring thirty to forty people to harvest the olives during this season. He was like a feudal lord, the wealthiest man in the village. Much of the olive oil sat in beautiful, colored-glass bottles set on straw in a warehouse and around the grounds of his house. It was traded locally, but in the '60s and '70s, he started to export the oil to Saudi Arabia, Kuwait, Abu Dhabi, and Jordan. As wealthy as he was, he never wanted his children to depend on him, so my mother did not see any of the money. He gave so much to charity or to build schools, but to his children he rarely gave anything. He offered to paint our house, pay the tiller to till our land, or help my mother improve our place. He gave us olive oil if our trees did not yield enough fruit. But rarely did he give money, as he did not want my father to get lazy and rely on him.

Though the olive season was so central to their lives, Um Yousef only had around eleven trees in Sireen's youth, and it was only later that her family began to grow more of them, after many seasons of Sireen's life had passed and she had left Palestine.

When she returns, she always maintains a relation with one Roman-era tree. It is the tree she used to climb in her youth, on whose branches she would then lie to rest and, from her perch, look out into vast fields. Now in her middle age, she climbs it as if she were fifteen, as if she has reconnected with a childhood friend. And when she lies on its branches, the two seem beautifully entangled. The tree and the land are no longer as secluded as they once were. A road runs nearby; one can see new houses in the vicinity. Sireen looks on at the olive tree and reflects on this spirit living through a long-troubled history, with its crinkled trunk rooted in the soil and long, winding branches pointed to the sky. She cannot help but think of all the other trees the Israelis have yanked from the earth to confiscate Palestinian land and of all the farmers who remain stubbornly faithful to this land that they have cultivated for centuries.

As seasons turned and winter blew into Palestine, we reoriented our relation to the land. By February, it was za'atar leaves that consumed us.

Oh, how the scent of za'atar has followed me throughout my life! It has been the one constant. I remember having it for breakfast every day of my youth, and even now, it is always present on my kitchen counter, ready to be dipped in olive oil. In Kufr Ra'i, za'atar and olive oil were both free and came from the land around us. My mother would lay a plastic sheet in the middle of the room and set it with a stack of clean plates and cups. She would place a bowl of za'atar with olive oil in the middle, then a plate of *labneh*, another of olives, and a third of tomatoes and cucumbers. If we were lucky, she would add a large bowl of eggs and potatoes once a week on Fridays, but that became rare as our family grew.

Even *labneh* was not readily available because we didn't have goats. And when we did bring *labneh* home, it was so sour. We didn't have refrigeration, so we would dry it, mash it, roll it into balls, and pack it into jars with olive oil. It could sit like that for a whole year. But when we ate it, it was so sour. I didn't like it back then.

Milk was scarce too. We took a little Arabic coffee kettle to Dar Abu Munther, whose house was a few minutes away by foot. He had cows and sold milk and would fill the kettle up for us. We drank milk on rare occasions—maybe if someone was sick—and it wasn't pasteurized. We drank tea, not milk, with our breakfast.

But the one thing that was always guaranteed was *zeit ou za'atar*. And as much as I love oil and za'atar, I used to hate the za'atar-picking season.

In the hills around Jenin, za'atar grew between the rains in February and March. The land was still wet and muddy when we took to the fields, carrying our *shwal*, the same large canvas sacks we used to store flour. Us girls—the boys never picked za'atar, even when they were older—went out in old clothes that we could no longer wear in public. One day it might be old school clothes, another day an old dress over pants. And our heads were adorned with headscarves like a bandana.

The time of za'atar picking would almost have been a picnic if not for the hard labor. We packed *tabouleh* and other food for lunch and then took off. The trip took a few hours on foot because my mother felt that the farther and deeper into the hills we went, the more za'atar we would find. All the older ladies collected za'atar near our village. We left in the morning and returned by sunset, and all day we picked za'atar.

Sometimes, we would bring Arselene along in a sling if our mother was joining; other times, Arselene remained with the neighbors. Ihab and Iyad joined as well; Yousef too, especially if our mother was forceful enough with him. My sisters and I enjoyed looking after our brothers and playing with them in the fields at that young age. Then, when we had to do the serious work, we let the boys play on their own and run around freely.

We didn't use gloves back then. We cut the za'atar from above the roots with our hands, and by the end of the day, they were full of thorns, dried, dirty, and green from the za'atar leaves. Once we trekked back home, the process continued, as we had to pluck the leaves off the stems we had picked in the field. We had to do this on the same day because once the za'atar begins to ripen, it becomes too difficult to make it the way we traditionally like. Ah, I remember those bittersweet nights. I remember sitting under the stars in our courtyard, the village lights barely shimmering, us plucking away. The za'atar was visible only from a single lamp powered by our village generator. My mother made mint tea, and women came over to help us. They sat through late nights plucking leaves with us.

The next day, we dried the leaves in the sun. If it was raining, we dried them inside. We laid a large table cover on the floor and left them to dry. At the beginning of the season, when the za'atar was still fresh, instead of drying it, we used the fresh leaves to make *za'atar fteer*, or flatbread, almost every weekend.

Once the za'atar dried, my mother crushed the leaves with the *jarousheh*, two old grinders made from granite stone, and packed them up in bags and placed them in storage under the stairs. The amount we picked between February and March lasted us for a year.

Every time we needed za'atar, my mother opened a bag and brought some out. We mixed it with sumac, roasted sesame seeds, and a dried lime powder called *ruh el-hamod*. This is what consumers typically see in the market. A small plate of ground za'atar takes about two hours to make if we consider the whole process because one needs to pick a large quantity of za'atar to produce the tiniest amount.

No part of our za'atar-picking routine changed after the Israelis made it illegal to pick wild za'atar in 1977. They gave the plant a protected status, but it was really just another way to control us and our culture. That year was also when the Israeli government first established the colony of Mevo Dotan by confiscating land belonging to the town of Yaʿbad. It could have been our land that they took, and it was terrifying observing how settlers could so easily colonize land.

That summer, Abu Yousef took his three sons to the road in the valley on the outskirts of the new colony, which was still a construction zone. The boys looked on as their father stood in silence, the despair and heartache visible in his glazed eyes. For Abu Yousef, the loss of this hilltop to a settlement was a continuation of the loss of 1948, all happening a stone's throw from his children's village. He worried about them growing up so close to a settlement while he toiled in Abu Dhabi. He worried the lands around their village would be next.

"Promise me you will stand your ground should that time come," he said without giving a thought to the lasting resonance this would have on his sons.

10

1981

"Iyad! *Yalla.* Come inside the house," Um Yousef called out. She was tired and had no energy to chase after her son, having just given birth to Baha a few weeks before. Iyad, now seven years old, was filthy from playing in the alleyways with kids from the neighborhood.

"*Ya Iyad, inta m'afen.* You stink. What happened to you?" Um Yousef yelled, frustrated, as Iyad returned, head down. "Why do you do this to me? Why do you have to come back home all filthy? How many times have I told you to be careful? Your clothes are a mess!" she howled, with Baha cradled in one hand and her other hand waving and hoping to get a piece of her son's bottom as he kept his head low and rushed through the front door. What Um Yousef hadn't noticed was that Iyad had returned to his mother's usual refrain with tears in his eyes. A friend had pushed him and snatched from his hand the dill he had picked on the side of the road and was about to savor. Iyad had not let his friend see him in tears, but they came gushing when he walked through the front door. After he passed his mother, he came upon Sireen, who noticed his tears.

"What happened to you today, ya *biss biss*?" I asked, referring to him as a kitten in a playful, gentle tone. It was the nickname we had given him in those days.

Iyad simply whimpered. He hated being bullied, he hated his erratic emotions and the way he couldn't control his tears, and he was starting to feel like he needed to stand up for himself. Sireen consoled him and sent him to shower.

On such days, after his shower, with hair still damp, combed and parted to the side, he would walk into the living room, which doubled as his mother's bedroom, and sit on the floor playing with plastic building blocks. It would be early evening by then, around six o'clock.

Sometimes, in the evenings when we had electricity, we watched television on our black-and-white 13-inch TV set. The reception was bad. Often, we had one person on the roof positioning the antenna, another on the stairs, and a third in the room, all screaming at each other to know when the reception was fixed. We could only catch one Jordanian channel and an Israeli Arabic one. Palestinians were not allowed to broadcast their own TV channels or to set up any other form of telecommunication—radio, TV, phone, all of it was controlled by the Israelis. And all the channels shut down at around 7:30 p.m.

If there was no electricity, we ate and might sleep early. In those days, we got our electricity from a generator owned by a neighbor, but it meant we were at their whim. When they slept, they turned it off. They might have agreed to let us keep it on longer, but we were too terrified of stray dogs and Israelis to go out at night and turn it off ourselves before we slept.

Some evenings, if Iyad was playing on his own, Yousef might try to bother him. He would tease Iyad or snatch a block out of his hands. Iyad didn't put up much of a fight. He was nonconfrontational and could be pushed around. He'd sit in his corner whimpering before moving on when no one came to his defense. Sometimes, Ihab stood up for him. The two of them got along better. They could often be found playing in the courtyard with a stash of marbles or pretending to be in the Palestinian resistance fighting the occupiers.

Iyad enjoyed watching his three eldest sisters knead dough and put it aside overnight to rise. The sisters took turns, and Sireen did it every third night. Then, after the morning prayer, Um Yousef took it to Um Fareed's *taboon* to bake it.

When Sireen wasn't kneading dough or performing other chores, she would be on the balcony upstairs, working on an assignment if it was a school night or listening to music on the radio and doodling in a notebook if it wasn't. Iyad would scuttle over to the balcony and snuggle next to her on the floor where she was seated on a cushion, her back and poofed hair leaning against a wall. She'd play with his hair, and he would ask her to tell him a story. On those mostly candlelit evenings, she mustered all the spirits of the *hakawati* to take him to different worlds.

Iyad loved a good story, and I was good at telling them. I made up such elaborate stories that the next day, when he'd ask me to tell them again or to continue them, I would have forgotten most of what I told him.

In such moments, Iyad sat mesmerized by Sireen. The stories brought him calm, no matter the type of story. And her voice! It created a sense that there was nothing else in the world. Sireen reveled in her brother's attention. Someone was hanging onto her words.

The balcony was the focal point of our youth. It extended across both upper rooms and looked out over the valley. But in 1984, my mother turned it into another room by putting up glass panels all around it.

In the summers, we used to eat and play on the balcony, and we even slept outside on many nights. I remember I cried when she had the panels installed.

My mother then furnished the balcony and the second room upstairs with seaweed-green sofas and armchairs, a walnut-brown oval dining table—that no one was ever allowed to use unless there were guests—and a large off-white china cabinet.

That same year, in 1984, my sisters Maysoun and Suzanne graduated from college in Amman, finishing at the same time because Suzanne had been held back by my mother to help around the house. My mother traveled for the graduation and my father, coming from Abu Dhabi, met her in Amman. She took with her my youngest brother, Diaa, who was just two years old, and left me with seven siblings to care for. By then, Suha was also around, born in 1978, and Sawsan in 1980. I remember I wanted to name Sawsan "Salam," after the previous year's Egyptian-Israeli peace treaty that I thought would usher in peace. Instead, it began a process of isolating the Palestinians from their Arab neighbors.

I used to wake up in the morning, make breakfast, and set it out for my brothers and sisters on a newspaper on the floor. I had to care for Baha but didn't have time because I had to study and take exams. I would give him to the neighbors and go to school. When I returned, I had to wash and fold clothes, give the younger ones showers, and cook. Of my oldest brothers, Yousef and Iyad were of little use. Only Ihab helped with the cooking.

I remember that my parents came back two days before the *tawjihi* exams taken in the last year of high school. They returned not speaking to each other, angry over something my mother's brother had said. That night I couldn't study because of their screaming and went to bed early. I told my mother to wake me up when she woke for the sunrise prayer. I needed to study because I got nothing done at night.

My mother didn't wake up early that morning. She was too tired and depressed from fighting the night before. I woke up startled by the school alarm of the boys' school near our house where they were administering all the exams.

I hurried to class and took my history book with me, ripping a chapter from the book. I answered all I could, then opened the ripped pages and began to cheat. The instructor caught me. I pleaded with him and explained that I had not been able to study. I had gotten a perfect score during the mid-semester exams and my grades were excellent. The instructor did not budge, and the incident ended up dropping my total grade from a 90 to the low 80s.

I followed in my sisters' footsteps after that, starting university in Amman. My father even met me there to get me ready for college. I remember going downtown together and choosing several colorful outfits. It was all unusual for a farming family. I consider myself and my older sisters lucky for *felaheen* in those days. My parents wanted us to study at a teachers' college in the West Bank, but we managed to convince them to let us study in Jordan instead.

It was important to Abu Yousef that all his girls get a proper education. At the time, the Israeli government's "open bridges" policy meant it was easy to come and go to Jordan, and the Jordanians still administered education in the West Bank. Thus, when each of the girls graduated from high school, their parents did not put up much resistance to the idea of them studying in Jordan. This was especially the case when Sireen left, for the situation in Palestine was quickly shifting and becoming less secure.

With the PLO's defeat and its departure from Lebanon in 1982, Palestinians in the West Bank and the Gaza Strip realized that *sumud*—steadfastness and perseverance—was not enough to liberate Palestine. They no longer had the option of waiting for others to wage the resistance on their behalf. Although there had always been acts of resistance, they increased markedly in 1982 with the mobilization of women's organizations, labor unions, professional and relief organizations, and students.

In the coming years, confrontations with the Israeli occupation forces intensified, reaching a breaking point in 1987, by which time the three eldest boys of the Sawalha family were teenagers. These changing conditions, occurring as they did as Yousef, Ihab, and Iyad were coming of age, would propel the family into a new chapter, one that would spiral it into the center of the struggle for Palestine.

Part II

"DON'T LEAVE ME HERE"

11

1987

"*Ya battal! Bravo 'aleyk!* I think you hit that soldier's shield," Yousef told Iyad with a smile, calling him a hero, one hand up in the air drawing a fist, as they both scurried out of view of the troops. Iyad was a great stone thrower for his age and felt proud when he got the respect of his eldest brother.

"Let's go. The troops are moving in, and they'll start making arrests and break up this protest soon," Yousef instructed. They were in the nearby village of Rameh whose streets Yousef knew well. Iyad followed his brother down an alleyway. Yousef had participated in at least ten protests that year and had a good sense of when it was time to run and when one could throw rocks. Iyad was still charged with adrenaline and felt invincible.

They bolted back home and arrived to Um Yousef's stern face examining them for clues of where they had been. She yelled at Yousef and asked if he wanted to continue to be reckless: "*Biddak tsee*'? Fine! I don't know what you're doing, but don't take your brothers." Iyad remained head down and silent behind his brother.

Um Yousef worried about her sons as demonstrations in Palestine became more frequent. No less than three thousand protests were recorded in the Gaza Strip and the West Bank from 1986 to 1987. The year 1987 began with the deportation of student leaders who were members of Fatah, the main political faction. They had been arrested during protests at Birzeit University in December of 1986. Fatah, along with other political factions, including the Palestinian Islamic Jihad and the Popular Front for the Liberation of Palestine (PFLP), protested the deportations. In some West Bank cities, the Israeli army tried to thwart the demonstrators with tear gas, live bullets, and university closures.

Yousef had been hearing of the protests, of people mobilizing to resist the occupation forces here and there in Palestine, and he got swept up with his older friends. Luckily for Um Yousef, the protests in Kufr Ra'i that Yousef took part in were smaller and were met with less force. But she struggled to contain him. She kept pushing him to come with her to the fields, but he went along less and less that year. At first, they argued often, but she couldn't keep him home. She just hoped her other two teenage sons would not be swept up by the same romantic thoughts of revolution.

Palestinians also began to take more action to rein in other Palestinians who were collaborating with the enemy. They particularly went after members of the Harakat al-Rawabet al-Filistiniyya, or Village Leagues, as they were called. The Israelis tried to pass off the Village Leagues as a means to peace and an alternative to the PLO. But the leagues were, in fact, an attempt by the Israeli military administration to win over collaborators among Palestinian peasants. It was, after all, an Israeli obsession to find native surrogates to manage the occupation as a way to make the conditions of colonization seem friendlier.

In the early 1980s, Um Yousef watched with great consternation as the leagues recruited members from the villages and installed village chiefs with the help of the Israelis. The earliest Village League was first declared in al-Khalil, الخليل, Hebron, in 1978, and expanded into an organized movement by the early 1980s. One branch was formed in nearby Qabatya, قباطية, a few towns northeast of Kufr Ra'i. This especially terrified Um Yousef, as she understood that between the nearby league and the collaborationist camp in Fahme, her village was sure to be overrun by its own traitors. The fact that she was alone, without Abu Yousef in the house, troubled her further. Without their father, she worried that other men might influence her boys. Abu Yousef, for his part, lived his days in Abu Dhabi with looming guilt. Um Yousef hoped her sons and daughters were raised with enough dignity to not fall for Israeli traps. The Village Leagues had considerable trouble finding any support, though. People in the villages militated against them, with several village heads facing assassination attempts.

As much as Um Yousef was afraid of anyone working with the Israelis in any capacity, she and other parents were not too keen about their children engaging in confrontations with the occupying army either, and the youth often found themselves caught in between the disciplining slaps of their parents and the fatal shots of Israeli gunfire. The more the youth read the various revolutionary pamphlets, the more the elders grew afraid, and it was not uncommon to hear Um Yousef and others scream, "You think you are going to free Palestine? Here, from this village?"

But the youth already knew the histories of their villages and the power of peasant resistance in the past. They had heard the stories from their ancestors who were involved in past armed revolts. Sireen's grandfather himself took part in hiding revolutionaries during the Arab Revolt, and it was from the nearby village of Ya'bad that the sparks of that revolt were ignited in 1935.

Beginning in August 1987, a series of Islamic Jihad operations by escapees from the Gaza Strip's central prison ignited the popular imagination, triggering lengthy curfews, house-to-house searches, and large-scale arrests. Sireen remembers parts of it, but she was mostly knee-deep in the monotony of her banking job—commuting between home and work, trying to stay proper, dealing with being a single woman away from home—and more concerned with her mother's invisible gaze than with the events unfolding back in Palestine.

On October 6, four Islamic Jihad prison escapees opened fire on an officer from the Israeli internal security forces, known as the Shin Bet or Shabak, and killed him. All four Palestinians were pursued and killed. Ten days of popular strikes and riots ensued, most confined to the Gaza Strip, but some also in the West Bank. Israeli forces responded by firing tear gas and live ammunition and demolishing houses of Islamic Jihad members in the Strip. In Kufr Ra'i, despite Um Yousef's attempts to run a tight ship at home, Yousef, Ihab, and Iyad were participating in a few smaller demonstrations. Yousef also spent long hours in political meetings with other young men from the village.

Two months later, an Israeli truck crashed into a station wagon carrying workers near the Jabalya refugee camp in the Gaza Strip at the Erez Crossing, killing four and wounding ten. It was seen as retaliation for the stabbing and killing of an Israeli businessperson in the Strip two days earlier by an unknown person. Some say this last episode lit the flames that were carried into the West Bank, igniting more sustained and coordinated action for the next five years. Yet the tinder must be gathered and properly set. While the truck crash may have been the spark, the years of protests and acts of resistance, and the long organizing prior to 1987, stoked the fire of what may have looked like a spontaneous uprising.

Um Yousef tried to ensure that her sons remained at a distance from the explosive uprising—what was soon referred to as the intifada, an uprising or "shaking off." Each day brought important turns, mobilizations, and milestones, some events intensifying in meaning, others receding in the overall retelling of history. One event remains particularly ingrained in people's minds: the formation of the Islamic Resistance Movement, Hamas, one month after the incident near the Jabalya camp. Hamas was established as the activist arm of the Muslim Brotherhood in the Gaza Strip, but it departed from the parent organization's traditional goal to re-Islamize society, foregrounding the Palestinian struggle and resistance instead.

While it could be said that confrontations between the Islamic Jihad and the Israeli army opened the gates to the intifada, it really began with people of all ages protesting. Rock-throwing teenagers on the front line captured the world's attention—they were known as *atfal al-hijara*, children of the stones. Soon, the uprising became more coordinated and was directed by a Unified National Leadership (UNL) composed of Fatah, the PFLP, the Palestine Communist Party, and other leftist factions loyal to the PLO leadership. The PLO was now based in Tunisia, and it issued communiqués but could not control internal events in the Occupied Palestinian Territory. The Islamic Jihad and Hamas remained outside the UNL as they were not part of the PLO, but they too sustained the uprising.

Alongside these groups, a vast network of organizations—unions, village collectives, professional organizations, and refugee committees—resisted mostly through mass actions involving demonstrations, general strikes, boycotts, and tax strikes. The UNL itself called for general strikes on the ninth day of every month. Soon, armed elements also entered the fray. One group, the Fahd al-Aswad (Black Panther organization), would emerge as an armed wing of Fatah, combating the occupier but also taking it upon itself to weed out collaborators. Because of Kufr Ra'i's proximity to both the collaborationist camp in Fahme and the Village League in Qabatya, Yousef believed that the Fahd al-Aswad was going to be crucial to the success of the uprising. Iyad would soon adopt his older brother's views but take them a few steps further.

Sireen followed the events of 1987 from Amman, but she knew next to nothing of how her brothers were involved. She also knew little about most of the political parties, except for the more prominent Fatah party led by Yasser Arafat. Boys in the village, including her brothers, were supporters. The demonstrations gave Sireen and her friends in Amman hope. But she found herself more concerned with how to carve out a space away from the prying eyes of her mother than with the events back home.

In Jordan, I studied Islamic banking, and after graduating in the spring of 1987, I began work in Amman for Bank el-Iskan in public relations and marketing. The Housing Bank for Trade and Finance occupied one of the biggest buildings, a landmark in the Shmeisani neighborhood. I worked there for three years.

Even though travel to and from Jordan became more difficult that year due to the protests, my parents haunted my everyday life—my mother especially. After finishing university, she wrote me almost every week and sent letters with someone coming from Palestine. In them, she told me how she had nightmares of me meeting men.

"I saw you liked someone; I saw you got engaged; I saw you ran off with someone." I had a whole box of these letters. I threw them all away when I got married because I hated them. They were her nightmares, but they haunted me every time I was out, every time a man talked to me.

Sireen felt as if she were under constant surveillance, tormented. Once, she went on a trip to the gold market and received a letter from her mother a few days later. Her mother's cousin had spotted her in the market with a group of her friends, which also included men. Her mother's presence, an apparition, beset her life and paralyzed her. She reflects back on herself and how much she cared about and feared what Um Yousef might think.

Stupid me!

Yet, still, Sireen strongly resisted wearing a headscarf. She preferred her shoulder-length hair blow-dried, curled, and loose. She often wore skirts right below the knee, or long dresses with short sleeves, always full of vibrant colors.

In Kufr Ra'i, it was an absolute sin for me to go out and hang laundry without covering my head. We had a green steel gate that was almost taller than our house, but still, if I went out to the balcony on the second floor, people could see me, and I would get into arguments with my mother over that. Even the roof had a fence, but if my head showed, then it needed to be covered.

I thought this conversation would end when I married, but it has followed me relentlessly all my life. It didn't help that I was the only one in the family who refused to wear a headscarf. When Suzanne and Maysoun finished high school and went to Jordan, they both began to wear it. I was expected to do the same when I finished my *tawjihi* exams.

As a compromise, my parents both insisted that if I did not wear the headscarf in Jordan, then I had to do so at least whenever I returned to the village. During my winter visits, I wore a cap and a shawl. In the summer, I wore a shawl wrapped very loosely over my hair.

We fought so much over this. If I prayed and fasted, and I didn't do anything wrong, why should people force me to do something that I was not convinced of? This is not something from our religion. Islam is not like this.

But that was it . . . I spent six years in Jordan, and beyond refusing to wear the headscarf, I never did anything rebellious. Imagine that! On most days I regret it.

12

Early 1988

In Kufr Ra'i, a group of boys from Yousef's circle of friends joined a nearby Fahd al-Aswad cell. The Fahd al-Aswad had just come into existence some months earlier and began mobilizing in Qabatya, where a Village League had been formed years ago. In its early days, the Fahd al-Aswad restricted its operations to the district of Jenin, targeting the Israeli military and those Palestinians who collaborated with it. But soon, the organization grew, and cells were formed across the West Bank and the Gaza Strip.

The definition of a collaborator was quite broad, and the charge could be leveled at anyone suspected of undermining the national struggle. A *simsar*, or real estate agent, who facilitated the selling of Palestinian land to settlers or the Jewish National Fund was considered a collaborator. The less dangerous *wasit*, the intermediary who facilitated services rendered by the occupation forces, was also a collaborator. Another kind was the far more dangerous *'ameel musallah*, or armed collaborator, who often accompanied Israeli army special forces on raids of homes of political activists. The *jasous*, the spy or informant, was anyone who provided the occupier with information about political activities in a particular area. There were lesser-discussed types of collaborators too, such as the economic collaborator who pushed Israeli products into the Palestinian market, the political collaborator who implemented long-term Israeli policies, and the infiltrator, who might infiltrate national organizations. What to do with collaborators was a source of great debate within Palestinian society. But while Palestinians debated, the Israeli internal security forces, the Shin Bet, were eager to use Palestinians in any way they could, and they would never miss an opportunity to recruit a Palestinian collaborator.

While the Israeli prison system was one avenue for recruitment, the permit system was another. Palestinians needed permits for virtually everything. They needed one to travel abroad, to print and publish, to start a business, or to build a home; the list went on and on. In order to apply for a permit, they needed a collection of forms and stamps for the application, and the process took forever. Thus, it was no surprise that collaborators could be recruited from among parents desperate to obtain a permit so that a severely ill child could go abroad for medical attention. University graduates eager for permits to secure employment formed another vulnerable group.

The Fahd al-Aswad around Kufr Ra'i and elsewhere in the Jenin District decided to finally deal with Palestinian collaborators, systematically and severely. Every few weeks, they took collaborators into the hills and interrogated them in secret caves. They would tie up suspected collaborators, beat them, and record a confession tape. The next morning, they would go to the mosque and play the tape on the loudspeaker to let the town know that the person was an 'ameel. The traitor would then usually run away and go live in '48 Palestine or try to defend themselves against these accusations. In many cases, the suspected collaborator was killed before they had the opportunity to do either.

Sometimes, the Fahd al-Aswad got it wrong, and the family of the presumed traitor, or sometimes the person themselves if they were allowed to live, received a letter from the PLO stating that this person was innocent. This created internal tension between people. Some began to wonder if people were using the charge of treason to settle personal scores.

Yousef was not a member of the Fahd al-Aswad, but he did accompany a group of boys on one operation against a suspected collaborator. It was his first, and would be his last.

"Osama Saleh, the *mukhtar*!" announced Firas, one of Yousef's childhood friends. He was referring to the head of a nearby village.

"What?" came a response from another boy in the group.

"These are the directives I've been given."

"But he's almost seventy years old," someone exclaimed.

"All the more reason. Who would suspect him, no?"

Yousef agreed, but his skepticism was visible on his face.

"The *mukhtar* has to deal with Israelis all the time," said another of Yousef's friends. "He has to deal with them to get permits and other paperwork authorized for everyone in the village."

"But he's not the only one to deal with Israelis. We can't suspect everyone who has dealings with them. This is what they want us to do!" one of the boys said, trying to put up a fight. But it was timid—no match for the older, more confident Firas.

"Osama Saleh always goes to the Israeli-Palestinian coordination office nearby, and he's there all day. What do you think he is doing in the coordination office? People come in after him to get paperwork done, and they are out before he leaves. What is the *mukhtar* doing that takes so long?"

People were talking. Firas was not alone in his general suspicion of village leaders. Many in the West Bank had questions about them. It wasn't the first time such talk circulated, and the Israelis knew this well. They often kept people in their offices for longer than they needed in order to plant seeds of doubt among other Palestinians who would walk in and notice the person. Or they deliberately called someone to the military administration office during lunch breaks and at peak times, so people would see a person going to the office and suspicion would be born. And suspicion is like rumor, and rumor like wildfire. Once it spreads, it consumes any possibility of truth, and the suspect, like the forest, is defenseless in its path.

Some days passed since the boys first mentioned Osama Saleh, the village chief. Yousef and his friends continued to discuss the man's life. "My father saw the *mukhtar* whispering to the lieutenant at the coordination office when he went to renew a work permit," one of the boys announced. Another added that the *mukhtar* was friendly with a known collaborator. A third mentioned that someone had seen him in a car with an Israeli. The more they talked about him, the more the group got excited, and the larger the plot grew. The boys began to suspect the *mukhtar*'s friends, believing he had organized them into a cell of collaborators. They decided they would confront him.

That day, my mother had prepared *maqloubeh* for lunch. The family was all together when Yousef heard a voice from outside, a signal. In an instant, he jumped up and shot out of the house. He darted past Iyad, who had not yet joined the lunch table. He passed our donkey and the rabbits in the yard, stopped for a second by a pile of *shwal* in the storage area, and grabbed one and kept running.

My mother called out to him, but he did not turn around. My father—back from Abu Dhabi for good that same year—rose to chase Yousef, but he was too slow. Ihab took off after his brother, and Iyad followed. But they were no match for Yousef's pace, and he outran them both.

When Yousef and his friends congregated, there were at least ten boys, all dressed in black masks and gloves, with plastic bags on their shoes to obscure their footprints. Yousef had ripped the *shwal* and slipped it over his head so the sack covered his body. But in his haste, he had not flipped it inside out. Our family name, which my mother printed on them, was visible on his back. What amateurs! Imagine how funny he looked trying to be in disguise! Ha!

The boys started on their way to the *mukhtar*'s house. Yousef was at the back of the group. They reached a fork in the road that led to the *mukhtar*'s house in one direction and to the *mukhtar*'s friend's house, Taha, in the other. At that intersection, Firas stopped.

"We should go to Taha's house instead. He's a traitor as well, I didn't tell you earlier. Yalla, let's go."

The boys were stunned. Several of them did not like this change. They protested, but Firas was determined, as though he had planned this all in his head. But why? The boys didn't ask. They were too excited and caught up in the moment. They had to act fast.

"Okay. Yalla, let's go," one of them shouted. This was enough to prevent any second thoughts. The boys followed Firas.

Minutes later, they arrived at Taha's house. Ihab and Iyad followed, but they remained in the distance so as not to blow their cover. They watched as the events unfolded.

Taha was with his son and some relatives. It was shortly after Friday prayer, around lunchtime, and his son—top of his class—was back from his studies at law school in Jordan.

Four or five boys from the group barged in and screamed Taha's first name with none of the formalities or respect the young normally have for an older man in his sixties. His son jumped out at them in defense. "What do you want from my father?" he yelled.

"Your father is a traitor, and we are here to interrogate him."

"My father is not a traitor. Your fathers are traitors. You sons of dogs!"

After those words, from outside, Yousef could only hear a clamor—a crashing chair, a table grinding against the floor, smashing plates, the staccato "No! No! No!" of people shouting, and the sounds of a struggle. Then commotion suddenly turned into one penetrating scream.

"Baba!"

The boys exited and scattered. Taha stumbled out, holding his body, blood spilling everywhere. A relative came out next, his eyes maddened and seeking revenge. In his hand was the bloody knife one of the boys had used to stab Taha.

As the relative walked out into the sun, he came across Yousef, who, for a moment, stood frozen. The relative collided into him.

Yousef ran, huffing and puffing but not feeling the blood nor the pain that came from the open wound in his side. Adrenaline carried him until he was far away from the commotion. And even when he finally stopped running and saw blood on his shirt, he thought it was someone else's. He looked around to see if anyone was following. He knew he was still not out of danger.

As soon as word got out from the screams of Taha's son, an informant in town told the Israelis that there was an altercation. They would encircle the village in a matter of minutes. Yousef had to get out or his fate could be death or imprisonment. As he stood panting, back bent, and now clutching his wound, Ihab and Iyad, with jaws dropped, sprinted over to him. They had witnessed it all and recognized him. Yousef wasn't exactly incognito with his family's name visible on his back, plastered on the canvas sack, the *shwal*, for the whole town to see.

Neither brother asked any questions. They each grabbed one of Yousef's arms and put it over their shoulders. Ihab carried most of the weight while Iyad struggled. They walked a short distance with him to the main road.

There, they hailed a car, bundled him in, and took off in the direction of Nablus. Even though the hospital was farther away, the boys felt it would be safer there because the Israelis would expect them in Jenin. Iyad helped Yousef apply pressure to his wound. He had seen blood before as people were shot in protests, but this was the blood of his oldest brother. Shock and distress appeared on Iyad's face as he told his brother to hang on until they arrived at the hospital.

Yousef's wound was deep. The knife had penetrated my brother's kidneys and come close to puncturing his stomach. The Israelis were searching for him and the others involved in Taha's stabbing. In the hospital in Nablus, doctors cleaned him up and stitched up his wound quickly, then his friends arrived and smuggled him out to the village of Saida, near Tulkarem.

Soldiers came looking for him in Saida.

Yousef's friends hid him in a house somewhere near the village and tended to him for almost two months. They changed his bandages and fed him regularly, but he lost a lot of weight. As soon as he was able to walk, my father sent him to Jordan.

He remained in Jordan for a year after the wound healed. We finally arranged for him to make it to a university in Kansas. It was much easier to get to the US in those days. He had finished high school and was top of his class, so with a university acceptance and an affidavit of funding support from my uncle in Jeddah, he made it to America.

Meanwhile, the actual assailant, masked and unidentifiable, escaped while family members and neighbors rushed to aid Haj Taha, who lay on the floor, grabbing his chest in agony and slowly losing consciousness. A group of men lifted him and scrambled to get him in a car to the hospital.

Haj Taha was dead on arrival. The nurses and doctors tried to revive his arrested heart but could do nothing. Later in the afternoon, the family held a funeral for the old man, with townspeople unsure whether to attend the burial of a suspected collaborator.

The boys were heroes. At least, they must have thought that. They had killed Taha, the traitor. To understand him as a poor shepherd, a man who had nothing, would have shattered them. He had to be the traitor. Thus, he was.

And often, the people they suspected were indeed traitors. But in this particular case, Taha wasn't. Some days later, a brief investigation by village elders found no evidence of collaboration, and the Fatah party also exonerated him. It was a case of misinformation. Yet the Fahd al-Aswad was too feared by then for anyone to take revenge, lest the act of revenge be seen as treason.

Haj Taha's son, struggling with the open wound of loss, turned into a successful and respected man. But lost spirits have a way of holding onto our mind and body. Thirty years later, he would reserve comment about that day save for a few words:

> Much time has passed since the death of my father. And I have no desire now, or no ability actually, to search into the past. It is enough that I remember that event continually, no less during his yearly memorial. And each time I cry. I cry at the thought of injustice Palestinians commit on themselves and on their Palestinian brothers.

13

Late 1988

Iyad woke up with the rest of his siblings at the break of dawn, but he was always slower to move, dreading the idea of school. He stumbled to the sink and washed his face. His three older sisters had all left the house by now, either married like Suzanne and Maysoun, or off at college in Amman, like Sireen; Yousef, too, had left a few months earlier. Still, the house was brimming with the energy of eight kids.

Ihab yelled out for his younger brother. The morning was clear and chilly, and his voice pierced the silence like the blare of a tractor at dawn. Iyad walked out calmly, banana in hand, as if he had all the time in the world. Ihab and Iyad were inseparable, the best of friends. Ihab was often frustrated by his younger brother's attitude, delinquency, and impulsiveness, whereas Iyad found his elder brother to be too timid and a mama's boy. They both helped their mother with the harvest, but Ihab did so more often than his little brother.

The brothers were different in a few ways. Ihab saw himself as the one who always tried to keep the peace, and Iyad was the one stirring up trouble—oftentimes in misguided attempts to protect his older brother. Ihab remembers his brother's recklessness and ability to insert himself into fights even when they had nothing to do with him.

Once, they were playing in an alleyway when Ihab encountered two boys, and they began to talk. Iyad soon noticed the boys laughing at his brother, who looked upset, so Iyad rushed over. Without warning, he jumped between them and pushed one of the boys, putting him in a headlock. There was a little scuffle, and Ihab and the other boy jumped in to break it up.

Over time, Ihab came to expect his younger brother to step in to defend him whenever a confrontation arose.

Every morning, the two boys set off in silence. They wore blue jeans and T-shirts. Iyad had black shoes that were visibly worn—hand-me-downs from Yousef. When they arrived at school, the boys split up, though not for long. They typically spent all their recesses together, often playing basketball.

Iyad joined his friends in class. The mood on this November day was particularly somber. School had not been in session for a week after the Israelis had imposed closures in retaliation for student strikes and kids in town protesting daily despite curfews. During that week, Iyad, Ihab, and many of their friends had taken to the streets, confronting Israelis with rocks that were met with live gunfire.

A large protest had broken out at the outskirts of the village. There were boys and men of all ages, some women too. Iyad and Ihab were there, as were Fouad al-Ashgar and Jalal al-Aris, two friends of Sireen's from her school days.

I remember Jalal, our neighbor's son. He used to like me. In high school, he once brought a megaphone and started shouting the answers to an exam so I could cheat. Imagine—this was considered flirting! We were in different buildings, so when the boys finished their exams early, they ran out with a megaphone and shouted out answers to the rest of us. We couldn't date or even look at each other in the street, so this was their way of showing they liked us.

Iyad followed Jalal and Fouad close behind, admiring their bravery as they faced dozens of armed soldiers and threw rocks. Not long into the protest, as Fouad threw a rock, a soldier shot him in the leg. Fouad darted across the street and into an alleyway. Iyad and Ihab remained out of sight, unable to cross the street, and watched the soldiers give chase. Jalal tried to give Fouad more time to escape by distracting the troops. He began throwing rocks with more intensity, empowered rather than afraid.

Jalal did not last more than a few moments before being shot by an Israeli soldier. The wound was fatal, and he did not make it to the hospital. My brothers, helpless as bullets rained over them, saw him fall that day.

Fouad had managed to run to Jamila the seamstress's house and hide from the soldiers. Jamila was a 1948 refugee from Haifa and lived alone with her cats. The Israelis followed Fouad to her house. When they found him, a soldier pushed him to the ground and beat him. Another soldier choked him with a boot to his neck. Fouad struggled; he tried to push the soldier's foot away, but he had lost too much blood and was too weak. The Israeli held his foot there until Fouad suffocated.

Fouad and Jalal were my age. We graduated together. And just like that, they were gone for throwing rocks. And I heard about it over a phone call while in Jordan.

A few days later, Iyad sat in class, subdued like the protests. He was day-dreaming, searching for clues about his future, while a teacher conducted a lesson as if the protests of the previous week were a normal part of life. Maybe the teacher was right—maybe they were a normal part of life.

With his fingers supporting his chin, he wondered about his role in the latest protests. He wished he had done more. Was it seeing Yousef injured that made Iyad more determined? Was it several years earlier, when he saw Fouad and Jalal throwing rocks in a protest? Was there even a single moment he could point to? Later, whenever anyone asked, he would always say that his path was determined when they kicked his father out in 1948. But in that classroom, all Iyad knew was that after the Israelis killed Fouad and Jalal, he would not remain helpless the next time Zionist forces suffocated his village.

🌿

Three months later, four boys from Kufr Ra'i were on their way to the nearby village of Fahme to play football. Ihab was one of them; Iyad had stayed home that day. It was a cool morning, and the sun's rays kept the boys warm, hugging their bodies and caressing their faces. On the way, the boys kicked pebbles, goofed around, and teased the youngest, fourteen-year-old Salameh Sbeih. He was a tough kid with a large radiant smile. He enjoyed being in the company of Ihab and the other older boys, so he laughed at their jokes. One of the boys ruffled Salameh's hair and looked at him with a gentle smile.

They had been walking for some time on the road between the two villages when they heard gunfire from the direction of Fahme. The view to the village was unobstructed from where they stood, just a long hilly road ahead of them. Some teenagers were throwing rocks at soldiers who looked like they were retreating into their vehicle. In their excitement, the four boys decided to get closer and continue to Fahme. As they neared the scene, two Israeli military jeeps came speeding from behind them. The boys turned and saw the vehicles headed for them. Alarmed, they left the football to bounce down the path and ran for cover in the village streets. Salameh was fast, but he lagged slightly behind with his shorter legs. "*Yalla*, come on, run! We need to hide!" Ihab instructed.

As the jeeps drew closer and came into a clear line of sight, several soldiers began to shoot at the boys. "Guys, run faster! Run!" one of the boys screamed, his steps becoming lighter as he tried to pick up speed.

Several bullets struck Salameh. He fell to the ground. The others slowed momentarily. Was there something they could do? They saw the soldiers get out of their vehicle near Salameh, who was rolling in agony and crying. The boys picked up their pace.

When the Israeli soldiers got out, they beat and kicked Salameh, and when he lost consciousness, they dragged his limp body into their vehicle. Before they took off, villagers from Fahme had already made it to the scene and a Palestinian doctor had wanted to treat the boy's wounds. The Israelis had refused.

Later, village council members found Salameh's lifeless body at a local military headquarters. He had three gunshot wounds, several bruises, a bloodied mouth, and a broken nose. His funeral drew a huge crowd. Men and boys came from the surrounding villages to express their anger. The intifada had yet another martyr.

Of the three other boys that day, one managed to escape, the second was shot in the back, and the third saved the injured boy's life. That third boy was Ihab, who deceived his injured friend by telling him the wound was from a rock and to keep running.

When the first sounds of gunfire were heard in Kufr Ra'i that morning, Iyad jumped to his feet. It took him a few moments to determine the direction of the shots, but when he realized they came from Fahme and that his brother was on his way there, he dashed out of the house. He passed his mother in the courtyard, who shouted for him to get back inside. He brushed her off with his arm and yelled that he was off to check on Ihab. He was partly overcome with worry for his brother and partly motivated by the excitement of confronting his enemy.

When he arrived in Fahme, villagers were still arguing with the soldiers

to get Salameh medical treatment. Iyad saw that it was too late for any confrontation and, hearing about Salameh, panicked that Ihab might also be
injured. He went in search of his brother, asking neighbors if anyone had
taken cover in their homes.

He finally found Ihab and his injured friend hiding in an alleyway. They
had been waiting for the army to clear the village, afraid they would otherwise be pursued and denied medical attention. Iyad put the boy's arm over
his shoulder and, together with Ihab, got the attention of a passerby who
found them a car. They loaded the boy in and rushed him to a hospital, where
the boy underwent surgery and survived.

The episode was a turning point for Ihab. He would not remain in Palestine for much longer. Iyad, on the other hand, was determined to fight back.

14

Late 1989

فلسطين حرة

"Palestine is Free"

Iyad and three other friends were standing on the lookout for Israeli soldiers while one of the boys painted those words on the wall of a house that lined the street running through Kufr Ra'i. Raising the Palestinian flag or writing the word Palestine on the wall could land you three years in jail. The boy wrote with an unsteady hand, with black paint that dripped down the side of the wall. It competed with several other slogans and a Fatah party poster peeling at the sides and faded by the sun.

There were no lit lampposts. The boys found shelter in darkness, though the half-moon on a clear night made them more conspicuous than they liked. How many times had they done this over the last year? How many times had they escaped the grip of patrolling Israelis? Iyad had lost count. He never let his guard down, but he grew more confident. Although it was rare, other kids had been caught by soldiers for painting walls. The Israelis didn't treat this act of protest lightly, as the slogans and graffiti turned the occupied walls into spaces of free expression. Graffiti was used to vent frustration, to communicate news and directives, to assert existence, to mobilize the people, and to threaten the enemy.

When the boy was done with the graffiti, he gave them a signal. Before they scattered, Iyad looked on at the message. It was defiant, refusing to recognize the occupation. He was gratified by this. The aspirational meaning of the words gave him a sense of dignity. They intimated a way to fight for a free Palestine by acting as if one, as if Palestine, were already free.

Iyad's house was closest, and he sprinted to the slightly open front gate. He squeezed through, barely moving the partly rusted joints that might have woken up his parents.

It was a futile attempt. Um Yousef heard his footsteps, opened her eyes briefly, then shut them tightly and humphed. She had stopped waking up at night to throw her fits after several months of the same routine. She waited for the morning, leaving Iyad to guess what daylight might bring.

At dawn, always first to wake, Um Yousef walked over to Iyad's mattress and kicked his behind. "Where were you last night?"

She kicked him again. "Where!"

Iyad startled and sat up. She smacked him on the head several times as he tried to get cover, unsuccessfully deflecting her attacks. "I was out with friends," Iyad remarked, accompanied by a giddy laugh.

"Where?"

"Out!" He said again, snickering, and jumping away as his mother tried to catch him. Her efforts to whip sense into him were as futile as Iyad's efforts to evade her blows.

"Mama, leave him alone. He's a teenager," Suzanne interjected. She was now living in Dubai and was back home for a visit. But Um Yousef was relentless. She sensed Iyad was politically involved and knew better than her daughter the mood on the streets. She saw what the boys in the village were doing—how they were confronting Israelis, standing up to their military machines as if they were invincible. And she had been to their funerals and had already almost lost a son. She was not about to risk another one. She would rather accommodate injustice. So she tried to discipline liberation out of his blood to save him.

Abu Yousef was right beside her. The loss of his home in 1948 was a deep scar, and he recalled his heartbreaking visit back to his village over a decade earlier with Sireen. But he was older now, and although he believed in the need to resist, he was unwilling to give his son to the resistance. It was all futile, though. Ihab had left for Amman five months earlier after graduating from high school, and ever since, Iyad shut his ears to whatever his family had to say. Standing lookout was just the beginning.

Several days later, Iyad marched out into the school courtyard with a megaphone in hand. He stood as if he were on a stage, precisely in the middle, as though he had previously marked the position with a spike. Without pausing, he announced to the students that a protest was taking place at the entrance to the village. This was the only way he could have any chance of getting students to participate, because Israeli military rule forbade gatherings in groups. Talking to children in school, where they already congregated, was the easiest way to mobilize them. And sure enough, when students at recess heard Iyad's announcement, many rushed out to join the protest.

Only minutes earlier, Iyad had barged into the headmaster's office with a mission. "What do you want?" the headmaster exclaimed. Iyad said nothing. He went straight to one corner, grabbed a megaphone that was resting against a wall, then started to head out.

"What are you doing?" the headmaster asked loudly. "Put that down! Give it back to me!"

Iyad was almost out of the room. At the door, he paused, looked at the headmaster, then pulled the office door keys out of the lock, stepped outside, slammed the door behind him, and locked the headmaster in his office. The headmaster ran to the door and pulled at the handle, but it was too late. Iyad had locked him in. "Iyad! You're making a big mistake. Come back and unlock the door, and I'll forgive you," he said. But Iyad did not look back.

That day, he gathered around forty students and led them out of school to join a protest at the edge of the village to oppose the establishment of a new settlement near the town of Qalqilya, قلقيلية. There, for two hours, Iyad and his schoolmates threw rocks while others chanted, all of them dodging rubber bullets and trying to stay alive.

The next day, the headmaster called Iyad and his mother into his office. The conversation was short. This was not the first time he had created problems at school. Iyad no longer cared about his grades and was failing. He was expelled.

At the age of fifteen, Iyad was sent off to Qalandia Technical Institute to learn to be a mechanic. It was there, in Qalandia, قلنديا—between Jerusalem and Ramallah—that he really began to get involved in resistance activities and developed his political network and connections.

Iyad was often harassed by Israeli soldiers who were on patrol. They stopped him once near the Grand Mosque of Qalandia. Another time, they questioned him as he was walking onto Ramallah Street from the refugee camp. They asked him where he was going, where he had been, what he was doing out on the street. They asked him simply because they could. And because he had no choice but to answer.

In Qalandia, he also partook in weekly protests, taking to the front line to throw rocks at soldiers. In the evenings, he engaged with new friends in discussions about the future of the intifada and debated who in town might be a collaborator. Among these friends was a teenager named Daoud, who Iyad knew from Kufr Ra'i and with whom he developed a closer relationship. Daoud was two years older, a smooth talker, and one of those people who seemed to know everything about everything, or at least thought he did. Together, they formed a cell of the Fahd al-Aswad, an armed group associated with Fatah. It seemed like the obvious choice because Iyad knew of them through his brother and everyone in his circle was a supporter of Fatah. Iyad went along with them.

At first, he organized in Qalandia, but then much of his activities focused on Kufr Ra'i and the surrounding areas. He recruited Noor from Kufr Ra'i, a young man slightly older than him, street smart, with connections acquiring weapons—mostly handguns and M16 assault rifles. Over the next two years, while Iyad and the Fahd al-Aswad confronted Israelis in various towns and villages, he, along with Daoud, Noor, and others in his cell, developed a reputation for meticulously hunting down collaborators—informants, spies, and traitors of all types. To free Palestine, they believed they had to clean house first to avoid infiltration, to avoid being surrounded. But the business of identifying collaborators was messy, and more mistakes would be made along the way.

15

1990

Iyad was on the run. As part of the Fahd al-Aswad, he had been involved in several armed confrontations with Israelis. In Tulkarem, he managed to escape through back roads into nearby hills after they injured an Israeli soldier. Near Qalandia, he and his comrades shot at an Israeli patrol vehicle and killed a soldier. Again they escaped unharmed, this time making it to a safe house in a nearby town as the Israeli army searched for them in Qalandia.

Abu Yousef and Um Yousef had long ago lost the battle of trying to steer him toward his studies and getting a regular job. Now, when he spent time at home, they were mostly happy to see him and worried for his safety. They didn't ask about specifics, but sometimes Abu Yousef and his son talked about the larger political developments of the day. Abu Yousef had been inspired by the intifada and was still hopeful it would bring about his return to his village of Taybeh. Iyad always reassured them and insisted he was safe and studying at the Qalandia Technical Institute. Um Yousef wanted to believe him, but she also knew she could not rein in her son's commitment to freedom. A part of both his parents admired his passion. They believed more Palestinians needed to have this determination. But they feared the cost and hated living in anticipation of it.

By May of that year, their family was complete—maybe not as they might have imagined it, with half their children dispersed around the world, but it was a family nonetheless. Their final two children were girls. Salam was born in 1984, and Esraa, the youngest, in 1990, the year Saddam Hussein invaded Kuwait and promised the liberation of Palestine.

By the time Esraa arrived, none of the older girls, Maysoun, Suzanne, or Sireen, were living in Palestine, nor were the three older boys around. Suzanne and Maysoun had both married, the former moving to Dubai and the latter to Jeddah. Sireen was still in Amman, Yousef was in the US, and Ihab was in Russia. Iyad was mostly away from home, in Qalandia, and later, when he was done with technical school, he spent time in the surrounding towns and villages of the northern part of the West Bank—mostly Nablus, Tulkarem, and Jenin.

Sireen returned from Amman in May to meet her newborn sister, Esraa. She was only planning to be there for a few days and was hoping to spend time with Iyad.

Because of my brother's activities with the Fahd al-Aswad, the Israelis started appearing at our house more often in search of him. These visits became so frequent to the point that my mother could spot military jeeps from a distance when they were headed for our village.

Once, while Suzanne was in town visiting, my mother hid Iyad under the bed of Suzanne's newborn son. A second time, he hid behind the front door. When the soldiers barged in, he lodged himself into a space behind the front door and the wall, and they could not find him. They searched every room, tore up mattresses, and opened our fridge, only to find it filled with books and loose papers. It made them pause and break down in laughter. My mother had bought it for show, but that day, it served yet another purpose. It distracted the soldiers, who walked out of the house empty-handed a few minutes later. Sometimes Iyad would just escape from a backdoor that led into the hills where he could quickly hide, and they wouldn't pursue him.

Iyad came home on the second day of Sireen's visit. They met with warm smiles, a comfortable affection in the crinkling of their eyes. They hugged tightly, and Iyad kissed her forehead. Um Yousef had made Sireen's favorite dish for lunch, *maqloubeh*, and they spent the rest of the afternoon catching up.

Later that night, everyone went to sleep except for Sireen and Iyad. The house was quiet as they sat under a dim flickering kerosene light in the glass-enclosed balcony, enjoying a June breeze through two of its open windows. Iyad was wearing a gray tracksuit and bent over to fix his crew socks. He then turned to his sister and asked, "Can you make me dinner?"

"Really?" I exclaimed. "No way, it's too dark!"

"Yalla . . . you barely ever see me." Iyad was persistent. "Please don't make me get up. I miss your food." He gave me a smile and was being annoying.

"No, you don't," I said. "Khalas, I'm tired."

"Yalla. Please. For me," he continued to nag.

In the end I caved and said fine. But I told him it wouldn't be anything fancy. Just fried eggs, *labneh*, and a plate of *zeit ou za'atar.*

Then, suddenly, we heard dogs bark in the distance.

Sireen startled, and the barking grew much louder. Iyad looked into his sister's eyes. She could see the worry in the lowering of his eyebrows and the biting of his lip. But his steady shoulders showed the confidence of a man who had been in this situation many times before.

The barking was followed by the sound of engines revving as vehicles gained speed. Iyad and Sireen looked out and saw lights flare from two military vehicles rumbling up the road.

Iyad slipped on his shoes, double knotted the laces, and clicked the back door open.

I had just enough time to dip two pieces of bread in za'atar mixed with oil. I slipped them into my brother's hand. He grabbed a banana, his favorite fruit, and set off.

From the back exit, he passed Um Farid's house and the houses of two other neighbors. Then it was just him, a long winding path, and the dark hills ahead, with no homes and not a soul in sight.

Soldiers knocked on the front gate, disturbing the jasmine tree. Sireen took her time to open it. When she did, they questioned her briefly, but when a neighbor's dog barked behind the house and further up the road, they knew Iyad had snuck out. They hurried back to their vehicle in chase.

Iyad sprinted up the main path, then slipped out of sight, using shrubs to hide his path. He melted into the rugged landscape, gliding in the darkness through rocky paths he had used many times before. In a few short minutes, he had scrambled down the hill on which his home was perched and made it halfway up another hill.

Military vehicles hunted him down the dirt path, moving slowly. The soldiers scanned the area, but their view was limited, as they were unwilling to trek into the valley.

Iyad came to a cave within one of the surrounding hills. He entered and covered the opening with rocks and branches. There he waited, passing the time trying to pick zaʿatar out of his teeth and hoping snakes in the wild would let him be. By the time the military had finished scanning the area from afar, he had dozed off.

The next morning, he walked into the family house covered in white dust, and Sireen could breathe again.

16

Fall 1990

Sireen was in Amman working in parent relations at the newly formed Rawdat al-Maʿaref Schools and College, which was owned by a family from Jerusalem. She had left her position at the bank the year before. Her job didn't usually involve greeting parents, but it so happened that she was at the front desk filling in for a friend on one particular day.

Two days later, a man called my workplace. He was direct. He told me that he had noticed me when he came in with a friend who was picking up a child. It was the day I had been working at the front desk. He was looking for a wife and asked me if he could get to know me better.

My parents would never allow it. They had been trying to find me a suitor, but so far all their efforts had amounted to nothing because every time a man was suggested by a relative or friend in the village, he was not good enough for my parents—not educated enough, not respectable enough, not from a well-to-do family, not from the right region in Palestine. There was always something. They would have a heart attack if word got back to them that we had met. And word always got back.

I told him that if he wanted to see me again, he had to come to my work. The next day, he came by toward the end of the workday, and we spoke briefly. He had come from the US and wanted to date first as they do there, but I explained that I could not go out with him in the way that he wanted.

He stayed for less than an hour, but the walls have ears, and her parents found out.

It felt like my father was in Amman the next day with an ultimatum: I could either get married or return with him to Palestine.

Earlier that August, Saddam Hussein had invaded Kuwait. There were worries that the Israelis would retaliate against the Palestinians if Saddam attacked the Israelis. My father said that it was unacceptable that I stay in Jordan. "You can't stay here, and we don't know what is happening with this war," he told me.

In the short time between the man's visit to my school and my father's arrival, my father had learned enough about him to make an informed judgment. His name was Mohammed. He was an educated man from a good family in Nablus. Now I was being forced to choose: marry and leave to the US with a man I had barely seen, let alone known, or return to Palestine, single, to face the possibility of chemical attacks and have my dreams buried in the ongoing popular uprising.

I decided to get married. But I don't know how my parents made these decisions about marriage. A month or two before, my cousin had asked for my hand, too. He was educated, yet they said no. My mother didn't like his mother. She said she was too strong. But they had no idea about Mohammed or his family; they knew only that he lived in the US, and that seemed to be enough for them. And, oh, the irony! His mother turned out to be a hundred times stronger than my cousin's mother.

Between the uprisings in Palestine and Saddam's threats to the Israelis, the situation was very tense, and we held the *katb el-ktab*, the signing of the marriage contract, followed by a dinner that was more or less our *farah*, our wedding. It was all rushed and not a wedding in the traditional sense. We had a small gathering at a restaurant in Amman with twenty people. My father was there, but no other family from my side. Not even my mother attended. Everyone put on a smile that night. I laughed and enjoyed myself. My father too. People danced a little *dabkeh*, which was traditional for a wedding. Mohammed looked happy, and I thought I'd grow to love him. I was sure of it.

Only a few pictures remain from that day. In one photo, they are holding each other on the dance floor. Mohammed is looking at the ground with a slight smile; Sireen is staring at his hand holding hers, also smiling. Mohammed is in a tuxedo. Sireen is wearing a black top exposing part of her back and a black-checkered green skirt, falling slightly above her ankles, with a large bow of the same pattern on her waist. Her look is typically eighties, with large, fluffed bangs.

Behind them some friends are sitting at tables. It is hard to determine whether they are enjoying themselves. Except for what looks like a first dance, the image resembles a casual night out at a restaurant more than a wedding scene.

Sireen has little to say about the evening. Although she remembers being happy, there is bitterness in her voice as she recalls the event. Bitterness that is born not from her anger at her parents who denied her a proper wedding celebration but from the marriage that began in a restaurant.

Although Sireen didn't know it at the time, that December marked the beginning of her estrangement from Palestine. She was excited. Excited to leave the grip of her parents that extended even into Jordan. Excited to not have to return to the precarity of an occupation said to be temporary. An occupation that in reality was so difficult to dismantle, that, like a serpent, it regenerated itself after each blow.

That year, she moved to the land of great possibility with her husband. She left her world, her culture, her language, for New York City. Despite its reputation as a melting pot, she soon realized it was a place with hard lines between communities, where survival depended on knowing English.

Before leaving for America, I traveled from Amman to Kufr Raʿi to say goodbye to my family. I was only there for five days. I expected to see Iyad more often, though my mother warned me that he rarely spent time at home anymore. He was wanted by the Israelis and was always on the run.

"Iyad, *ya mʿafen, esh sarlak?*" I asked him with a raised voice when he first walked into the house on my first day, covered in dust from head to toe. I asked him what had happened, showing concern and getting motherly with him. But despite the fact that he was filthy, I gave him a hug and a kiss as always. He reciprocated but ignored my comment, said hello, and smiled as he pulled away. I smiled back.

Iyad was over six feet tall by then. He was slender and tanned, his forearms hardened and biceps defined.

He sat with me for less than an hour. My mother made tea with mint. Then Iyad left through the back door and didn't return till the next morning. I was worried that night, but my mother had long given up. She couldn't live day in, day out expecting something to happen to her son, so she put him in God's hands and prayed silently for his safe return every time he left the house.

The next morning, the Sawalha family woke to the news of the death of Mustafa al-Ramman, a taxi driver. His pregnant wife was expecting a baby boy. Mustafa was found hanging by his feet from an electricity pole in the village. His ripped shirt hung over his head, revealing lacerations on his back and stomach. The shirt was remarkably bloodstained, partly from the deep cuts on his wrists, indicating he had been allowed to bleed to death. His face was bruised, one eye unrecognizable as such. Mustafa's body was exposed in town to remind everyone of what happens to collaborators. There was a kind of intensity to the killing born out of the intimacy between victim and executioner, between neighbors.

Um Yousef heard the news and looked outside to see people running, wanting to see the body. She remained seated on the floor, legs crossed. She buried her face in her hands for a brief moment and whispered for God's help: *"Allah yisa'edna!"*

When she stood up, she walked to Iyad's room and searched his dresser for a dagger that he often carried with him. She wanted to inspect it for blood, but she couldn't find it. She spent the day silent, waiting for him to return.

Iyad finally came through the door at sunset. Um Yousef looked up. She looked terrifying in the glow of the single fluorescent light in the room. She screamed, accused him of killing Mustafa, and made him swear, swear a hundred times over, that he did not harm the man. Iyad asked for God to forgive her for the accusation. *"Allah yisamhek, Hajjeh,"* he said. She slapped him across the face. Silence descended upon the room for several long seconds. Then Iyad turned around, walked out of the house, and slammed the front door behind him.

This incident happened two nights before I was to travel. On the eve of my departure, I went to bed, reassured that he would be back to say goodbye in the morning. He returned only briefly and was gone before I was up at 4 a.m. to catch my ride to the Jordanian border. He snuck in and took my gray leather jacket. It was a feminine looking jacket, but he told me later that he loved it and wore it often.

Later, the story that circulated in town was that Mustafa was not a collaborator. It was a wrongful death, though some were not convinced by this new narrative. His wife and child were redeemed, nevertheless, but that was hardly consolation for the pain and suffering they had gone through. Mustafa could not return from the dead. The humiliation his family endured at the public display of his body could not be unfelt.

*

In America, Sireen and Mohammed lived in a one-bedroom apartment in Brooklyn. This was in the days before the borough became the "in" place for the young up-and-comers who later came in droves, driving up rents. Sireen juggled going to school while working to keep the family afloat. The city was lonely, made more isolating by her limited English. It was difficult leaving the house and going to the grocer, terrifying to navigate the streets. Even the sanctity of her own home had stopped feeling safe not long after they had moved in.

Only days into her new life in the city, while on a walk to meet Mohammed's friends for dinner, he chose that moment to criticize her appearance, bluntly describing her as a peasant lacking in elegance. Upset, she returned home. He followed, and for a fleeting moment, she thought it was simply because he didn't want them to part on that note.

When they arrived home, and as soon as she opened the door to their apartment, he shoved her inside, threw her to the ground, and stepped on her neck. He then forced her back out to the planned dinner and, seeing no other choice, she complied. She performed well for the hosts that night, exchanging pleasantries and smiling at the right moments.

These encounters with her husband grew more frequent. No one ever saw the bruises, not because they weren't there, hidden under her clothes, but because they were often imprinted under her skin, in her mind. He put her down when she was smiling and tore apart her confidence when all she needed was an anchor.

Mohammed had encouraged me to get another degree, complaining that my Jordanian one was not good enough. So, I enrolled in English night classes at Baruch College. Soon after, I signed up for a degree in marketing and was in school for another five or six years.

A year into my marriage, I began work at the Jordanian mission to the UN. It was an exciting job, and I was lucky to land it through connections I had. My main task was to sit at the Jordanian seat to represent Jordan during the Security Council and General Assembly meetings. My title in this role was that of "advisor," which allowed me to represent the Jordanian mission at the different UN committee meetings. I did not speak up, though. My job was to be present and, at the end of each meeting, to send the transcripts to the Jordanian Royal Court or to the Foreign Ministry.

It was a wonderful feeling to have a job that had a global impact and to watch global events unfold in real time. It was an intense and demanding job because I was there during the nineties, when the sanctions on Iraq and the Oslo peace process in Palestine were hot topics. It was an exciting and glamorous time as well. But between work and school, I was exhausted and drained most days. I woke up at 6 a.m. to get to work on time. At lunch, I sat on my own in the conference room or at my desk, with a sandwich and juice, and used my break to study.

Since divorce was too complicated, and since her parents would not approve of it, in 1993, two years after Mohammed first assaulted her, Sireen finally came around to the idea of having children. Her parents were certain it would improve relations with her husband. And so, the next year, Bassel was born.

Even after Bassel's birth, Mohammed wanted me to continue my schooling and UN job. I don't know if it was some kind of twisted feminist vision he had in his head or if it was to lift his social status, but regardless of his reasons, he never provided me with the support I needed to juggle everything. Luckily, I was able to leave Bassel with my mother, when she was visiting, or with a neighbor who had a kid my son's age.

After work and classes, I used to sleep on the train for an hour on the way home. When I arrived, I had to do all the chores around the house and take care of Bassel. After putting him to sleep, I continued my homework. At times, I felt like my time as a student and working in Jordan was just a brief pause from the continuity of life between my mother working us hard and all the burdens that fell on me in my husband's house.

Sometimes, I think back on what my husband told me in the week before we got married, and I wonder if I should have paid more attention to his words. He told me that, as a bachelor, he used to cook well and throw large parties and feasts. "I've been used to living on my own for seventeen years and doing everything on my own," he said. "If I ask you to get me a glass of water, you need to tell me to get it myself because if I get used to you doing things for me, then I'll get too lazy."

In Sireen's words, one can hear echoes of the first days when two lovers try to court each other, when despite trying to impress upon each other their better sides, they still reveal little truths, little signs, little confessions. If only Sireen had listened more carefully. Indeed, her husband stayed true to his word. The more Sireen did for the house and for him, the less he lifted a finger when he got home. She spent too long blaming herself for not seeing the red flags.

17

Late 1991

A year after Sireen left for New York, a terrible incident shook Kufr Raʿi and its surroundings. Iyad, Daoud, Noor, and several other comrades kidnapped four young men at gunpoint from different locations over the course of an afternoon. They put a hood over their heads and dragged them to a cave in the hills that they had prepared for interrogating their captives. The young men were between seventeen and nineteen years old. One was the son of the village baker; another was Iyad's neighbor. All four young men were fruit sellers and day laborers. To make a living, they crossed over the Green Line to work for Israelis.

"I can't breathe!" the baker's son screamed desperately. He was starting to cough, and Iyad could see the boy was close to convulsing. He knew the boy. He knew he had asthma, so he removed the hood from his face and let him breathe. After regaining his breath, the baker's son looked at Iyad, who was himself masked, and thanked him. Maybe he hoped that acknowledging this kind act might soften his captor and get him released. Iyad dismissed him.

Soon after, Iyad was relieved of lookout duty and went home for dinner while others stood watch. Daoud went home as well.

When they returned later that night, they found the baker's son on the floor by the entrance of their makeshift base in the hills. Stone had turned crimson from blood. They looked further in. Iyad's neighbor was also on the floor, his head torn open—executed by a bullet to his head.

I heard two versions of what happened next. In both cases, when Iyad returned, the baker's son was dead. In one version, one of the Fahd al-Aswad members had taken the lives of all four young men. Iyad marched up to him and demanded to know what happened: "What did you do? What did you do?" The young man said that all four of them had confessed to a range of treasonous actions.

But I think he had it in for the baker's son, and there was an altercation in which the Fahd al-Aswad member beat him to death. The three other young men were likely then killed so there would be no witnesses.

In this version, I heard that Iyad and Daoud listened to their colleague who had been standing guard and questioned his story.

"Where is Noor?" Iyad asked.

"He had to leave. He had some urgent issue. I don't know," the young man responded.

"Why didn't you record the confessions?" The person standing guard was younger, new, and inexperienced. When he said he had forgotten to, it was plausible. They didn't believe him, but what was done was done.

In the other version I heard, it was Noor who performed the execution. Rumor was that Noor was left alone with the boys and one of them was able to identify him. Noor felt he had no choice but to get rid of them.

But if the baker's son were here, perhaps he might have told us that this was a personal vendetta under a political guise. If we could ask him, he might also hold Iyad responsible. There is, in any case, a third version, where Iyad, upon returning with Daoud, had clear orders from superiors in the Fahd al-Aswad operating in the town of Qabatya to execute the boys. No personal vendetta, no political guises, just definitively proven collaboration. And Iyad was the one to pull the trigger.

The next day, the Israelis heard the news and went looking for the bodies. They did not take killing collaborators lightly. People were talking about our family.

In some quarters, people were encouraging and could be heard saying all kinds of things. "Iyad is a hero!"

"Yes, he is a man above men. We need such brave men to rid us of collaborators."

"They deserved what they got. *Ma khirib baytna ila al-ʿumala.*"

"When you see a snake, you have no choice but to kill it."

Others were of a different mind. They were afraid. They saw these killings as arbitrary; they thought they were taking Palestine in the wrong direction.

But the first group pushed back: "Mistakes are made in redeeming Palestine. *Fida Falasteen.*"

My family was caught between people's pride and fear. I don't think Iyad killed those boys, though. But he did not snitch on the boy who did. He maintained that these kids were collaborators and deserved what they got.

In the intense years of the intifada, around 822 people were killed for being suspected of collaborating with the Israelis. What was to be done with collaborators, after all? Like many, Iyad held the view that punishing these people was a political and noble act in service of Palestine. But it was a difficult question no one could answer, an issue that created open wounds within the Palestinian community. Iyad himself would eventually come to regret the zeal and ease with which he went after collaborators.

18

June 11, 1992

There was a house at the end of a winding street on the outskirts of the city of Baka al-Gharbieh, باقة الغربية, or Western Baka, a Palestinian city within the borders of the Israeli state straddling the Green Line that demarcates the West Bank. Baka was divided at the start of the Nakba in 1948, with its eastern half remaining part of the district of Tulkarem in the Jordanian-controlled West Bank and the western half, Baka al-Gharbieh, brought into the Haifa District under Zionist control. Iyad Abu Shqara knocked on the door of the house at the end of the winding street.

Iyad's nickname, Abu Shqara, had become a kind of nom de guerre and the name the Israelis often used. In fact, in Kufr Ra'i, the family was known as Dar Abu Shqara, the house of Abu Shqara, which came from the word *shaqra*—of fair complexion. One story is that the family acquired this nickname because Abu Yousef was born so blond and blue eyed that people joked he was a descendant of a British general.

Iyad knocked again, and Qassem, a boy with stubble under his chin whom Iyad knew from Kufr Ra'i opened the door and greeted him with a smile. Iyad entered into a room with simple furnishings—a wooden table with four matching chairs and a blue loveseat with floral prints at least a decade old. A bare bulb hanging from the ceiling gave the place a hospital-like feel and cast a glow onto peeling paint, which had weathered years of humidity. The loveseat was occupied with jackets, and scattered across the table lay several handguns.

Noor had sent Iyad to this house on this moonless night to acquire weapons from Baka al-Gharbieh. It was a common smuggling route. The two boys had been through so much in the last two years. They had escaped imprisonment together. They had covered for each other as Israeli tear gas rained over their heads. They knew each other's every thought and movement.

Two chubby, youthful men walked out of the kitchen with beers. They introduced themselves to Iyad as Ahmad and Imad and offered him what they were drinking. He declined.

He could hear sounds from a television coming from another room. It had been so long since he'd even seen one, let alone watched anything. They told him to follow them into that room. He took off his shoes, leaving them by the front door with all the other pairs, and saw that no one was carrying a weapon. Imad noticed Iyad looking at the guns they had laid on a table by the entrance.

"You can leave your weapon on the table, it's fine," he said casually.

Iyad reached behind his back, pulled out his weapon, grabbing it tightly. He paused as if unwilling to let it go, and finally laid it down on the table. It was an act that took a mere moment, but it is in these unnoticeable, insignificant moments that life is made and unmade.

He walked into the next room and sat on one of the cushions on the floor, and the other young men sat next to him. They exchanged pleasantries, spoke about the weather, and someone asked if Iyad had experienced any difficulties in making the trip over. No more than five minutes had passed when he heard footsteps interrupting their conversation before they had even gotten to the subject of the weapons deal. The old house rumbled with heavy thuds that were easily recognizable as military boots.

Iyad's stomach dropped. This was not how the night was meant to end. His eyes shot around the room with a deep sense of disbelief. He had no time to collect himself or his thoughts because the momentary silence was interrupted by hard knocks on the door followed by a call from outside: "This is the Israeli Defense Forces! Everyone surrender yourselves. Don't resist. There is no need for anyone to die."

A second round of hard knocks followed.

Iyad glared at his comrades, Qassem in particular, because he had known him to be a nationalist. The Israelis were seemingly there for all of them, but Iyad was sure there was a mole in their midst. How else could the army know of this meeting? His heart pumped faster in anticipation of the encounter with the soldiers. His cheeks stiffened and turned red as he continued to look around at the others, eyebrows pinched together, searching for clues about who might have informed on them.

He tightened his fists and leaned forward as he prepared to dash off. He had nowhere to go. His temples burned with rage. He could feel something inside him about to explode. And in the moment before the soldiers barged in, he thought of his friend, Noor. Was he involved in laying this trap?

As the thought settled in and Iyad's mind raced to calculate his next move, the front door slammed open.

There was no struggle.

They grabbed the four men, took them outside, and threw them to the ground, more than a dozen soldiers surrounding them. Iyad and the other men curled up as they received several kicks and were bound with plastic handcuffs.

Iyad was taken, kidnapped, captured—call it what you will—in a house on a winding street in the city of Baka al-Gharbieh. And in the moment of his kidnapping, he struggled with who and what he was to become. Although he had long ago accepted imprisonment as a repercussion of resistance, it was his parents he was most worried about. He thought of how they would be treated if they tried to visit him, and of their sadness at having to endure their son being locked away in an Israeli prison.

My parents didn't hear about his capture until the next day, with little information about where, when, or how he was taken. News traveled slowly in those days, so I only heard of his capture a day or two after that. I was home in New York when the phone rang. I was terrified of what the Israelis would do to him. I cried, I was inconsolable, but I don't remember being surprised. I had known that sooner or later they'd catch him. Iyad trusted people too much and was too public in those days. He'd buy from and sell weapons to just about anybody. Too many knew he was involved with the Fahd al-Aswad.

Daoud was caught two days after Iyad, and they were imprisoned together. Noor, on the other hand, escaped to Jordan, returned some time later, and got married, but he was eventually caught. He served time only briefly.

In Kufr Ra'i, neighbors of the Abu Shqara family came to pay their respects, to share the family's pain, and to grieve for their collective reality. Abu Yousef sat on a white plastic chair in the courtyard, cigarette in hand, receiving guests with glazed eyes that were constantly fixed on a moon that shone in the daylight. His mind held on to the image of Iyad, his son's soft smile, his worried look, and Abu Yousef asked himself if he had not done enough to rein his son in. His mind also raced to his village, Taybeh. To that visit two decades ago, to dreams of return. Neighbors tried to console him. Palestine would be liberated, return was around the corner, Iyad would be released soon, they said. He would persevere and bring dignity to the house; he was in God's hands.

Abu Yousef just nodded till he got tired of nodding. Then he retreated, tormented by his own powerlessness—the harrowing realization that there was no string he could pull to free his son from prison.

Iyad's physical and mental suffering was mirrored in Um Yousef's face. The initial torrent of tears had now dried up, and in their place appeared blackened circles around her eyes as dark as a starless night. She too had an empty stare, lost in imagining the scenarios of her son's interrogation, lost in contemplation of what she needed to do.

For Um Yousef, the grief was a moment of conversion. She had to accept the path her son had chosen. Her task now, in the prison visits she planned to make, was to do all in her power to ensure his *sumud* in captivity, to ensure his perseverance and that he was up to the ethical demands of the struggle. He must survive at all costs, lest captivity be seen to break one's soul. And he must not confess, not even under duress.

A few days after Iyad's abduction, I wrote a letter to Amnesty International requesting their help in finding Iyad. My parents had no idea where he was and were told not to search for him. Amnesty International was not helpful and only responded to me three months later, after my parents had already located and visited him.

Iyad was thrown into the back of a green army pickup truck. It was covered with layers of mesh to prevent anyone from being able to see in. He sat with legs chained and hands cuffed behind his back. They blindfolded him with an old rag that transformed his world, and nothing, from then on, would be as it had been. Immobile, and in pain from the plastic handcuffs digging into his wrists and the blows he had already received, he felt his anguish, like that of every captive, begin then, at the moment of his kidnapping. As the world went dark, save for military boots he could spot in the tiny gap where the blindfold met his nose, and as he heard strange voices laugh and a female

17 June 1992

Amnesty International
322 8th Avenue
New York, N.Y. 10001
ATTN: Ms. Soraya

Dear Ms. Soraya,

    My mother just called to tell me that my brother, Ayyad·
Ahmad Yousuf, who is eighteen years old and is in the Occupied
Territories, was arrested by the Occupying Israeli Forces on
11 June 1992 in Kafa Rai, Jenin. As usual, the occupying Israeli
Forces accused him of ill-doing, and as you well know, they
detained him without telling us where he is, what he was accused
of, and without allowing him to contact his family. We were just
told not to follow-up on him. How can we do that? He is just an
innocent 17 year old who just turned 18. God knows what crimes
they will accuse him of. I am willing to do everything to free
my innocent brother – to save him from torture, detention,and
suffering, as well as to help my parents who are beside themselves
with worry, unable to sleep every night and unable to cope with
this dilemma. They still have to worry about their 13 children
who are dependent on them.

    We have no one else to turn to for help. I know that your
organization has been helping various families and people from
different countries, I write to you now to ask for your help. All
I want to know is how my brother is faring, his whereabouts, or
any kind of information that could tell us how he is. Please
contact me as soon as you can get hold of some news regarding my
brother at this telephone number and address;

                    Ms. Sireen Ahmad Yousuf
                    3620 Bedford Avenue, # E9
                    Brooklyn, N.Y. 11210
                    (718) 253-1714

    Your immediate attention on this matter will be highly
appreciated.

    Thank you very much.

                            Sincerely yours,

                            Sireen Ahmad Yousuf
                            Sireen y

Sireen's letter to Amnesty International after her brother was captured.
SOURCE: *Family collection.*

soldier taunt him, he could only take solace in his anger and in his unbroken will to resist.

Although Iyad was prepared for this moment, prepared because imprisonment or death are the only two options for a resistance fighter, he was still afraid. Fear approached him from the outside, in the form of a soldier's voice and footsteps. Fear emerged from inside him, in the feeling of his sunken stomach and the heavy thumping of his heart. Fear was in between. And, oh, how he wished it weren't so! How he wished for it to be locked inside him, inaccessible to the world.

From *fida'i* to *aseer*, from resistance fighter to political prisoner, all in an instant. Iyad struggled with who and what he was to become. And when he was met with curses and beatings, he asked himself again and again, What next? And where to? And what will become of me?

The engine started. Four soldiers jumped into the back with Iyad and pulled down a layer of mesh behind them. He could no longer see or hear what happened to the other men in the house. On the way to the detention center, he got no reprieve. The soldiers cursed at him, called his mother and sisters lewd names, punched and slapped him, and beat him with the butt of their rifles. They drove for a half hour, then the vehicle stopped. Someone grabbed his arm and yelled at him to get down, "*Yalla, inzal!*"

Iyad dragged his chained feet and stumbled out, held up by two guards. At this point, no one who mattered to him knew where he was or what had happened to him. No one knew if he was being directed to the entrance of Jneid Prison in Nablus or Salem Prison near the village of Salem, سالم, northwest of Jenin.

When he entered the prison compound, he was forced to strip and give up his clothes and a watch given to him by his sister. There were other prisoners standing with him. All of them, like him, were designated "security prisoners," and he took comfort in knowing that he was not alone.

The guards removed their blindfolds. Standing naked in front of female soldiers, the captives were given simple orders to turn around, sit, and stand, in what was a shaming exhibition. Then, in their nakedness, they were beaten with sticks and chains while the women laughed and insulted their bodies. In their nakedness, despite being with other prisoners, they experienced their first moments of isolation, pulled away from the only world they knew.

Questions were thrown at the captives. "Who are you?" the guards asked. Who am I? the prisoners wondered. But they remained silent, as if uttering their name would take it away from them forever and open the gates to all the answers the guards sought.

Iyad was questioned briefly, processed into the system, and then left standing until a guard approached him, blindfolded him, grabbed his arm, and pushed him down a long corridor to his cell. They did not warn him of the steps on the way, leaving him to trip and fall on his face. Blood splattered on the floor and gushed from his nose. Laughter filled the room, its source unknown. Several guards were surrounding him now. He could hear their shuffling and steady breathing. In their presence, he experienced his second moment of isolation. He was alone, at their mercy, and the interrogation had not yet begun.

No longer Palestinian *fida'i*, the new *aseer* is tossed into a cell fit for five but housing fifteen inmates. The other inmates greet him as if he has entered their home. They make him feel comfortable. Without solidarity, they are all dead. They tell him to rest on a plastic mat. He does as he's told. In this moment, he discovers that sleep is an escape from confinement. But the jailer has learned this too and has perfected sleep deprivation as a mechanism of torture. The prisoner closes his eyes, exhausted, only to wake almost instantly to the sounds of screams and beatings. To whom do the voices belong? He tries to guess if they are coming from a nearby cell, someone he's met, or just a recording. It's all the same. There will be no respite from incarceration today.

The inmates warn the new prisoner that the interrogation may start soon. They mean to prepare him. But "soon" is a period of anxiety defined by waiting.

The guards came for Iyad. He was handcuffed again and dragged out of his cell. They put him in the back of a military jeep. Where were they taking him? To Jalameh? Petah Tikva? Or the "slaughterhouse" of al-Moscobiyeh? He was told they took the serious cases there, or else they would have interrogated him down the corridor.

The engine started.

In these moments, fear strikes the prisoner's every membrane in a body he wishes he could dispossess. He can feel sweat rising, his body getting weaker, his head lighter. Yet through it all, he must show strength.

As he was taken away, Iyad repeated to himself the last words his prison cell comrades whispered to him: "Beware the birds." He had heard of their presence in the prisons before, but now the birds—*al-ʿassafir*, the collaborators—would be after him. *"Ismud,"* they urged. "Don't give them what they want. Persevere."

19

An Israeli Prison, Late June, 1992

The floor of Iyad's prison cell was so cold he could feel his bones shivering when he lay on it. The air was rancid and smelled of the fluids of a thousand prisoners who had come before—a cocktail of sweat and blood and urine. Eventually, this wretchedness would become a source of strength, and he would build immunity to his occupier. But in this moment, all he could think of was how to hold together the remaining pieces of himself.

There was only darkness his eyes steadily adapted to. He looked around his enclosure of 2 meters by 1.5 meters. There was a 5 cm-thin mattress to sleep on—the *barsh*, as the prisoners called it—and two sheets that could be used as a pillow and cover. None of it was enough to cushion the icy floor.

The bare, cracked cement walls that surrounded him left him suspended between life and death. He shut his eyes and tried to dream. Every now and then, a hatch in the door opened and a tray dropped onto the floor, and for a moment, a shiny ray of light brought the cell to life with all its ugliness.

He had not seen a soul besides his interrogators, and they made him prefer to be left alone in this world, in this solitary place with the rats, with the prayers he had etched into this concrete confinement, with two buckets of feces and urine.

He tried to keep track of time by the meals he was served. On bad days, he was given a slice of stale bread, half a spoonful of yogurt, and a scoop of what looked like rice and lentils but, in fact, was *byka*, the stuff of cattle feed. On good days, they sometimes tossed him a bowl of boiled black beans with jam. In an act of defiance, he would tell them it was delicious. Sometimes, the guards forgot a meal or decided to switch his breakfast for dinner, and time was sent into a swirl.

In this place, even as he struggled to mark the passage of days, nothing seemed to exist in time, and there was no past or future.

By the time the prisoner appears at the first interrogation, he has already been subjected to the long, tormenting years of Israeli occupation. Every aspect of the occupation, from its checkpoints and curfews, which increased during the intifada, to the way it facilitates corruption, impoverishment, and unemployment, has been carefully orchestrated to instill a feeling of failure and futility in the prisoner—to break his will and fragment him ideologically so a confession can be easily extracted when the time comes. All of it is done to instill self-doubt and despair, to turn nationalists into collaborators. But one article of faith the prisoners believe in is that the nationalist, the *munadel*, the one who struggles, will not succumb. And so, it is through sealed lips that prisoners try desperately to frustrate their interrogators.

The prisoner has only one purpose in that moment: to refuse to cooperate with his interrogator by eliminating his own fear. All other aspirations he leaves outside the prison walls. The pain might seem unbearable, the violations against his body brutal, but he promises himself that he will persevere. He lifts his chin and feels his shoulders roll back. His silence will sting the ears of his enemies. Whatever the prisoner tells them will already be known to all.

Iyad's first meeting with interrogators from the Israeli internal security forces, the Shin Bet, was pleasant. The inmates warned him he would be beaten, but the interrogators tried a different approach with him. They put him in an office. "Sit down. Do you need anything? If you cooperate this will be over soon, and you can return to your cell." He remained silent. They left.

Shortly after, they returned and took him to the *zinzaneh*—the isolation cell. He had heard a lot about this place. But still, he was not prepared for it. Fear surrounded him, and he retreated to his dreams, and from one dream to another he measured time. He would lose count of them in the months to come.

Iyad heard Hebrew words. Later, he learned what many of them meant. But on this day, the foreign language strummed discordant against his nerves, broken only by a terror-inducing command, in Arabic, to strip: *"Ishlah!"*

When Iyad refused, he was beaten by two interrogators. When he refused again, they kicked him till he couldn't raise his head any longer. Then they left him for several hours. When one of them entered again, he sat down, and there was a shift in tactics. "I know your mother is alive and you have eight sisters," the interrogator said softly, legs spread open toward Iyad, slouching in his chair. "I see you have not finished school." He continued to reveal information to let Iyad know that he had been studied, his life an open text for the jailer.

The goal of the interrogator was to extract a confession. The interrogator has multiple personalities, from creative abuser to caring friend. Iyad just needed to hold tight and remain silent. Silence was his only weapon, and it often worked to frustrate the inquisitor and make him halt the interrogation.

The prisoner knows that the interrogator can make him starve, break his arms, pierce his skin, and disfigure his body, but he also knows the interrogator cannot move his tongue. However abused, however close to death, speaking remains voluntary; the secrets of the resistance are for him to keep or share. His choices will determine how straight he walks, how powerful the belief in his cause. Dignity and faith. These are the intangibles the interrogator is after and is seeking to break.

Another of Iyad's interrogators entered the room with hesitation. He was insecure. His job, as any job, depended on his character and determination. But the success rate in this line of work is not so high, and this interrogator questioned if he was up for this next task.

The interrogator has to file reports and answer to his superiors, who expect to receive constant updates and new confessions. Sometimes, he will believe in his work: it is a matter of national security. Sometimes, he might take pride in his work, especially on the days he is successful. But other times, he hates his job. Is he good at it? Is this the best way he can serve his people? Is there somewhere else he could be?

If Iyad were to survive the interrogation with his dignity intact, he had to understand this: the interrogator is weak.

I remember sitting awake on the couch those first nights, knees to my chest and arms wrapped around them, thinking of what they were doing to my brother. I felt a knot of helplessness in my throat, and I could not swallow. I prayed that they would spare him the worst of the interrogation.

*

The sound of skin striking skin reverberated in the room.

Iyad received a slap to the face like a bell signaling the beginning of this round of interrogation. He was ordered to get on his knees. He refused. The interrogator grabbed his shoulder and kicked him behind the knees. He fell for a moment, then stood. This was repeated several times, until the interrogator finally grabbed him, shook him violently, and threw him to the ground.

He rolled over and lay on his back in a plain white room with nothing but one bright light and a photo of Theodor Herzl hanging in a wooden frame. From the stories he had heard, he knew that electric rods would be brought in shortly and administered to his testicles. Until then, he did what he could to defend himself against slaps to the face and kicks and punches to the stomach. Sometimes, prisoners are interrogated with foul-smelling bags over their heads that can make them vomit on themselves. In that moment, though, Iyad was made to see everything. And as they continued to beat him, his head flung from side to side, and his eyes circled the room. When his eyes met theirs, he laughed hysterically. He whispered to the Lord for patience and mercy, *"Allah a'teenee al-sabr, a'teenee al-rahma."*

In these instances, the prisoner knows he has to concentrate. The man before him has powerful implements but is weak in spirit. Powerful and weak. The prisoner must not lose sight of this if he intends to avoid falling for the traps that lead to becoming a collaborator.

This period is also accompanied by mind games. The interrogators use what they know about the captive to strike fear in him. His mother and sisters will be raped, they threaten him. They will do it in front of him, in front of his father. Then they leave, and other interrogators enter. One smiles, touches the prisoner gently, and promises money and opportunity if the captive complies. One man leads the interrogation, but others appear and disappear. It continues like this for eighteen days, a month, one hundred days, more.

Iyad was given bathroom breaks of three to four minutes at a time, which also doubled as his time to eat, when he consumed rotten and cold food— forty-five grams of fish or meat with a rancid stench, hot colored water passing as soup or tea, and just enough calories to keep the human rights organizations at bay. And in the lull, when Iyad was not being questioned and beaten, he was made to wait with a bag over his head, standing on the tips of his feet, held by a rope tied to his hands behind his back, and forced to hear the echoes of beatings and the screams of prisoners from the chambers next door.

But he knew what they were doing, and he knew the captive must maintain his focus. He must be ready for these tactics lest he be consumed by fear. Any response he gives, any word he utters, will be used against him, especially in the first sessions when the interrogator looks for benign information to learn about the captive's personality—what he likes and dislikes, what he eats, even what newspapers his family and friends read. All this will be used against him. Except for the laughter. And so, the captive laughs, and at some point, he is not sure anymore if he has gone mad from laughter. And when he is not laughing, he retreats into a faraway place where he cannot hear the ugliness of this world or feel the pain it inflicts.

Thus, when they hung Iyad upside down from his ankles, when they chained and tied him in a distorted position in the "closet," when they meted out the worst of it, he took refuge in the yard of his village home with the scent of jasmine filling the air. He imagined the reception for him by comrades and family if he did not confess. He took sanctuary in dreams that got him through the period of interrogation.

It was a standoff between two unequals, a mismatch—Iyad with his dreams and laughter, and the interrogator with his vast implements and varied techniques of torture. Through *sumud*, Iyad and the prisoners maintained a fighting chance.

In the end, Iyad only confessed to acts he allegedly committed, but without handing over names or revealing useful information to the prison authorities. His confession might have come under torture, or in between, when they put him in a cell with trusted comrades from his political party who gave him a hero's welcome, comforted him, and tended to his wounds. He bragged about one or two of his resistance activities around them, only to discover days later that these were not comrades but collaborators who "sang" all they had learned to their captors. After days or weeks of silence and no one to speak with, this was an effective tactic that allowed prisoners to feel at ease and let their guard down. When the jailers took Iyad back for interrogation, they confronted him with his own words.

20

1993

For most of Iyad's first year in captivity, Um Yousef was rarely able to visit him, and when she did, they were separated by a glass window, except at the time of his initial court hearing. He looked so ghastly that day, she couldn't control her gasp. Iyad, hands and feet shackled, shouted out to her, "*Hajjeh*, don't you dare cry in front of these dogs!"

This breathed life and defiance into her, and she shot back, "Never! If I could, I would give birth to ten like you. Prison is for heroes!" And it was this same spirit that she mustered on the eve of each visit.

Her life revolved around these visits. She was absorbed in thought of how to secure her son's release. She had grown more bitter. It was noticeable in the frequency with which she snapped at her children and in the slowed rhythm of her life. Her land was her only refuge, and she continued to tend to it as before.

Um Yousef's children took turns accompanying her on the prison visits, as only a limited number of family members were allowed at a time. Arselene went to see Iyad most often, and she recalled how the separation was difficult on both of them, how he worried about her when her mother visited alone, how she missed him when she traveled for six months to see her sisters in Dubai and Jeddah.

In between visits, Arselene thought of Iyad often, remembering him most when she ate Um Yousef's *freekeh*, his favorite dish of smoky cracked wheat. And even though the two-year difference meant they fought often as children, Arselene looked up to her older brother. She spoke of how he used to take care of her before he was taken away, of how, once, he rushed her to a doctor, carrying her while running, when she was stung by a scorpion as the two of them walked to their land. And then, when they were separated by prison walls, they grew closer.

The encounter with Iyad was often a tug-of-emotions for Arselene and everyone in the family. Usually, when he was weak, they were strong; when he was strong, they cried, though the initial weeping quickly subsided to quiet tears. But Um Yousef did not play this game. She was always stoic in front of him and looked prison guards in the face with sharp, unflinching eyes.

In prison, after the interrogation period, Iyad was, as ever, consumed by the question of how to liberate Palestine. What was to be done?

He participated in prison study circles. In some, he debated politics with comrades; in others, they read the Quran and texts by religious scholars. He took plenty of notes. He also began to accompany cellmates to prayer. And slowly, as he reflected on who he had been, and on the changing political scene all around him, he turned away from Fatah. His thoughts began to align more closely with the political ideology of the Islamic Jihad. He never officially dropped his membership with Fatah, though. It was a calculated decision he hoped would pay off in time.

In the early days, in study circles in prison cells at night, Iyad sat back, arms and legs crossed, focusing intently on debates by more experienced prison mates and elders. They differed in their understanding of how the Islamic Jihad had evolved. Some said that leaders in the Egyptian student activist scenes in the 1960s and '70s had inspired the organization. Others argued that it was tied to the growth of the Muslim Brotherhood in the Gaza Strip and emerged directly from the Palestinian desire for more intentional resistance against the Zionists.

Back in 1973, the Israeli authorities allowed the Brotherhood to run charitable organizations, and this facilitated the growth of the movement. As the Brotherhood grew, it developed into a counterweight to the PLO, but it took a reformist approach and remained reluctant to engage the question of Palestine. "In 1981," lectured a member of the Islamic Jihad and a fellow prison mate as Iyad listened, "some of our members, disenchanted with this reformist approach, split from the Gaza branch of the Brotherhood and formed the Islamic Jihad." Unlike the Brotherhood, they embraced armed resistance alongside the PLO.

Iyad was there to learn, but he was less interested in the origins and more in how the group could answer the question of how to liberate Palestine. His political turn was not particularly unique. More so than other political factions, the Islamic Jihad, and the Muslim Brotherhood more broadly, had traditionally attracted members of Fatah. The common understanding was that Fatah had no real ideological depth. It was held together primarily by a shallow nationalism and by its call for armed resistance—an armed resistance whose legitimacy no one doubted.

What was different, Iyad found, was that the Islamic Jihad combined the revolutionary approach of Fatah, in calling for national liberation, with a religious turn. Its slogan: Islam, jihad, and Palestine. Islam as the starting point, jihad as the means, and Palestine's liberation as the goal. If a Fatah member were religious, and the Islamic Jihad was concerned with Islam and Palestine, then it was an easy leap to make. And it did not take Iyad long to do so.

While the Brotherhood insisted on the Islamic transformation of society as a prerequisite for the liberation of Palestine, the Islamic Jihad envisioned this happening simultaneously and prioritized Palestinian liberation in the here and now. Iyad believed in this approach. He found the Islamic Jihad's strategic engagement more convincing than the reformism of the Muslim Brotherhood and its Hamas wing. He was also persuaded by the Islamic Jihad's analysis of Arab governments. Unlike the Brotherhood's cozy relations with various regimes, the Islamic Jihad leadership criticized these governments for guaranteeing Israeli security and being authoritarian stooges of the West.

Iyad was drawn to the Islamic Jihad's vanguard and its resistance to the entire settler-colonial project, and he was taken by one of its charismatic founders, Fathi al-Shiqaqi, who came from a family of refugees from the village of Zarnuqa, depopulated in 1948. Iyad buried himself in the many pages of al-Shiqaqi's writings. He read of the man's genius and of what he was building. He hoped one day he would be free to meet this man who was quickly becoming everything Iyad wanted to be.

Al-Shiqaqi had learned from his village history that surrender would not prevent erasure. He had been inspired by the Iranian Revolution and saw it as a successful model for comprehensive revolutionary change. This was a sticking point that caused the Muslim Brotherhood to label the Islamic Jihad in sectarian terms as a Shi'a movement beholden to Iran. Iyad came to understand al-Shiqaqi, admire his thinking, and share his views on the Iranian Revolution as well as his respect for Hizballah, the Islamic Resistance Movement in Lebanon, which was effective in dealing blows to the Israeli military.

Like al-Shiqaqi, Iyad asked himself more and more why the Palestinians had been defeated. And why now? And like al-Shiqaqi, he was driven to a critique of colonialism. Palestinians were not locked in a battle between the West and Islam. Theirs was an anti-colonial struggle, where the Zionist movement served as a direct extension of Western colonialism. Iyad read and reread al-Shiqaqi's works; he continued to engage in study circles in prison, and, awed by the man, he came to follow his belief that the struggle was not an apocalyptic battle between Good and Evil but a historical one between oppressor and oppressed. It was an illuminating moment when Iyad came across al-Shiqaqi's analysis that Western philosophical claims about the freedom of man simply meant the freedom of Western man. Not his freedom, not that of Palestinians, not that of the whole of humanity. It was this idea, he felt, that was an obstacle to the freedom of his people.

In al-Shiqaqi and the ideology of the Palestinian Islamic Jihad, Iyad found a rejection of *takfir*, or excommunication, as a weapon against internal enemies. Ramadan Shallah, who succeeded al-Shiqaqi as the group leader after his assassination in 1995, once said that "the weapon of excommunication [*silah al-takfir*] is in our view the most dangerous weapon that kills the *umma* from the inside today, and our faith in it." These teachings influenced Iyad to reconsider whether he had adopted the best approach against collaborators.

Iyad's transition to the Islamic Jihad began in 1993, around the time that Arafat met with Yitzhak Rabin, Shimon Peres, and Bill Clinton in the Rose Garden of the White House and the Oslo Accords were signed. Iyad, among many others, rejected the accords and the public displays of peace. Like many Palestinians, he felt that Arafat had surrendered his people to US and Israeli diktats in exchange for nothing.

The handshake in the Rose Garden changed conditions in prison. Those prisoners most affected by the handshake belonged to Fatah. Some of them felt betrayed, as they felt they endured unimaginable torture for a cause that had just been relinquished. Others felt defeated and began to voice that the resistance was over. Unlike Islamic Jihad and Hamas members, the deal promised Fatah prisoners their release. This led to tensions among the prisoners, and divisions in a once almost-united prison population began to arise. Yet even as their ability to resist collectively took a severe blow, prisoners went to great lengths to look out for each other against an ultimate enemy who was desperate to find a way to exploit these new divisions.

Hamas and the Islamic Jihad were opposed to the Oslo Accords from the very beginning. Soon after the handshake at the Rose Garden, the Islamic Jihad formalized its military wing under the name of the Saraya al-Quds, also known as the al-Quds Brigades or the Jerusalem Brigades. Iyad heard of the formation of the brigades in prison. He also heard of their various operations. Among them were several *'amaliyat istish-hadiya,* or martyr operations, in 1994 and 1995, that had killed a number of Israeli soldiers and civilians. In these operations, Islamic Jihad operatives, strapped with an explosive belt, blew themselves up at specific locations that struck fear into the Israeli public.

In a news report on a prison television, Iyad caught images of the destruction left in the wake of one such operation. He and others clapped in the moment. "Wow! Look at that!" he exclaimed in disbelief and excitement, pointing at the screen. Another screamed with joy. "They've given us back our dignity," he said. The prisoners felt these attacks as acts of solidarity with them, that people on the outside were still resisting while they persevered in prison. Still, Iyad and others discussed the strategic utility of these operations and whether it was acceptable to target civilians—and whether settlers in the West Bank, the Gaza Strip, and Jerusalem were even civilians or whether they served a military purpose. Iyad was ultimately impressed with these acts. They were far more organized and effective than anything he had ever done with the Fahd al-Aswad. He felt they were a powerful tool in the absence of traditional weapons. Between Fatah's subservience to the diplomatic track of Oslo, which appeared to be full of false promises, and the Saraya al-Quds's resistance operations, it was clear to him which movement he would support.

I watched the handshake and the entire ceremony on CNN from my Brooklyn apartment. I remember I was part weary, part elated. How could peace come with no definite timeline for the release of my brother? With no vision of what the Palestinian state would look like?

Still, the moment was exhilarating, and Sireen couldn't help getting swept up by the dramatic, Hollywood-esque staging of the signing ceremony, with the White House in the background, the statesmen under the sun, the three thousand honorable guests, and the pomp and circumstance at the end. So much so that she missed the opening words of Rabin's speech highlighting Israeli victimization above all else.

The Oslo Accords were billed as an agreement that would create a Palestinian state in the West Bank and the Gaza Strip alongside an Israeli one, ostensibly paving the way to peace. Often, the two terms, Oslo and *peace*, became synonymous, and soon people called it the Oslo peace process. Yet the document made little mention of peace and was more concerned with establishing a process for an interim self-government. Everything was interim, a time in between. But there was no common understanding of in-between, of until-when, or of where-to this was heading. Oslo, wrapped in the veneer of a solution, produced more questions about what the future would look like.

The Oslo Accords outlined how the new Palestinian Authority (PA) would collaborate with the Israeli government on political and economic matters, on developmental projects, and on security coordination. The PA was to become a native surrogate managing the occupation, something the Israelis had been seeking since 1967. For the Israelis, Oslo also heralded much more intense US-Israeli security cooperation and the upgrading of Israeli technological capacities. It also signaled to companies worldwide that they could invest in the Israeli economy despite continued occupation. In the intervening years, while the process dragged on and the "interim" became the status quo, markets opened up, and Israelis and their state grew richer.

The writing on the wall should have been clear. But the image of the handshake in the Rose Garden kept broadcasting in people's minds, and it was more potent than the words etched in the agreement, which, anyway, very few people read.

A year after the Rose Garden handshake, Sireen traveled to Palestine in June to introduce her son, Bassel, to the family. Several months had passed since the Ibrahim Mosque massacre in al-Khalil, when an American Israeli settler gunned down 29 Palestinians and injured 125 others while they prayed. Two martyr operations were carried out in response during the month of April. The handshake still held, but people were skeptical of the future. If the Israeli military occupation did not differentiate between combatants and civilians, did Palestinian resistance need to?

I was so excited to finally see Iyad again, and I was undeterred by all the events going on in Palestine.

Um Yousef tried to temper her expectations. "The prison guards can turn you away without reason," she warned. But Sireen was determined to introduce her son to her brother. Iyad was being held in Jneid Prison, in Nablus, which was still under Israeli control. Transfer of the city to the PA would not take place till the year after, in 1995. So it was not terribly difficult to commute between Kufr Ra'i and Jneid Prison, save for a few mobile or "flying" checkpoints as a result of the Ibrahim Mosque massacre and its aftermath.

A few days after arriving in Palestine, and after a restless night, Sireen woke up at dawn to prepare for her trip to Nablus. She felt disoriented in her emotions. She was happy to be back home. This house contained her past, and it seemed alive, continuing to change and grow with her. There was a bittersweetness to waking up early. In New York she missed the morning dew of Kufr Ra'i and the chilly breeze before the sun warmed the air. She missed the sound of her neighbor's rooster and the gentle hooves of her mother's donkey while farm machines were still in slumber. She even missed the sound of Um Farid's broom swishing dust off the front steps and the voices of her siblings as they got ready to follow their mother to the land. But the morning also reminded her of all the work she didn't miss and of the blisters she'd return home with after the harvest of the different seasons of her childhood.

Sireen rubbed her hands and bit her lip gently as she thought of what it was going to be like to see her brother. While being on another continent meant she would go years without reconnecting with her family, the experience of having a brother in prison, and imagining the ways he was suffering brutal punishment, captivity, and torture, magnified her feeling of separation from him. His incarceration often weighed on her as she walked down the streets of New York, smiled among friends, or stared out at the city lights at night. Guilt often consumed her happier moments. Distance was no longer measured in metric units but in the space between incarceration and freedom. She longed to visit her younger brother.

Sireen tiptoed in the dark around her sleeping siblings. Bassel was sleeping too, peacefully. All the siblings and their kids (those who had returned for the summer, at least) were in one room on mattresses laid out on the floor for the night. She showered quickly, dressed in blue jeans and a short-sleeved shirt, and spent some time styling her short, wet hair. She then joined Um Yousef, who was already in the kitchen boiling tea. By then, the outhouse had been turned into a proper room, but the toilet remained a hole. The outhouse was attached to a large kitchen, which was built after Sireen left to the US and in the place of a room that used to house their donkey and rabbits. The kitchen had expensive wooden cabinets and appliances, like an oven and a fridge, but they were rarely, if ever, used. The kitchen and outhouse were also now attached to the rest of the house, making them less frightening to use at night.

Mother and daughter finished their tea and got ready to depart. Um Yousef had her headscarf around her shoulders; her eyes looked dark and heavy with bags that were not there the last time Sireen saw her.

My mother examined me before we left. She noticed my outfit, and her lips tightened, her eyes sharpened. "Go change. Wear something looser. And bring a headscarf," she shot out.

I grumbled. All my clothes were tight fitting, so I borrowed a silk long-sleeved shirt from my sister. My mother took another look at me. "Get a headscarf!" she demanded. This time I refused.

Um Yousef wasn't going to make an argument out of it this morning. Perhaps her daughter would listen to Iyad.

The taxi that was to take them to Nablus arrived. Sireen gently picked up Bassel, who hadn't woken yet, and grabbed her diaper bag with the bare essentials. Um Yousef lifted and fastened her white headscarf, which matched the mustard *abaya* she was wearing. They both hurried into the taxi. An hour later, it dropped them off at the main entrance of Jneid Prison—an incomplete hospital the Jordanian army had begun constructing until, in 1967, it fell under Israeli control and was refitted as a prison in the 1980s.

Um Yousef walked confidently to the guard at the entrance; Sireen followed with Bassel in her arms. They pulled out their IDs. The guard searched them and let them into the compound. There, they made their way to a holding area where other families were waiting. They waited for another ninety minutes because the prison authorities only let in a few families at a time and each visit lasted half an hour. This was the closest Sireen had come to seeing her brother in four years. Time seemed to expand in this room.

My mother warned me about what I should expect and how I wouldn't be able to hug or hold my brother. I tried to wrap my mind around this to make the moment easier. Just then, a guard called out for us to enter the next room.

My mother walked in first, and I followed right behind her. We stood inside, waiting.

The room was split down the middle with a fence and a thick screen separating visitors from prisoners. A door opened from the other side of the fence to let in the prisoners. Iyad was third to walk in. Sireen spotted him and felt tears stinging her eyes almost immediately. He smiled and struggled to remain composed, but a few teardrops formed around his eyes as well. They put their hands up against the screen, their emotions entangled through the quantum space that held the glass together. She could not find her words. The inability to touch her younger brother, the feeling of being so close and yet so far, crushed her ability to make sense of the world.

My brother finally broke the silence between us. *"Keyfek ya ukhti?"* he said.

"I'm good," I responded, smiling while wiping away tears.

Iyad looked down at Bassel, who was in my arms. He flashed a huge smile at my son. But I could tell it pained him not to be able to hold his nephew. Even children were forbidden from contact with prisoners at Jneid. He turned to me, "What have you been up to? Tell me about New York."

A question like this would normally get me talking, telling long stories about my life, but in that moment, all I could muster was, "What do you want to hear?"

"Tell me about your life. All I have heard are bits from our mother. Tell me one of your stories. The last time we saw each other, we didn't have time to talk for long, remember?"

I nodded. He continued, "I miss your stories. It's been so long. Do you remember those days?"

Of course I remembered! I chuckled. I could feel tears at my lips.

"You know, when they caught me, I was wearing your gray leather jacket," he recalled.

"Really?"

"Yes. I hope they return it when they let me out," he smiled.

I tried to feign optimism. He had been in prison for several years and still hadn't been sentenced. In the absence of a verdict, I was always hopeful, but in that moment, it was difficult to expect he would ever be released. "Yes, *inshallah*," I said.

"So, tell me how you've been."

I spoke fast, trying to catch my brother up with my last two years. I rushed him through my life in New York City, my work at the UN, and my English classes at Baruch College. I also spoke of my married life because he asked, but I left it superficial and kept out the darker side. His older sister, I told him, was in good hands, and he needn't worry. He too, spoke of his time since I went away, and although it looked like he had lost weight, he assured me he was doing well.

"Sireen, why aren't you wearing the hijab?" he said, changing the topic.

I laughed off the remark.

"Really, Sireen. You shouldn't dress this way. And you should wear the hijab if you are going to come see me."

Sireen was frustrated, but she wasn't going to show it then. She let out another nervous laugh instead.

Now, everyone wears the hijab. Every single woman in the village. This all started after the intifada, when people began to feel that the Israelis were winning because Palestinians had become less pious. We didn't have this religious strictness before, and groups like Hamas and the Islamic Jihad were not part of our daily lives. The Friday prayer, for example, was more of a communal event. The men would fix themselves up, shave, and wear suits to head over to the mosque to catch up on politics and social affairs. I remember when our family started to feel pressure to conform to religious norms, first from my sister after she married and moved to Jeddah, and then even more from Iyad once he became religious. He didn't even want me visiting again that summer unless I came dressed in a hijab.

They were approaching the end of visitation time, so Iyad dropped the issue. Sensing this was all about to end, his eyes went from tight to tired; he pulled back, slouched, and his voice softened with despair. He needed to get out. He implored Sireen to hire a good lawyer and do whatever she could to free him.

When the thirty minutes were up, the guard who had been watching over the visits called out for everyone to leave and escorted the prisoners out of the room. Iyad was the last to leave. Sireen watched him walk away. He turned around and looked at her and Um Yousef with a large smile and a chuckle before he passed out of view. For Sireen, departing prison was more difficult than arriving. It felt as though she were leaving behind an append-age, or even her entire soul. The guilt of continuing with her life was insuf-ferable. But she had a child, she had a life in the US, and so she was forced to compartmentalize it in her mind a day or two later as her heart refortified its walls and life trudged on.

21

1995

All around Sireen in New York, people continued to be optimistic about the Oslo agreement, Palestinians and non-Palestinians alike, and only a few critical voices emerged. Sireen felt more conflicted—at times swept up in the wave of hope and then calling home and getting a different perspective. In those days, the calling card she used was quite cheap, so she called often. Rates for calls to the Israeli phone grid were like those to Europe rather than Arab countries, and thankfully for Sireen, the calling card companies did not discriminate between Palestinian and Israeli numbers on the same grid.

She often found herself arguing on the phone with her mother or father about the ongoing situation. Sireen felt she had insights into Palestinian politics because of her work at the Jordanian mission. She was supportive of the accords, wanting her family to give them time. Abu Yousef was less combative with her and resigned himself to telling her, "We'll see." But as far as he was concerned, as long as his son was in prison, there was no moving forward and no peace.

Um Yousef was more stubborn in the face of Sireen's optimism. She tried to get Sireen to see how the Oslo Accords were upending people's lives and how they were being implemented on the ground. "They do not say anything about the settlements or any plans to freeze or dismantle them," she argued. "Oslo is legalizing the settlements!" They were doing so by signaling to the Israelis that they could do whatever they wanted until everyone could agree on how to define the end of occupation.

I knew the Israeli government had been given permission to continue to build more settlements. But I was just trying to be hopeful.

Sireen had no way of knowing at the time that in the next seven years, the settlement population would grow by 42 percent (to 115,000 settlers), a greater rate than in the seven years prior to the accords.

The agreement was meant to be a step toward creating a contiguous Palestinian state. Yet almost two years later, in 1995, in a second stage of negotiations as part of the process, the two signatories agreed to further divide the occupied territory into three sectors. So, while in South Africa, apartheid Bantustans were disintegrating, in Palestine, Bantustan-like areas were being carved out and cemented with walls, checkpoints, guard towers, and an efficient system of surveillance. For Um Yousef and Abu Yousef, the further fracturing of the land only brought more heartache and difficulties, more obstacles to visiting their son in prison.

I heard about the changes on the news and at the Jordanian mission. I read excerpts of the agreement, but it all felt unreal, the language sterile. It was as if I was reading about another place, not about my land, my people.

The agreement would result in three Palestinian sectors: Areas A, B, and C. Area A was the smallest, divided into eleven separate blocks, and under full Palestinian control. It was to include most of the major Palestinian city centers, except for Jerusalem and 20 percent of the city of al-Khalil, which is located in the southern part of the West Bank and had approximately five hundred Jewish settlers. Area B was divided into 120 separate blocks. These were placed under Palestinian civil control, but their security was jointly controlled by Israelis and Palestinians. This sector included 440 villages and their surrounding lands. In both Areas A and B, public order was to be maintained by a Palestinian police force.

The largest sector, however, was Area C, a single contiguous block comprising 60 percent of the West Bank, including Jerusalem, and it was to be under full Israeli civil and military control. This ensured that Jewish settlers in the West Bank remained under Israeli jurisdiction. Inside Area C, the Israelis prevented the construction of almost all new Palestinian structures.

"Do you see what's happening here, Sireen?" Um Yousef once asked with frustration. "They're permanently dividing us." The new areas were formalizing a structure that had developed informally during the intifada. More checkpoints would be constructed to maintain this new structure. And Um Yousef understood this. "Already, last week, a friend in Tulkarem traveled by car on dirt roads and then still had to stop at a checkpoint on the way to visit us. How is this peace?" It was Sireen's conversations with her parents that gave emotion to all the newspeak. And in those moments, she felt confused, unable to see the future.

"As long as we stay within Area A, nobody says anything," her mother continued. "We can go to Arraba and return with no question. That's about it. You'll see, slowly, they will strangle us! Lucky that Arselene is studying in Nablus and so far the wait at checkpoints is not long. You should see what happens to those who want to go to Birzeit University! They are always running into 'flying' checkpoints. It's unbelievable! It makes you just want to stay close to home." Sireen could hear the anger in Um Yousef's voice.

"Inshallah this will be temporary," I said, trying to console my mother.

"Temporary? Like everything they do?" she shot back. *"Majnouneh!"* she said, voice raised and calling me crazy. I really had nothing to say.

"I'm telling you, they are cementing what has already been our reality for the last few years!" her mother continued. "Instead of opening the border with '48, they are making it even more difficult to cross. The checkpoints we stopped at on the way to Nablus last week are not going away, they will become more permanent so they can control us within our areas. It's ridiculous!" More and more frequently, they also had to navigate around the growing system of Israeli settler bypass roads. These were roads that zigzagged through the West Bank. Roads that were forbidden to Palestinians.

Residents of Kufr Ra'i faced many restrictions, but they were luckier than those of Ya'bad, just a few kilometers away, in the area designated as Area B. To get there from Kufr Ra'i, people had to make long detours and pass through checkpoints. They were also luckier than residents of Deir Abu-Da'if, دير أبو ضعيف, or any of the other villages lying to the east of Jenin. Those villages were cut off from Jenin by one of the forbidden settler roads. These roads would grow and develop into an infrastructure of around 795 km of roads that snaked through the West Bank, cutting deep within it with surgical precision, dividing towns, and confiscating over eighty square kilometers of Palestinian land that had been the agricultural livelihood for many families.

"Khalas Sireen. *Samdeen.* We're persevering. Don't worry about us." Um

Yousef said when there was nothing left to say. Sireen paused. Then she followed up with reassuring words that God was protecting them. After they hung up, Sireen felt weighed down by worry.

As Palestine was carved up and I heard of the struggles of my parents on a weekly basis, my optimism was dampened, and I came to see Oslo as a land grab disguised as a treaty. But it was several more years before I experienced the restrictions it placed on my family and how these restrictions further separated them from their incarcerated son, from Iyad.

22

The Israeli Prison System, circa 1996

Iyad spent his first two years in Jneid Prison, but in 1995, the prison was handed over to the Palestinian Authority following the transfer of Nablus from Israeli to Palestinian control, as Nablus was part of Area A under the terms of the Oslo Accords. At that point, Iyad should have been released, as was required by international law when territory is "liberated." Instead, the Israelis relocated everyone in that prison to prisons in '48 Palestine. They sent Iyad to Shatta Prison, right outside the northern end of the West Bank, near the lands of the erased Palestinian villages of Shatta, شطة, and Bisan, بيسان. It became more difficult for family to visit him over there. After Shatta, where he spent several months, the Israelis transferred Iyad much farther from home to a desert prison in the south, in the Naqab, النقب, called al-Naqab Prison. They transferred him, and were constantly moving prisoners to prevent strong and deep relationships and to fracture any prison organizing or mobilization. From there, they shuttled him back up north to Meggido Prison, located on the site of the depopulated village of al-Lajjun, اللجون, near Shatta, before forcing him back south to Shikma Prison in the depopulated town of al-Mijdal, المجدل, now known as Ashkelon or 'Askalan, عسقلان.

After the first months of interrogation were over, Iyad entered into the daily routine of prison life, but because he refused a plea bargain, it took years before he was convicted and learned the length of his sentence. The process was torturous, and he switched defense teams several times. A man could lose his mind in limbo, dragged back and forth from prison to court, transferred from one prison to another. Each transfer, each courtroom visit was accompanied by an interrogation meant to shame, weaken, and break him. At first, he hoped these commutes would be good for him, that he'd see the country and smell fresh air. But if he had any hope, it quickly disintegrated when he experienced the vehicle used to transfer prisoners, the *bosta*.

Each transfer began with an encounter with the Israeli Nahshon army unit. Guards from the unit met Iyad in a holding area on the morning of each transfer. They were strongly built, Krav Maga–trained men of steel, and they made sure to use their muscle. They forced prisoners to strip, checked their bodies, slapped them around, cursed at them, and beat them.

"Tomorrow I have a court session," Iyad told his prison mate.

"*Allah yi'eenak*," came the reply. Iyad nodded in silence. He would certainly need God's help.

He tossed in bed more than usual that night, knowing the humiliation he was going to suffer. The next day, a prison guard escorted him to the Nahshon unit guards. They strip-searched him and several other prisoners. After Iyad dressed again, the guards pressed handcuffs hard into his skin and pushed him and the others along. "*Yalla! Yalla!*" the Nahshon guards said impatiently.

Iyad huffed in frustration. This was enough to get a baton smack to the back. Hands behind him, he lost balance and fell. A guard lifted him up from his elbow and pushed him along.

Iyad and the other prisoners—these wretched of the earth—were handcuffed and shackled together to cold metal seats in a vehicle that, from the outside, resembled a tourist bus or truck with a large steel frame. From the outside, one saw large, tinted-glass windows, but in reality, the windows inside were fitted with metal sheets, with pin-like holes to let in air and light. The interior was divided into cages, with a section for the Nahshon guards with their equipment and police dogs, a section for over twenty prisoners, and a last section with cells for the most dangerous, who were isolated. This was the *bosta*—what came to be known as the mobile grave.

Shackled, with their seats placed so closely together, prisoners had few positions in which they could sit comfortably. Every time Iyad tried to shift, he felt his cuffs sting his wrists. He looked around him and saw a comrade trying to overcome the moment's agony by closing his eyes; another had his head down and was lost in thought. Iyad began to move his lips, reciting verses from the Quran in silence.

What could have been a two-hour ride as the crow flies took around eleven hours, during which Iyad could not eat, drink, stretch, or relieve himself. And this was not the end of the road. It was merely a pitstop. It was this way for most prisoners who were taken to other prisons, courts, or hospitals. Iyad's court session in Salem, north of the West Bank, meant that the journey from Shikma Prison in ʿAskalan took him first to Ramle, الرملة, where he had to spend a night in Ramle Prison's temporary holding, and then to the site of the erased village of al-Jalameh, الجلمة, near Haifa, where he spent a night in al-Jalameh Prison. In these *mi'bar*, or temporary holdings, Iyad could be put in isolation or piled into a room fit for four that held twenty. Bitterly cold in the winter and suffocatingly hot in the summer, these underground cells, because they were temporary, were unkept in ways worse than the interrogation cells. They were overrun by rats and cockroaches and overflowing with the remains of human feces from a sewage system left in disrepair.

Iyad spent the hours angry that he had not received a sentence yet. If they just got it over with, at least he would be spared these torturous trips in the *bosta* that could take as many as three days with all the stops. And each stop came with multiple strip searches and beatings.

When he arrived at court in Salem, he was placed in another holding cell, this one a cement block of 2 meters by 1.5 meters with a small window, crammed with as many as twenty bodies. He stood with the others in this confined space from the early morning till around 3 p.m., surveilled by a guard who forbade him from visiting a bathroom, praying, or talking to his comrades. Any attempt to communicate with another prisoner could result in a beating, or collective punishment by closing the only window into the cell.

Iyad then had to make this trip back to Shikma Prison, so the total time of a trip to court took around five days instead of a few hours. Remaining without sentencing for years meant he had to make these trips countless times, the only consolation being the possibility of seeing his parents during some of these court visits.

When he was not being shuttled around, Iyad lived the daily routine of prison. It was a routine well regulated by the jailer but also by the various Palestinian political factions. Perhaps what was most precious about the days of routine in the static life of prison was that he could eat more decent food again. He and his comrades could cook what they liked and bought food from the prison canteen that was managed by prisoners. They shared their food. It was the ability to respond to the prison conditions as a community that helped them overcome those very conditions.

Prisoners received deposits of money from their families to be used at the canteen. But this money was managed collectively by the leadership of the factions so as not to create income disparity. At the canteen, they could buy meat, chicken, vegetables, cigarettes, soap, tea, instant coffee, sugar, and candy. It was a far cry from the rot Iyad had eaten during his months of interrogation.

On most days, he kept to himself. It was hard in 'Askalan's overcrowded cells in section 12, where he was one of ten, or section Dal, which he was transferred to later, and where he was one of eighteen. He knew everyone, and everyone knew and liked him, but he was selective about whom he mixed with. He remained reserved, observing more, talking and sharing less. His ambush in Baka al-Gharbieh was always at the back of his mind, as was the encounter with supposed comrades in the "bird room."

In a previous prison, in Jneid, Iyad met someone who was part of the Islamic Jihad, and there, he began to delve further into religion as part of a complete revolutionary practice. He woke each morning well before dawn, prayed the Tahajjud—the voluntary night prayer—waited briefly till dawn, and followed this with the Fajr prayer. The early rise meant he went to sleep at night earlier than most and passed up watching TV and other late-night social activities.

Before he gave up those activities, he learned that prisoners were not saints. The image he had of them from the outside was brought into perspective. In prison, people loved and lied, betrayed and stood up for one another—it was like life on the outside, minus a good dose of freedom. And despite Iyad's shyness and reservations, the prisoners tried to involve him in their horsing around. Sometimes, they attempted to trick him into watching an image of scantily dressed women on TV. He tried to avoid this because these images created urges in prisoners that had no way of being relieved. In prison, this became the dilemma of dilemmas and the other great obsession. Prisoners dreamed about sex. Even the saints dream about sex. And this obsession served as another tool in the system of control.

After the Fajr prayer, and after the guards came around to perform the prisoner count, Iyad went out to exercise for an hour. This was followed with an hour of free time outside, the time the prisoners called the *fawra*, where they were allowed into a small courtyard covered with a net. A net, lest they forget that the Israelis stood between them and the sky.

During this free time, even after his morning exercise, he sometimes played basketball or volleyball. Other times, he walked with friends in circles around the courtyard and gravitated to the more religious, regardless of party affiliation. With them he dreamed of freedom—to leave the prison cell and live under military occupation. Freedom! Freedom becomes another preoccupation, as the prisoner struggles to remember what life outside is like. Yet, even as he dreamed, Iyad understood that freedom was out of reach, and his only ticket out was a prisoner-exchange deal.

Once the free time was up, he returned to his cell, where the monotony of his day was broken in different ways. He took up work doing laundry for a brief time. It wasn't for the work itself that he or most others did this, but as a mode of resistance. Prison work provided a kind of postal system. Communication depended on these workers because they could come and go freely within the prison. These workers carried verbal messages. They were the veins of the prison community, and they were extremely careful in ensuring that information did not end up in the wrong ears. Iyad wanted to contribute to this communication between prison sections.

When he wasn't working, he passed time in *fiqh*, or Islamic philosophy classes, where he produced pages and pages of notes and interpretations of religious texts. He also buried himself in his Quran, reciting verses, taking more notes, and fasting often. In time, he became calmer and more patient, soft-spoken, and serious—a far cry from his earlier days of confinement, when he was rebellious and short-tempered, getting into trouble with prisoners and the prison administrators.

And then, in rarer moments, in the blind spots of surveillance, alongside other comrades, he also found time to take lessons in military tactics and the use of explosives.

🌿

In 1997, five years after his initial incarceration and many *bosta* journeys later, Iyad was finally sentenced.

Records from the military court proceedings claim that Iyad was charged with killing five collaborators, among them the baker's son and three other boys in the cave; with membership in the Fahd al-Aswad organization; with kidnapping, interrogating, and assaulting many residents suspected of collaboration; and with possession of weapons. The proceedings also suggest that he confessed to at least some of these charges, although he and other witnesses gave conflicting accounts that were revised multiple times. The confessions were extracted under torture, and the conviction was reached without proper proof or normal judicial process. Alas, these are the occupation's military courts, where normal itself is redefined.

None of this matters. What matters is that in the proceedings, the court stenographer recorded that "at the extension-of-detention hearing from 04-08-92, following the submission of the bill of indictment, the defendant says: 'I confess to the charges attributed to me.'" And based on these utterances, on this confession, Iyad Abu Shqara received a sentence that would ensure he spent the rest of his life in prison. A sentence of 215 years.

23

1999

I traveled back to Palestine again because my husband's father was terminally sick. My husband would not have agreed to my travel otherwise. It had been around four years since my last visit. This time, I went with my two sons—Bassel, who was now in kindergarten, and Zeid, who was still too young for school. I was there from early spring until the end of summer, arriving in Palestine a few weeks before my husband.

By this time, the web of the prison system had transformed due to the changes brought on by Oslo. Iyad was in Shikma Prison, which was over the Green Line in ʿAskalan. It was much more difficult for Um Yousef to visit because, each time, she needed to apply for a prison visitation permit to allow her to exit the West Bank—a permit that took weeks to issue, if it even came at all.

I wanted to make sure I could visit my brother while in Palestine, so I worked the contacts I had developed with the Red Cross and Amnesty International while working for the Jordanian mission to the UN. Before my travels, I faxed them to ask for special personal visitation rights to give me more time with my brother. My request was granted.

That spring, Sireen flew with her children from JFK to Amman, spent the night there at a friend's place, and took a taxi to the Jordan Valley the next day. She arrived early at the large parking lot of the bus terminal leading to the Allenby Bridge—the bridge to Palestine, the bridge that connected the east bank with the west bank of the Jordan River—but already masses of people were lined up with suitcases, duffle bags, and woven plaid plastic shopping bags, packed with whatever goods they couldn't find in Palestine, waiting to cross the bridge.

The beginnings and ends of lines of people were hard to find, if there were lines at all. Everyone was left to fend for themselves. Each traveler had to pass their luggage through security, have their papers stamped, pay the fee to exit Jordan, and pay for their spot on the bus and for each piece of luggage they carried. At every counter, there were crowds of people stretched out in an almost-inverted pyramid, waiting. Although the crisp breeze of the March morning offered some respite, Sireen could hardly enjoy it, as the rising sun and the suffocating presence of the terminal guards seemed to overwhelm the air.

I finally managed to get on one of the JETT buses, the ones operated by Jordanian Express Tourist Transport. It took two minutes from the base of the bus terminal to arrive to the exit on the Jordanian side. There were buses ahead of us as far as my eyes could see, all waiting. The driver turned off his engine.

Sireen and her children waited for three hours to cross the practically walkable arid river—the river her mother walked across with Sireen all those years ago, when gushing waters still flowed through it.

The wait was painful. It wasn't the pain of being so close to home and a rock's throw from her ancestral lands. This pain was far more mundane. It emanated from a feeling that the body was slowly decomposing in the heat. Sweat, bodies in intimate proximity, bad breath, dust, engine fumes, and restless children.

Soon, people began to wonder if they would even be allowed to pass through to the Israeli side of the bridge that day. And if they crossed the bridge, would they be allowed into Palestine, or would they be sent back on a technicality? To be allowed in or not—this question kept those on the bus preoccupied. The Israelis, on the other hand, remain obsessed with gates and locks to maintain, reinforce, and reassert the reality of the border, lest it be swallowed up by the dried river below and the shrubs on the surrounding hills.

The bus began to trundle slowly across the bridge, over the river—if it were not for the line of buses, this would be a journey that took less than a full thought to complete. Sireen looked out at the no-man's land between Jordan and occupied Palestine. She saw shells of homes that families were expelled from in June 1967. The homes appeared archaeological, of a time past. They are not. They are the living remains of a dispossession that is ongoing.

The bus approached the Israeli-controlled side of the bridge. For the traveler, the border guards are their first contact with Israelis during this journey as they watch them through the JETT bus's large windows. The border guards, a young woman with curly hair and a big smile and two boys with red cheeks, looked more like flirtatious teenagers skipping school than soldiers heavily trained to protect the nation's security. After a brief exchange between the Jordanian driver and the Israeli officers, the bus was allowed to enter Israeli-occupied Palestine. Sireen looked behind her at the gate that led to Jordan and saw a sign that welcomed travelers into the Hashemite Kingdom. Ahead, a sign welcomed her to the Allenby Bridge Crossing Point. That is all it read. There was no sign to indicate where the bridge led. It was all so vague, as if it connected Jordan to the unknown, to a land not yet named. The Israeli government had not annexed the land yet, so they could not name it. And the Palestinians had not succeeded in enforcing their right to name it, despite the Oslo agreement's illusions of promised statehood.

Sireen's bus finally pulled into the Israeli bus terminal. There were already hundreds of people waiting outside, and she had to wait on the bus till they were processed. When it was time, she exited the bus. People rushed to identify their luggage, and then held onto their carry-on bags while watching larger suitcases go through security. Their belongings would enter long before them.

Sireen made her way into the terminal almost two hours later. Her skin felt sticky. Her children were sweating, squirming, and begging to be carried. It was a struggle to keep from losing her temper with them; she gave them candy to buy time. She went through the first security check, was patted down by the officer, and then handed him her *tasreeh*, along with her children's. The officer flipped through the pages, then returned her children's travel permits but held onto hers. He gave it to an armed officer in plainclothes who put it in a pile with several others. After fifteen minutes, the officer called out a list of names. He handed back some travel permits without any questioning or explanation. With others, like Sireen, he questioned their reason for entry, where they lived, and what they did in life. After the questions, her *tasreeh* was returned to her, and she walked further into the terminal, where she had to give it to another border officer who told her to wait and left with a stack of travel permits.

Sireen stood, she sat, she paced, she stopped. She did this over and over. Her children whined and became irritable. She maintained her composure at all times, though. Hair unaffected by perspiration, shoulders firm, eyes narrowed and staring unapologetically at security personnel.

After a while, someone struck up a conversation with her. The conversation was reserved, made up of the usual introductions and formalities, but there was an air of suspicion about it. Here, at the border, everyone is cautious of planted collaborators searching for a cause to deny people entry. Sireen cut the conversation short, going against her usual chatty nature. She had to deal with impatient children. She bought water and chocolate from a kiosk at the entrance across from the immigration booth. Like at other West Bank checkpoints, the kiosk stood as a physical reminder of the inevitability of waiting at border crossings.

Sometime later, hours later, the officer returned, and Sireen was called to immigration counter number 1. The immigration officer was a woman named Orel. She was young, likely still a teenager. None of the officers that day appeared older than twenty. Orel faked a smile. Sireen raised the corners of her lips in return. Orel asked her mundane questions. What do you do? Why are you visiting? Where do you live? Sireen had already been asked these questions by the previous officer but had to endure several more minutes of the same line of questioning.

Eventually, the officer, who either ran out of questions or was finally satisfied with the responses, stamped her *tasreeh*, and Sireen was allowed to enter. When she walked past the officer, she exhaled deeply, just then realizing how long she had been holding her breath. She stepped outside only to make another realization: the Israelis had just stolen a day from her. Determined not to let them steal another second, she rushed her kids onto a bus to Areeha, أريحا, Jericho, where she now still had to pass through Palestinian border control, though this was quick. She then collected her luggage that the Israelis had sent long before on a separate bus, and, finally, took a taxi to Kufr Ra'i.

The day after I arrived in the West Bank, I called the Red Cross in Jerusalem, and they informed me that they had a copy of the approval for the *ziyara khasa*—the special or personal visit—and that I should go straight to 'Askalan.

The next morning, we woke before dawn—I don't think any one of us slept, to be honest. We were all anxious. Especially me, because I had placed so much hope on this visit. My mother and kids were going to join me, but my father refused to come along. He said there were already too many of us going, and he didn't want to go all the way only to be denied visitation.

Abu Yousef, seventy years old, cleanly shaven, still sporting a full head of honey-brown hair with only a few streaks of silver, was bitter that his health made prison visits so difficult. Besides the diabetes, he had a weak heart, and had already traveled once to the US a few years earlier for heart surgery. He mostly spent his days in his loose white gown, the *dishdashe*, smoking his cigarettes and taking turns visiting friends and having them over.

At 4 a.m., we rode in a van to Jenin. In the city, we caught an International Committee of the Red Cross bus with families from villages all around Jenin—it was the only way to be transported out of the West Bank for prison visits, unlike years ago, when we simply took a taxi to Jneid Prison in Nablus. It was total chaos. We had to push and shove our way onto the bus. My mother was used to it but having Bassel and Zeid with us made it more difficult. They were jet lagged, restless, and overtired, inconsolable when awake yet refusing to sleep. The whole ride, we were shoved left and right as the bus bounced and swayed.

We were driven to a checkpoint near a cornfield on the border of Tulkarem and '48 Palestine. There, we were left to wait on the bus for at least two hours. It was March, and dawn was terribly cold. The bus was decrepit, with no heating, jammed windows left open, and piles of trash. There were around one hundred of us on a bus meant for thirty to forty people. Girls were sitting on each other's laps, and men stood the entire time, even in the stairways that led out of the bus. There was a woman with a newborn wanting to show her imprisoned husband their child, and an old man, barely able to stand, wanting to visit his son.

After a while, they told us we could step off the bus while we waited to be let through the checkpoint. My mother came prepared. She had brought a large towel, and we laid it on the side of the road in the dirt and had breakfast. Other families did the same. She had brought bread, cheese, cucumber, and *fatayer zaʿatar*.

Around 8 a.m., we were finally let through the checkpoint, and the bus took us to the prison in ʿAskalan. When we arrived, there was a mad rush to disembark as soon as the bus slowed down to a stop. Whoever stepped off first registered first at the prison registration window. This meant that if you were last, you wouldn't see the prisoner till 4 p.m. and wouldn't return home till almost midnight. If you got in early, you could catch an earlier bus and be home before sunset.

The men and boys didn't care about anyone else. Some even jumped out of the windows; others trampled over the women and children. There was no way I was going to go through that process of waiting to register. I told my mother that we had authorization for a *ziyara khasa,* and there was no need to register. The women on the bus scoffed at me. Several dismissed me as naive. "They won't grant you the special visit. Just stand in line and don't waste your time," they said.

I cut the line and walked to the window at the main visitor's entrance with my American passport in hand, along with my UN ID and a letter from the UN proving I worked for them. The guard behind the window looked bored and uninterested in our presence. When he looked at me, he seemed somewhere between disgruntled and disgusted, like my presence polluted his air. I spoke in English and told the guard that I was there for a special visit. He swore at me and told me to get the hell out of his face. I got angry and said I had a letter from the Red Cross. But he told me to get in line and wait with everyone else. For a regular visit, I would have twenty minutes to see Iyad in a room with forty other inmates and their families. This was the standard way. With all the visitors, it was impossible to hear oneself speak in the packed room. Cameras monitored every move to prevent smuggling, and a guard watched over each family.

Imagine. Wouldn't you break down? I hadn't seen my brother in almost five years, and they were just going to give me twenty minutes!

My mother already had low expectations that this private visit would work, so she told me to stop crying and stand in line. I refused. The women who had warned me now looked at me with an I-told-you-so look, and I could barely make eye contact with them. I offered to give people at the front of the line one hundred dollars to switch with us, but they refused. I had to get in touch with the Red Cross. This was a nightmare!

We were in the middle of nowhere. A desert of dust and dirt, with only one road leading to the prison—the road we arrived on. I was told that there was a public pay phone near the prison. I rushed to it and placed a collect call to the Red Cross in Jerusalem. A Palestinian man picked up. Once I explained the situation, he said he was going to phone some people and told me to wait next to the phone for twenty minutes and call back. I was a woman at a payphone in the middle of nowhere, and he wanted me to wait! But I had no choice. I just couldn't believe this was happening!

I waited and waited. A half hour, I waited. Then I called back collect. The person on the phone told me that they had spoken to the prison warden and that I should go to the staff entrance.

I followed his directions. When the guards stopped me, I told them that I had authorization from the Red Cross in Tel Aviv and wanted to see the warden. This time they called for the warden, and she came out and told me to go around to the visitor's entrance. There, she let me in, took all our IDs, and apologized. She told me that anyone who was with me could come in and visit. My father was so upset when we told him this the next day.

My mother had not expected to be let in because the approval stated only my name along with my children's. My father had even told her not to bother when she began the trip that morning. She had tried to get approval using different lawyers, but nothing had come of her efforts. My mother was stubborn, though.

When my brother entered the private room, I felt my eyes pop out from the shock of his presence; he was right there, and I could touch him. I became giddy with excitement, tears streaming down through an enormous smile.

Iyad gave me a huge, tight hug when he saw me. It had been nine years. Nine years since we were in the same room without any barrier. Nine years since we had hugged.

He looked at me and said, *"Majnouneh!* You're crazy! My God, you're crazy!" He told us that when he heard the calls for private visitation and was not included, he started to cry. He couldn't believe that I wasn't able to get a personal visit with my connections and persistence. And then, when they called him later for a private visit, he thought, "She did it! That crazy sister!"

When we were done hugging, he examined me, the one who had always been taller. Now, after so many years had passed, the boy, the teenager I left behind, had grown into a man, and I was much shorter. He looked at me and said, "How does a mountain shrink?" He had become the mountain in our family.

Personal visits are special. We got our own air-conditioned room, a table, and several chairs. They brought us soft drinks, orange juice, and a bag with over twenty types of candy, cookies, and chocolate for the kids. And every once in a while, they came and asked us if we wanted anything. I have no idea what the Red Cross in Tel Aviv told them!

We spent two hours with my brother that day. He had the biggest smile, and my mother was over the moon. Iyad showered her with kisses on her hands and forehead. It was the first time in all his years in captivity, in all her visits, that she could hold him, hug him, kiss him. It was such an emotional moment seeing them connect, after all the prison visits where they were separated by a fence or a glass window.

There was some sadness in the air, though.

"Where is the Haj?" Iyad asked his mother.

"*Abuk kan ta'ban*. Your father was tired the past two days. He didn't think we would be able to see you," replied Um Yousef.

The visit was incomplete without my father. We told Iyad that my father's diabetes made him too weak for such a journey, and entry for all of us hadn't been guaranteed. My mother weighed in that she came mostly so we wouldn't get lost on the way, and she was shocked when they allowed her in. Still, it was as if Iyad searched the room, hoping his father would appear from the shadows. His absence was like a cloud over us.

Iyad had become quite religious, even compared to my last visit in 1994. He didn't used to pray or fast. Now, he was known as Sheikh Iyad. I noticed the changes, having not visited him in years. He spoke with a composure normally associated with religious figures, with the collected temperament of Hassan Nasrallah. He had so much religious knowledge. He had spent hours learning the Quran and taking notes.

We talked about many things that day. I tried to catch him up with my life without getting into too many details about my marriage. He spoke about marriage himself. And how he wanted to marry women who were in need. One of his friends was killed when his wife, a beautiful woman from Tulkarem, was two months pregnant. Iyad wanted to marry her when he got out. He talked about marrying another woman with children and a deceased husband, or a deaf woman. My mother joked, "Iyad, how many women can you possibly marry?"

I remember, despite the calmness in how he communicated with us, that he was also anxious about wanting to be free. He pleaded, "Don't leave me here. Do your best to get me out. Please!"

I felt he didn't want to rot away in prison. He wanted to do more with his life. I asked him what I could do, and he suggested I get a good lawyer. After we visited him, I spent much of that spring and summer, when I wasn't in Nablus with my husband's family, trying to find him a lawyer. We finally managed to secure him the famous Israeli lawyer Lea Tsemel to work on his case.

*

The summer months passed quickly. Midway into August, as Sireen was preparing to return to the US, the media began reporting about a prisoner's deal to take place in September, in which the Israeli authorities were to release around five hundred prisoners. She asked Yasser Arafat's office to put her brother's name on the list. A week later, they told her his name was rejected.

Sireen's last morning in Kufr Ra'i was on September 1. She woke up feeling unsettled about departing if there was still any chance for Iyad's release in the prisoner exchange that was scheduled in less than two weeks.

I made so many calls that day and finally got in touch with the office of the Palestinian Authority's minister of interior. I begged them to let me know if his name made the list. The names were to be announced in two or three days, but I couldn't leave without knowing. The minister put me in touch with the office that had the list of names, and they dealt me the final blow. Two hundred prisoners would be released, but Iyad was not one of them.

I cried in my last moments in Kufr Ra'i, thinking of my brother having to hope for the next prisoner's deal and wondering if it would ever come. I traveled that first day of September with my head down, not knowing if I would ever see my brother a free man again.

Maysoun, Sireen, and Suzanne, around the time the family returned
to the West Bank. Circa 1967. *Source:* Family collection.

Abu Yousef with Yousef, Ihab, and Iyad. 1975. *Source:* Family collection.

Sireen on her family balcony in the pink outfit her maternal
grandfather bought her, with Kufr Ra'i and the martyr's graveyard
in the background. Circa 1980s. *Source:* Family collection.

Iyad in his mid-teens. Circa 1990. *Source:* Family collection.

Iyad posing for a photo in his prison cell with a carpet for a backdrop. He is wearing a prison uniform under a leather jacket. *Source:* Family collection.

Iyad playing with his young niece. 2000.
Source: Family collection.

Um Yousef with Sireen's eldest son, Bassel. 2021.
Photo Credit: Jamal Aruri.

Sireen surveying her street in Kufr Raʻi, with many new homes
in the background. 2021. *Photo Credit*: Jamal Aruri.

Family photo, including, from left to right, Sireen, Salma, Bassel
(in back), Um Yousef (middle), five of Sireen's sisters, Baha (right),
and several grandchildren. 2021. *Photo Credit*: Jamal Aruri.

Sireen with her children Zeid (left), Salma (middle), and Bassel (right) at their home in Princeton. A painting of downtown Jenin hangs above them. 2022. *Source:* Family collection.

Part III

A PROMISE AND A PLEDGE

24

September 1999

The morning of September 9 was bitter for the Sawalha family. There was going to be a prisoner release, and Iyad would not be part of it. In the early hours, the Palestinian Center for Human Rights (PCHR) published a press release. It stated what Sireen had roughly been told before she left:

> *This morning, 9 September 1999 the Israeli authorities released 199 Palestinian prisoners from Israeli jails. These included including [sic] 98 prisoners from the Gaza Strip, and 101 from the West Bank. This release was carried out under the provisions of the Sharm El Sheik memorandum, signed on 5 September, which revised the Wye Accords, and set a framework for resuming the negotiations on final status issues.*
>
> *The memorandum states "the Israeli government will release Palestinian prisoners who committed their offences before the 13 Sept 1993 [sic], and those arrested before 4 May 1994." Today's release, which is the first stage of the releases agreed upon in the memorandum, was to be implemented within a week of its signing, and was to include 200 prisoners. One of the prisoners listed for release, refused to be released due to the fact that he has only one week of his sentence left to serve, and he asked that priority for release under the memorandum be given to someone else.*
>
> *A further 150 prisoners are due to be released 8 October. The memorandum also provides for further prisoners to be released before the month of Ramadan, i.e. by the end of this year.*
>
> *Though the memorandum clearly provides for the release of prisoners who committed their offences before 13 September 1993 and were arrested*

before 4 May 1999, the Israeli authorities excluded from release many prisoners who meet these criteria, on the following grounds:

1. *All prisoners from Jerusalem were excluded*

2. *All prisoners from within the Green Line were excluded*

3. *Prisoners from Hamas and the Islamic Jihad were excluded*

4. *Prisoners accused of killing Israelis were excluded*

5. *Prisoners accused of seriously wounding Israelis were excluded*

[. . .]

Abu Yousef woke up and walked silently out to the front yard. He was avoiding everyone. News of the prisoner release was heard everywhere; he was feeling helplessness as a father. Um Yousef got out of bed with a sense of disbelief that she had to continue waiting for her son's release indefinitely. She felt powerless. But the only way to live was to hold on to hope for Iyad, if not for herself. If she felt devastated, how did her son feel?

In Ramallah, two buses rolled into the Muqataʻa, Yasser Arafat's headquarters. In an eleventh-hour decision, the buses did indeed carry 200 rather than 199 prisoners, each in disbelief of their freedom, searching for their kin in the crowd of families waiting to greet them outside. Their relatives received them with bagpipe bands and gunshot volleys from Palestinian officers.

For that two-hundredth prisoner, whose family was uninformed of his last-minute release, looking out at the sea of unfamiliar elated people must have made the moment bittersweet, incomplete.

That two-hundredth prisoner, a member of Fatah, was Iyad. Given that the PCHR statement was explicit in who was denied release, clearly Iyad had not made his membership in the Islamic Jihad public.

For whatever reason, his name was not on the official list and not included in the press release. So, on the morning of this prisoner release, neither Um Yousef nor Abu Yousef, nor anyone in the family, had held out for good news.

Prisoners disembarked. Iyad finally stepped into the sun. All the prisoners were still in plastic handcuffs.

Released. Free. Despite the bitterness of comrades left behind, of liberation not yet near, of the larger prison into which they were being released. The euphoria of brushing against free air was fused with the anxiety of the unbelievable moment. And with thoughts of, Will the jailer reverse their decision? When will they come for me again? and with an eye over a shoulder at the surveillance all around.

Iyad stood at the center of it all, knowing he would not recognize any faces. He was hugged and kissed by strangers jubilant at the sight of their heroes out of captivity. He smiled, but he wanted to go home, to find a way to get this news to his family, to make his way onto the next bus to Jenin. The freed men around him raised their hands with victory signs, some chanting "God is great" and singing the Palestinian anthem about the warrior sacrificing for their ancestral land—"*Fida'i, Fida'i | Fida'i ya ardi | ya ard el jdoud.*" Relatives were crying and wailing with joy. Women in the crowd released high-pitched undulating sounds of celebration: "La-la-la-la-la-la-lee! La-la-la-la-la-la-lee!"

Again they let out a "la-la-la-la-la-la-lee, la-la-la-la-la-la-lee!" And again and again into the alleyways and the streets, and up at the sun, high in the midday sky.

The prisoners put on festive faces for their waiting kin and for the cameras, but in their hearts, they felt an ache for those left behind. Shukri Salema, after eighteen years in prison, was the longest-serving prisoner to be released. He gave voice to their heartache in his remarks to the press: "I cannot express my happiness, because I've left behind a lot of friends who have already served longer than me, some of them twenty-five years. The Israelis should release them, too." Iyad was among the angry prisoners unable to fully appreciate that moment of freedom, as only a tenth of the prisoners languishing in Israeli prisons were released. He was leaving newfound friends behind. At the back of his mind, he heard the whispers of his comrades remaining in the occupation's prisons imploring him, over and over, "*Ma tin-suna*, don't forget us!"

The phone rang. I picked up. It was my sister, Sawsan. Usually, conversations with her are flavored with a casual sarcasm and a striking sense of humor; now she sounded distressed and excited. In between sniffles and a cracked voice, she hurriedly told me to turn on the television. Iyad was on TV with other prisoners being released. It was such a weird feeling seeing my brother—imprisoned for life—now on TV as a free person, and to first hear about it on the news as any stranger would.

Iyad was the last one out. He had his head sticking out of the bus and I think this is how my parents found out. I was so excited I started screaming and crying from joy. But when I calmed down, I was so sad that I could not be there and had not waited another ten days.

When news broke in Kufr Ra'i, there was a celebratory atmosphere in town. People closest to Sireen's family drove their cars through the village, honking and cheering. The family dressed quickly and left with a long convoy to meet Iyad's bus in Jenin. It was like a wedding procession, the honking continuing all the way. But the celebration was short lived.

On the way, as drivers in the convoy of cars were swept up in the excitement, my father's cousin got into an accident, and his car flipped over. He was severely injured that day, and it put a dent in the celebrations. He passed away from his wounds six months later.

Shortly after his release, Iyad denounced Fatah and the PLO. He said they were all a bunch of collaborators and that no one kept their word. He told us he wanted to stay away from politics.

Later, we tried to convince him to leave Palestine for good, but he refused.

25

October 1999

Iyad had been out for barely a month and could still hear the pounding clank of his prison cell door shutting when he closed his eyes at night. He could still catch whiffs of dampness mixed with sweat and urine, the air still containing an aftertaste of decay, even as he walked to the edge of the village behind his house and stood facing the hills. He could not enjoy his mother's food, conversations with his father, or the warm embrace of his siblings. The tentacles of prison were still in his head, consuming his mind. Many of the memories, especially the image of gray walls, stay forever with prisoners.

He could not escape the suffocating concern coming from his family either, their sole focus keeping Iyad out of trouble. If he refused to leave Palestine, then he needed to get married. His parents figured that if he became a family man, there would be no need to worry about him. He tried to comfort them repeatedly. "I just want to get on with my life, find good work, and marry," he would say. And while there was nothing in his voice or in his daily routine to suggest otherwise, his parents still worried as long as he wasn't married or hadn't yet left Palestine.

Iyad had spent seven years in prison, so marriage was going to be difficult. His relations with my parents and sisters had also become somewhat tense. Our younger brothers, Diaa and Baha, were children when he left, and now they were in high school. They went out and smoked *arguilleh*, and Iyad tried to discipline them when they returned. He disapproved of their lifestyles. They didn't pray, and he wanted to make sure they did. He also questioned Arselene whenever she came back late from her work in Jenin. In the morning, he was the first one up and recited the Quran out loud on the balcony. On the one hand, he was good looking, made people around him laugh with his jokes and uplifting spirit, and his seven years of prison could be viewed by many as a mark of heroism. On the other hand, he had grown stern and strict, and the years of prison and trauma would surely cause women to have second thoughts.

In the months after his release, my brother spent much of his days watching the news, especially Al Jazeera, which was quite new then and brought twenty-four-hour news to the region. He also watched religious shows and prevented my sisters from watching TV series or music channels. I heard from my sisters how he fluctuated between being short-tempered and moody and being deeply compassionate. It was similar to stories we heard of other prisoners after their release.

In those early days, he also tried hard to apologize to the families of the victims he had wrongly accused of being collaborators and executed. He was heard cursing the Fahd al-Aswad and expressing his regret for his impulsive decisions and getting mixed up with the wrong crowd.

Among those he visited to make amends to was Um Yasser. He asked for her forgiveness for what the Fahd al-Aswad had done to her husband's brother. He told her that he had cleansed his hands of them, recognized that they had taken a mistaken path and committed wrongs, and that he had come to this realization in prison.

She turned him away and told him that it is for God to forgive.

He understood that his words were not enough and could not bring back the dead. He left saddened, vowing to her that he would do things differently.

Under pressure from his parents to marry, he tried to find a wife. He suggested names to his parents of women he was interested in and found suitable. But in the village, attraction was not enough. The match was as much about the families coming together and the reputation that had to be maintained. And so, with each woman Iyad suggested came a resounding rejection from his parents. No one was good enough.

My mother had not learned from her previous experiences matching her children. She remained picky with her conditions. "Yee, she is not pretty; yee, she does not come from a good family." A suitable wife had to meet all the conditions. And like that, each of my brothers, after trying to conform, got tired and married a non-Palestinian. Ihab married a Russian and Yousef an American. Iyad, still living under his parents' roof, could not find anyone.

*

Soon after his release, the Palestinian Authority (PA) employed Iyad, at least in name. He never cared much for money or fancy clothes; he wanted just enough to survive and be independent. The PA had offered prisoners modest work in the security services and with the police. In the first few months, he trained with them as part of their rehabilitation program. After the trainings, he collected a paycheck but rarely showed up to work. He did not want to have any part in managing the Israeli occupation. He was not alone.

There was another, lesser-known side to Iyad in those early days after his release—the Iyad that did not show up to his PA job. Like many others who lived near the border of the West Bank, he soon began to smuggle goods, including weapons that he sold on the black market. The Oslo agreement had been very specific about how many policemen and weapons each village was allowed, so if villagers, and Palestinians in general, wanted to arm themselves beyond these meager means, they had to find more creative ways to do so. Iyad received weapons from contacts in Jordan or from Palestinian towns in the region known as the Triangle, المثلث, northwest over the Green Line, and sold them in the West Bank. Later, he also came upon weapons stolen from the Israeli military and others that came from the Israeli underworld.

Iyad had gotten into the trade through one of his best friends, Mu'tasem, who was from the nearby village of Anabta, عنبتا, east of Tulkarem. Iyad's age, Mu'tasem had a receding hairline and large, droopy, green eyes that comforted those in his presence. Mu'tasem had also been active in the intifada. He was injured twice back then, jailed for fifteen days, released, and then, in 1991, sentenced to ten years in prison for activities against collaborators and the occupation forces. Iyad and Mu'tasem met in prison. Iyad saw a confident and loyal friend in Mu'tasem, a role model who was able to engage in resistance activities yet still complete school and enroll in college before the army captured him.

Mu'tasem served five years, after which he was freed in the first round of prisoner releases brokered as part of the Oslo agreement. After his release, he worked in the District Coordination Office, which handled Palestinian-Israeli security coordination during the Oslo years.

After several months working with the PA, Iyad found work in Nablus as a goldsmith and enrolled in a training course to learn to be a jeweler. He rented a room in Nablus so he didn't have to commute every day.

On the rare times that he did visit home, he came bearing jewelry for his sisters. On the phone, he told me how someday he was going to design a necklace for my children with the word *Allah* on it.

In the waning days of the first millennium and into the first months of the second, Iyad and his friends just hung out and enjoyed themselves, passing nights talking and joking, with Iyad's ever-present laughter. Iyad was not a man of many words, but he laughed often. He laughed to express himself and he laughed in the face of authority.

26

September 2000

It was a Thursday morning, the twenty-eighth of the month. Sireen was in the sunroom of her new house in Princeton, New Jersey. Her house was still cluttered with boxes because they had only moved earlier that summer. The house was actually in a town next door called Kingston, but she always referred to it as Princeton so she wouldn't have to bother explaining to people where she lived. Kingston was an unknown town, and there was more worth in claiming that she lived in Princeton.

She turned on the television and flipped through channels before settling on Al Jazeera. Then she began tidying up the room.

She moved about slowly. Her back and knees were stiff and in pain from all the work her husband made her do on the house. After they bought the place, he refused to hire professional contractors. He wanted to do all the renovations himself, not because of any romantic ideal but because he was stubborn and wanted to prove he could do it, with Sireen's help, like an exploited apprentice. He told her that all they needed to do was tear off the wallpaper, paint the walls, and move in. But after removing the wallpaper, they found five other frayed layers underneath the first. It took them three weeks to remove it all. They had to come from New York on weekends and some evenings, with their two kids, to get the work done. She put up with it because she had warmed up to the idea of moving out of New York. She hoped the change would do them some good. By then, the abuse had gotten more intense. Once, a request of his for tea went unanswered and would have resulted in a broken arm had she not grabbed a knife and threatened him in order to break from his hold. Perhaps they needed a fresh start.

*

Sireen had barely picked up a few items from a box when she caught the broadcaster on Al Jazeera reporting on Palestine. It was evening in Palestine, and when she tuned in, Ariel Sharon, also known as the "Butcher of Beirut," had already visited the grounds of the Haram al-Sharif and was heard saying that he came with a message of peace. Of all the Israeli military and political figures, Sharon was the most despised among Arabs. He had been behind the Sabra and Shatila massacre in 1982. Unit 101, which he had founded, was responsible for the massacre in Qibya, قبية, in 1953. And he was one of the prominent early supporters of the Israeli policy of settlement expansion in the years after the 1967 war. For many Arabs, he was a different type of enemy, one deserving his own special place in hell.

When Sharon visited occupied Jerusalem, he was accompanied by hundreds of riot police that prevented Palestinians from accessing the al-Aqsa Mosque compound. After his departure, Palestinians threw rocks at the police to protest their presence. They were met with rubber bullets. It was at this point that Sireen tuned in to the live coverage of the events in Jerusalem.

She immediately called her parents. Abu Yousef picked up. They spoke briefly, and he reassured her that they were all fine in Kufr Ra'i. But over the next few days, the protests spread from Jerusalem to Ramallah and beyond to other parts of the West Bank and the Gaza Strip. Rubber bullets became live ammunition. Palestinians fell. Twelve-year-old Mohammed al-Durra was fatally shot by Israeli soldiers while hiding, crouching in his father's arms. And Palestinians fought back with whatever weapons they could get their hands on.

Iyad was in Jeddah when Sharon visited al-Aqsa. Earlier that year, he had gone for the *Umrah* pilgrimage to Mecca, and his family had been trying to convince him to stay. His sister who lived in Jeddah even offered to open up a small shop for him, but he was resistant to the idea. The Islamic Jihad, which he had joined in a fuller capacity after his release from prison, had long maintained that a US-Israeli-Saudi axis was central in sustaining Israeli control, so Iyad was not particularly interested in settling in the Saudi state.

The day the Jerusalem protests broke out, Iyad was sitting comfortably on the couch in a white V-neck undershirt and white cotton "sunnah underpants"—long white cotton pants often worn under a *thobe*. His mother was right beside him, having accompanied him to Jeddah. He jumped up in his seat when he saw the scuffles and ran his fingers through his inch-long hair. His jaw dropped. "Wow!" he exclaimed.

Soon he began to argue with his mother about returning to Palestine. "There cannot be liberation if we don't fight!" he insisted. Um Yousef could recognize in his eyes the same determination she had once possessed that propelled her to walk back to Palestine against the current of expulsion. But she stubbornly refused to entertain his ideas. Abu Yousef called from Palestine and father and son spoke with each other—or, more accurately, screamed at one another. "There is nothing for you here. You already sacrificed enough!" Abu Yousef said. "Isn't it enough what you saw in prison? Do you want to return there? You already did your time, *habibi*," he implored. But this was no match for Iyad's determination, and after hearing details from friends who relayed the situation on the ground, Iyad decided to return home.

My brother was really excited when he arrived back in Palestine. The spread of the protests to all parts of the country, the energy in our village, the Arab and international solidarity, gave him and all of us a sense of hope. Maybe we could achieve true peace.

He began to spend more and more nights out of the house, in Ramallah, Tulkarem, and Nablus. Once, he brought his friends over at night. They talked for hours about the political situation and probably planned protests during that time as well. He bossed his sisters around and demanded that they make his friends dinner. My father got angry. "You have five sisters in the house, how can you bring all these men over!" They fought, and Iyad began to spend more time away after that evening, mostly in Nablus. My parents were driving him crazy, and he was doing the same to them.

Shortly after his return, he, along with Mu'tasem, established a Saraya al-Quds cell, probably in Nablus or Tulkarem, under some direction from Nu'man Tahayneh. Tahayneh was a writer, thinker, and military strategist of the Islamic Jihad in the northern West Bank and is said to have been responsible for identifying leaders in the areas around Jenin, Nablus, and Tulkarem—people like Saeed Tubasi, Mahmoud Tawalba, and Thabet Mardawi.

Iyad's involvement grew further in Nablus. He was able to provide weapons to activists, but more importantly, he gained more experience building explosives. He also learned to take apart mines, grenades, and other devices and repurpose the incendiary material to make explosive belts and turn cars into bombs. By late November, he began to take great care in his movements, returning less frequently to his family home in Kufr Ra'i, and only on surprise visits.

Although his family suspected he was involved in political activities, they knew no details. They'd later learn of his various undertakings every time the Israeli army barged into their home searching for him and brandishing a long list of accusations. Iyad never told them anything and denied the Israeli claims.

In Princeton, Sireen lived through the intifada phone call to phone call and news hour to news hour.

At first, people around me thought—or hoped—the conflagration would die down in favor of negotiations and diplomacy. I argued with them a lot. "It won't die down," I told them. I had to explain how we had been through years of negotiation, and how in the meantime, the Israelis had stolen more land, and the settlement population was growing at the fastest rate it ever had. People around me pushed back. "If only Arafat would agree to the Israeli offer," they said. It was so frustrating to blame our leadership, which had already given up so much of our land. The Israelis wanted to take Area C, more or less, and give us just Areas A and B. And these people around me wanted us to accept this. I was frustrated, but I explained to them how ridiculous this was. Would they accept it for themselves? I told them how my family could barely leave their village without being harassed with checkpoints. With this level of land theft, resistance was inevitable.

As days turned to weeks, Sireen became more fidgety. She waited for the phone calls from home and moved back and forth between the garden and her house, her steps quick and intentional, as if she was trying to get somewhere. She began to put a lot of time into her garden, spending long hours planting, trying to get her mind off the situation. And whenever she phoned home, Iyad was never around.

On the news, I watched live as protests were broken up with tear gas and live ammunition, Palestinian boys were rushed away in ambulances, and Apache helicopters fired Hellfire missiles into civilian areas. As the death toll climbed, there was no question in my mind that the Oslo process was dead. There was no return to the status quo before the summer of 2000.

Watching the news, I thought about Iyad, expecting to see him at the protests, wondering what he might be up to—if he'd be throwing rocks, or if he was getting more involved somehow with others in the PA security forces. Why was he never home?

I spoke to my mother almost daily. *"Hayna 'aysheen,"* she would say. "We're here, living." She didn't have much news about my brother, but she'd tell me he was fine, that he had called, or that he had stopped by the house a day before.

The rest of my family rarely left the house. "It is too dangerous in Jenin," my mother would say. It was dangerous in all the cities with shelling and street battles. It was also difficult to leave the village because there were so many road closures. There were over a hundred checkpoints at the time in the West Bank between the permanent, semipermanent, and improvised ones. And there were curfews. These were mostly imposed in the cities. My brothers and sisters could not attend university in Nablus with all these restrictions. They all just stayed put in Kufr Ra'i, where my youngest sisters could at least attend school.

The uprisings in Palestine connected Sireen to a new community. She had no friends yet in Princeton, nowhere to go, and life was dull and confining compared to in Brooklyn. There, she got out more. Manhattan Beach Park was within walking distance, and she could take her boys to museums and for walks around the city. With the uprising intensifying, she started to get more involved with the pro-Palestinian Princeton community. Soon she made friends with community members and Princeton students and began accompanying them to small demonstrations in Palmer Square. She raised banners given to her by students and chanted slogans against the occupation. She also gained the courage to take to the stage and give speeches, and she felt in the moment like she was making a difference when she heard the applause or led the crowd in chants of "Free, free, Palestine!" But she didn't hold out hope for achieving the right of return or ending anything more than the occupation of the West Bank and Gaza. In those days, she believed she would feel content if even that happened. After each protest, as the flare that had come to be known as the Second Intifada continued to burn, her hope blurred with cynicism.

*

On Thursday, October 26, 2000, one month after the start of the Second Intifada, an Islamic Jihad operative strapped with an explosive belt blew himself up at an Israeli target in the Gaza Strip. It was the first martyr operation
since the Israeli military had started using live fire and killing Palestinians
a month earlier. One Israeli soldier was injured, and no one was killed. The
next day, the Israeli military killed four Palestinians, injured 250, and fired
at an ambulance, severely injuring the driver. A week later, there was another
operation by the Islamic Jihad at the Mahane Yehuda Market in West Jerusalem that killed two people and left more injured. Sireen's eyes sprang open
when she saw on TV the wreckage left in the wake of this explosion. She
placed her hand to her mouth when she caught the look of horror on the face
of survivors. She closed her eyes and rubbed her hands down her face, trying
to collect her emotions. She felt an initial shock. But like many Palestinians,
she felt more infuriated with the silence of the international community in
the face of Israeli aggression and frustrated by their calls to negotiations,
which went nowhere. She was angry. Embittered. At Palestinian deaths being
forgotten, at their continuing dispossession going unnoticed. And she, like
many, felt these explosions as a release of her inner powerlessness. It gave
her hope. It was exciting. But she also understood their ugliness. That in a
small way, these explosions mimicked the oppressor. That the world would
understand it as terror rather than the last avenue for the weak to resist.

27

Early 2001

One of Iyad's first missions was to set a roadside bomb activated by a cell-phone on an Israeli-only road frequented by settlers and military vehicles. A few of the young men he recruited descended from one of the hills near Ya'bad and successfully set the bomb somewhere on the way to the settlement of Mevo Dotan. Mu'tasem was among them.

They bolted for the hills, down into a valley, and away from the blast site. Mu'tasem stayed closer to give a signal to set off the explosion.

Minutes later, a military vehicle passed by. One of the young men called the number to detonate the bomb. It was all planned like clockwork, but he got a busy signal. He tried again, only to get a woman: "Please try again later. This number is out of network." Surrounded by hills, they looked at each other, stupidly. "*Yil'an abuk shu ghabi*," Mu'tasem cursed the young man.

Iyad was fuming when they returned, but at least no one was caught. "*Allah yisa'edkum*," he scolded, asking for God to help them. They definitely needed more training.

Mu'tasem's bomb preparations were not always successful either, and it was a miracle he still had the use of all his limbs. Once, while preparing a roadside bomb—something he did in his house, which was adjacent to his parents'—instead of plugging in his personal phone to charge, he absent-mindedly stuck a phone rigged to a bomb into the charger. The blast was heard next door, and when his brother scrambled to the scene, he found Mu'tasem lying bloodied on the floor. He picked him up to rush him to a hospital, but Mu'tasem refused. He was afraid to alert the authorities. Luckily, the injuries left no permanent damage.

*

Iyad was operating out of Tulkarem, and it was a challenge to smuggle explosives out of the city and past Israeli checkpoints because the PA was trying to prevent such movements, but he put his faith in God and pushed ahead. In one operation around late February, he prepared three explosive belts to be detonated over the Green Line.

"Are they ready?" Muʻtasem asked Iyad as he walked into his workshop.

"Yes. All set. Where did they say these would go?" Iyad asked.

"They're meant for a bus and two restaurants."

Iyad raised his eyebrows at Muʻtasem and paused. It was not often they targeted restaurants, so he knew that if this worked, it would be a big deal. But it also meant they'd become the most wanted. He could see his friend had also thought this through. "*Tawakal ʻalla-llah*," Iyad said reassuringly, asking Muʻtasem to put his trust in God as he passed him the belts. "*Tawakal ʻalla-llah*," came the response.

On a day of angry clouds, Muʻtasem met the three operatives chosen for this mission and gave them the belts and instructions. They set out in an old Volvo as rain began to fall. They managed to get out of the city, but not long after, their car broke down.

"We should have waited another day or two for clearer weather," Muʻtasem suggested to Iyad when he got word of their car troubles.

"We can't let the weather dictate our actions, *tawakal ʻalla-llah*," Iyad responded with confidence. "They'll come through."

The operatives spent an hour repairing their car, and then, having fixed it, persisted on their way. But they had not been driving for long when, on a beaten path, their car got stuck in mud. Two of them got out, cursing their luck. They pushed while the third gently stepped on the gas pedal. By the time they successfully pulled the car out, the two pushing the car were drenched from the rain and covered in mud, and there was no way they could continue. If it were God's will, then His will that day was not as they had anticipated, and the operation was postponed.

Several weeks later, as Israeli violence escalated and Palestinian armed resistance became more sustained, Iyad visited friends at the old campus of al-Najah University in Nablus. He was sitting on steps in between the buildings, joking around, laughing, and passing time before his friends had to return to classes, when a man approached him. He had a backpack and looked like a student. The man asked to borrow Iyad's cellphone battery to make a call. It was not a particularly unusual request. He explained that his own battery was dead, he didn't want to use Iyad's call units, and the number was saved on his phone.

Iyad hesitated briefly, eyeing the man. He felt he couldn't reject the request, but he feared the man might rig the phone battery. It was a tactic Israeli intelligence had used before. He looked at his phone for a few seconds, then opened it, pulled out the battery, and handed it to the man with only one word, "*Tfadal.* Help yourself." The man took it and moved away for a bit to make his phone call and get some privacy.

A minute later, he returned, thanked Iyad, and asked God to protect him. "*Shukran sadeeqi. Allah yihmeek,*" he said, as he was handing back the battery. Iyad raised his arm, signaling for the man to keep the battery, and responded, "*Allah yihdeek,* this is from me to you. Please, keep it."

The man was surprised and confused. He insisted that he return the battery, but Iyad would not have it any other way. The man tried to force the battery on him, but Iyad was persistent. In the end, the man left with a new battery.

Iyad couldn't be too vigilant. If you were going to resist the entire force of the Israeli military and intelligence apparatus, you had better watch your back at every moment, as they had many ways to strike. One of their more successful strategies was to employ Palestinians trained by the clandestine Unit 504. These collaborators identified targets for the Israelis, sometimes by splashing ultraviolet paint on cars to mark them for Apache helicopters. No one was safe.

Iyad reputedly had a keen eye for recognizing collaborators from his days with the Fahd al-Aswad. In one incident, one of his comrades in the Islamic Jihad had been told by a man that he could secure weapons for the organization. When the comrade approached his superiors about this potential arms deal, they asked Iyad about the contact. Iyad recognized the name from the First Intifada and warned them that this man had been a collaborator. Iyad had interrogated him almost a decade earlier. His comrade ignored the advice and said he would be careful. A few days later, as Iyad's comrade prepared to enter a car with the man, Israeli intelligence encircled him, shot at his feet, and arrested him. He was sentenced to thirty-five years in prison.

*

As the resistance continued, the Shin Bet put more pressure on the PA to rein in Palestinian activists in the Tulkarem and Jenin areas. Iyad and Muʻtasem were now on the run from both Palestinian and Israeli authorities, who were exchanging intelligence.

At one point, the PA forces learned that Iyad and Muʻtasem were in a safe house in Tulkarem assembling explosives. They encircled the house before the men got wind of what was going on. When Iyad discovered this, he made calls to comrades in the city. In a matter of minutes, a group of Saraya al-Quds fighters was outside the house confronting the PA police, creating a loud commotion. "Leave this place! There is no one in this build-ing," shouted a Saraya member.

"If there is no one, then why are you surrounding us?" came the response from a PA officer.

"This is our territory. You have no business being here." The two sides continued to exchange angry words, arms flailed in the air, and chests bumped. At one point, the Saraya al-Quds members threatened to use force if the PA officers did not leave. Though the confrontation did not escalate beyond that, it did provide the distraction Iyad and Muʻtasem needed to escape the building. They fled up to the rooftop and jumped to another roof. From there they made their way to another safe house. The confrontation was so successful—or the PA forces were not committed enough to their mission—that a few days later, Iyad and Muʻtasem snuck back in to find their explosives right where they left them. They collected them and moved them to a safer location.

That was not the last time they were chased by PA forces, nor was it the last time they so easily evaded them. Many in the police force were sympa-thetic to those carrying out acts of resistance. Orders from above were often executed with minimal effort and in a similar manner to the "botched" raid at the safe house in Tulkarem. One time, an officer in the Palestinian intelli-gence unit called Iyad to warn him in advance that police were on their way to arrest him. And it was like this, through a network of support, that he continued to evade capture.

28

April–May 2001

Iyad met a woman several months after his twenty-seventh birthday. Her name was Mariam, and she was his friend's neighbor. It was spring, and all around him the blood-red *shaqa'iq al-numan*—the anemone, the wind-flower, the Spanish Marigold—blossomed in the valleys and hills of Kufr Ra'i, but, of course, he had no time to notice them during that season he met Mariam.

Mariam's father was from Kufr Ra'i but had lived in Croatia for some years, during which he married and had three children. He was one of many Palestinians who went to study in Eastern Europe in the 1970s and '80s—a result of strong connections between the PLO and the Soviet Union. In 1999, he divorced Mariam's Croatian mother, won custody over Mariam, her sister, and her brother, and took them to Amman. He was unable to take care of the children alone, so he sent them to Palestine to be cared for by their grandparents.

When the son was a little older, he rejoined his father in Amman, and the daughters stayed in the West Bank. As teenagers, the sisters found life difficult. Mariam was reserved and not very confident, and it didn't help that she spoke broken Arabic. Village life under occupation was very different from life in Zaghreb, and she feared the Israeli army as it escalated its violence and tightened its control over the West Bank during the Second Intifada.

Mariam was petite. Her hair, straight and below the ears, was the color of muddy auburn earth, her complexion a matted white. With this mix of tones and her sharp nose, she had a look that captured the attention of men in the village.

When I found out Iyad was interested in Mariam, I objected. Suzanne did as well. From what we heard, the family had a bad reputation in the village, something to do with rumors of collaboration among family members. We fought with Iyad, but he didn't listen. "I marry her or no one else," he'd say.

Sireen could see why Iyad was captivated by her looks. Her brother Ihab believed that Iyad saw her youth as an opportunity to shape her into a pious Muslim and thus gain him *ajer*, points in heaven.

It didn't seem that Mariam herself was aware of the attention she attracted. She mostly kept to herself and remained obedient to her grandparents. Some people think this is why Mariam listened to her grandparents, who thought that Iyad, with a sister doing well in the US, could eventually take Mariam there too.

Iyad eventually convinced our father to accept Mariam. I was heartbroken, devastated. I didn't understand this relationship. Mariam had been raised overseas, with a different mentality, and Iyad was strict and wanted things in the traditional way that we were used to. How could that ever work? I thought the whole affair would shut in Iyad's face once her family was asked for their blessing. But we were all surprised when they agreed to the marriage. Iyad had spent eight years in prison; he had no education and no job. Why would anyone agree to marry their daughter to such a person? Why would she herself agree?

Her grandparents called her father in Jordan and made the case to him. He agreed. It felt as if everyone around me had gone mad. What was going on? Why would they marry their daughter to Iyad?

Sireen had heard the rumors of collaboration that circled Mariam's family members. Rumors of collaboration were like the plague. It was hard to find anyone untouched by this, even national heroes. It was especially easy to believe this about people you were not fond of or others who harmed you in some way. Did members in Sireen's family not want the union because of the rumors, or did the rumors materialize because they did not like the future in-laws? Um Yousef was not in favor of the marriage; it upset her. But she hoped that it would allow Iyad to settle or that it might be his ticket out of Palestine.

Many in Sireen's extended family were also against the union. They could not believe that Dar Abu Shqara was accepting Mariam's family as kin. But despite many arguments, Iyad's parents hosted a large gathering for the engagement, the *katb el-ktab*, where the couple signed their marriage contract. It was the first such occasion among their children to take place in Palestine. But it was all done reluctantly, and on the day of the engagement, Abu Yousef was heard prodding his wife to get up and be excited: "*Koumi! Yalla, imshi!*"

Iyad was dressed casually that day, in a short-sleeved light blue shirt and beige trousers. His beard was trimmed, and his smile stretched from ear to ear. His trademark laugh made up for many of the blank expressions surrounding him. Mariam looked more subdued in her velvet and sleeveless merlot evening gown with matching opera gloves.

The day after the *katb el-ktab*, Iyad called and asked me to talk to Mariam. I hesitated but agreed. I didn't know what I would say to her.

"Please, talk to her in English," he pleaded, almost childishly.

So we chatted for a bit. I tried to distract from the lump in my throat, that feeling of heartbreak, by pacing around the kitchen, wiping an already clean counter, playing with the ends of my hair, and trying to smile as we spoke. I must have come across as friendly because Iyad was so giddy afterward. I congratulated him and wished him happiness, but it was hard to hide my sadness.

Two days later, Iyad returned to Nablus. There, daily life intertwined with politics, and politics with military action, and he went on a mission to confront soldiers the next day. He did not answer Mariam's calls and disappeared for the next ten days. Then, two weeks after Mariam and Iyad had last spoken, Mariam's grandparents woke up to find Mariam, who was still living with them, gone. She was not at school or with any of her relatives. She had disappeared.

Rumors spread that she fled. There was speculation that Iyad's time in Nablus made her reconsider whether this relationship was a good idea. Perhaps she learned the extent of his political involvement.

It was not until two days later that her father called from Amman and said she was at her mother's home in Croatia.

They said an unknown car came to pick her up at the edge of the village, and she went to the Croatian Embassy in Tel Aviv. There, she told the authorities that her grandparents had forced her to marry a man she did not love. She stayed there for a few days before they supposedly flew her out.

Mariam's father sent a message to Iyad's family, agreeing to pay for all the expenses of the marriage—for the dress, food, arrangements, and *mahr el-muqadam*, the advance that Iyad's family had paid Mariam. He apologized, saying, "My daughter doesn't want this marriage, and she's left the country. I'm very sorry." Her grandparents, however, refused to pay back the money and said they were going to wait until Mariam returned. They never paid.

It was strange. Mariam had spent two months preparing for the marriage. It wasn't a quick or spontaneous one. She went to the markets with my sisters to pick out her dress and was involved in the whole process. My parents visited her several times. Her sister became friendly with my sisters, and Mariam expressed how handsome Iyad was.

I spoke to Iyad. He was hurt, destroyed, ashamed. What would people say now that his fiancée had run away?

And so it was that Mariam exited from Iyad's life as quickly as she had entered it.

29

July–September 2001

I remained bitter over Mariam's disappearance and was afraid of what it would do to my brother and the stress it would inflict on my mother and father. It was clear Iyad was overcome with humiliation because in the few weeks after Mariam's departure, he did not show his face in Kufr Raʻi, only once secretly returning to see my parents. But where was he? What was he up to now? I remained constantly on edge in Princeton, trying to be present with my children but often lost in worry about my family in Palestine, about Iyad.

In those weeks, Iyad was busy trying to stay a few steps ahead of the Israelis, who had stepped up their assassinations against Palestinian resisters, conducting fifteen attacks and killing twelve resistance fighters between July and August.

At the end of August, Abu Yousef made plans to travel to the US to visit Sireen, who was nine months pregnant and ready to deliver a baby girl within the next two weeks. Sireen was looking forward to his arrival; she hoped the time away from Palestine would be good for him, and she was happy to have him in her life again. She remembered the last time he was in the US, when she still lived in Brooklyn, and how they had sat together in cafés and he had shared with her snippets of his life and his thoughts on the world.

But when he arrived in the US, he could barely breathe from the immense pain he was feeling.

*

On the morning of his departure, Abu Yousef had risen before most of the village awoke. The air was still, and there was a haze over a settlement outpost on a hill in the distance. Um Yousef had prepared him a light breakfast, and she woke her children to say goodbye. They bade him a tearful farewell, having not been apart from him for so long now, but Um Yousef, like Sireen, thought it would be good for his health to be away from the tensions in Palestine. Iyad was the most relieved. With Abu Yousef away, Iyad would not have to worry about his father finding out what he was up to, and they would argue less.

Abu Yousef gave his girls hugs; they kissed his forehead in tears. His eyes watered, his cheeks reddened, and he eventually burst into tears, as he often did with his goodbyes. Then he gave his son Baha a hug and told him to stay safe and take care of the family. He hugged Um Yousef and got in the taxi van that had been waiting on the street, and the taxi took off.

It was still early morning when he arrived at the bridge and passed into Jordan. There was little fanfare save for the usual waiting that accompanies border crossings. He felt some pressure in his right foot but paid it no mind as he made his way to Queen Alia International Airport, 30 km south of Amman.

The wait in Jordan was long. He took his shoe off to check his toe. A cut? An ingrown nail? He could not ascertain what was causing him pain. He played with his toe a bit, flexed it, and put his shoe back on.

On the long direct flight to New York, he did not remove his shoes. Perhaps it was the pride of always needing to be proper in public, or the feeling of wanting to be dignified and patient around the judging eyes of strangers. But by the time Sireen met him at JFK airport, Abu Yousef could hardly bear the pain in his toe, and after a smile to his daughter, a hug, and kisses, he had no reason to hold back. In the car ride, he removed his shoe to reveal a bad infection. With traffic, it was almost a two-hour drive back to Princeton from JFK. He insisted he was fine. Sireen drove him home.

For the first two hours, nothing she did helped. A cold pack, ice, pain killers—nothing. She took him to the emergency room at Princeton Hospital. There, he was told his toe was infected and was prescribed antibiotics in a valiant effort to reverse the irreversible.

Sireen returned to Princeton Hospital with her father two days later. The infection in his big toe had worsened—oxygen in the toe's cells was slowly being sucked out and consumed by the poison, its nail turning yellowish and the skin green and putrefied. Two of his other toes had also begun to swell. He had gangrene.

They told us that they had to amputate the big toe immediately, hoping that this would resolve the situation and that they wouldn't have to remove more of his limbs. My father was sad and angry. But he had diabetes and heard these things could happen, so he understood. It was just a toe and could have been worse.

The procedure did not take long. They drained fluids and left the wound open to monitor the infection and covered it with a moist dressing. Abu Yousef had to remain in the hospital for several days.

After four days, my father's foot did not heal. It became blue and infected, and the doctors felt they had no choice but to amputate the tip of the foot and all my father's toes.

They amputated half the foot, but still it did not heal, and it was at this point that they told us the amputation would not succeed unless we amputated below the knee.

My father lost it.

Imagine losing a leg. Imagine the anger, pain, and frustration.

Alone, without a doctor present, my father began to shout and cry in the hospital room. I remember his words: "Kill me, but don't make me return handicapped to Palestine for people to see." Then he screamed at me, "Why, Sireen? What did I do to you, Sireen? Why do you want to cut off my leg?"

The daughter had become her father's guardian in a land that was not his, surrounded by a language he did not command. She had to sign amputation release forms—mere ink on paper that would torment her decades later. Such things should never be asked of a daughter.

The entire hospital ward heard the screams when I signed the paperwork for the amputation. What do you do when you have three or four doctors telling you there is no other solution, that the gangrene will eat his entire body, that he will die, and so it is best to amputate below the knee, and that the science of prosthetics has improved, and that he will walk again?

Abu Yousef found it hard to cope with the news, despite having undergone two previous amputation procedures that week, or perhaps because of them. A diabetic lives with the anticipation of amputation as a normal part of their psyche. But in Kufr Raʻi, Sireen did not recall ever knowing or seeing diabetics who were amputees. There were people tortured and others humiliated in front of the village by the Israelis. But everyone was whole, even diabetics. He would return with a part of him buried in the US—missing, dismembered. And so the shock of the news of the impending loss was mixed up with the shame he would feel in Palestine.

Sireen had already relayed the news to her brother Yousef in Ohio and to her family in Kufr Raʻi. Yousef spoke to the doctors, understood the gravity of the situation, and supported Sireen. Her mother's first reaction was to scream at her. "What are you doing! What are you doing!" But then Yousef phoned his mother, and it didn't take long for him to convince her. Someone relayed the news to Iyad as well, and he called Sireen immediately. Iyad was his calm self, though. "Sireen, are you sure this is the only way?" he asked.

She explained the whole ordeal in detail. Iyad felt a tinge of guilt that he had wanted his father to leave the country. He fell silent. Then, as if his approval mattered and the procedure were not a foregone conclusion, he said, "Okay." Sireen was already crying on the phone. He told her to take care and hung up. For a long time after, he remained afflicted by the thought that if only he had chosen a different path, if only he were not fighting to return his father to his land, perhaps his father would have been spared the loss of his limb.

They took Sireen's father to prep him for the surgery. She could only accompany him so far before they were separated. Abu Yousef disappeared behind swinging doors and entered alone, terrified, into a world untranslated to his ears while his daughter was left confronting the limits of her care.

Even if the doctors could easily communicate with him, what would they say? No jokes could be cracked; there was no consolation that he might return to the way he was, no reassurances or hope or promises.

The anesthesia began to take hold. He looked around in the last moments before slipping into the abyss. Feet shuffled, mouths uttered nonsensical words, there were sounds of laughter. And as he went under, he took his fear with him.

The operation itself didn't take longer than forty-five minutes. The doctor used a bone saw to cut and crack through the leg. Flesh at the tip of the knee dangled as if picked on by scavenging animals. For the surgeon, it was a defeat, a doctor's admission that all the techniques of medicine, modern and ancient, could not compete with a dying, gangrened limb.

When the surgery was over, Abu Yousef was left to lie unconscious in the recovery room, one-legged and alone. When he finally woke and was lucid enough, he was probably thinking it was better to die with the gangrene than to live with the pain.

He lay there with a drip to keep him nourished, an epidural to reduce the pain, and a catheter to drain his bladder because he was going to be immobile for a few days.

When they transferred my father to his room and he finally opened his eyes post-recovery, I was there next to him. The doctor came and reassured us that there were no more complications. Then he turned to me and said, "I think you're in labor."

I gave birth to Salma on September 2, 2001. And just like that, my father and I lay in the same hospital. I on the fifth floor, and he on the third, and he could not visit or see his new granddaughter. It was hard to feel the full force of the happiness of birth while knowing my father was suffering below.

With the help of my husband, my father checked out of the hospital and into the Merwick Care and Rehabilitation Center before I was discharged. They said that he couldn't be home because they couldn't assign him a nurse, and I was in no shape to attend to him right away.

After leaving the hospital, I went to visit him at the center so he could see Salma. I still remember the moment I saw him and he laid eyes on my daughter. He cried and begged me to take him home. "Please, please, I don't understand them, and they don't understand me. The food is disgusting. No salt or pepper."

It was hard for Sireen to watch her father break down and not have the power to do anything in that moment, and it shattered her to leave him that evening.

Things became even more complicated because when I returned home, the place was an absolute mess. My husband had not taken care of the house, and Zeid had developed a severe infection from untreated pink eye. I had to rush him to the hospital after just having returned home with Salma. We had to check Zeid into the hospital for three days. Mohammed stayed with him because I couldn't. It was stressful and exhausting, and I felt alone.

The next morning, she went to the Merwick Center and tried to have her father released. The nurses refused. It was not that simple, and the doctor had to check his leg. It was not till the sixth or seventh of September, in the evening, that he came home.

At home, he slept downstairs in the living room. It was easier for him, and we had a futon that was lower to the ground. We put a walkie-talkie next to him, and I kept one near me at night.

On September 10, we went to sleep early. At 4 a.m. the next morning, I heard him scream. I raced downstairs and found him on the floor. He had wanted to go to the bathroom, had tried to stand on his phantom leg, and had fallen.

The steel wire used for the flap that had been holding his flesh together at the knee had detached. By the time I came down, the floor, the sheets around him, and the white *dishdashe* he wore were all drenched in blood.

Mohammed and I picked my father up, got him to the car, and loaded Salma in because I could not leave her to wake up alone and go without food. I drove to the ER with Salma in the baby seat, luckily asleep. Mohammed stayed home with the boys.

When the doctors saw my father, they told me that he needed another surgery to restitch the flap. They didn't allow me to stay in the room with him because I had a newborn and I had to leave the emergency area. It took a long time before he was done. I remember the wait clearly because the television was on CNN in the waiting area, and I recall clearly that it was there that I saw the first plane crash into the World Trade Center that morning of September 11. And even though my mind was preoccupied with my father's suffering, I remember sitting with the hospital staff, shocked, glued to the TV, some worried about family in the city, and everyone filled with fear and panic.

With a newborn less than a week old, a father still dealing with the pain and confusion of a phantom leg, and now, Lower Manhattan buried in smoke and rubble, it seemed to Sireen that the world was conspiring against her. She could not even pause her daily life to reflect on events that were happening only fifty miles away in New York City.

After dropping off my father at home and making sure my husband was there to take care of him, I drove to Rite Aid to pick up medication for him. On the way, I was stopped by a police officer on Nassau Street for speeding. I still remember how I finally broke down and begged him to leave me alone.

Sireen was overcome with a flood of emotions at that point, the day and the week finally catching up with her as she tried to appeal to the cop.

Sometimes, appeals can work. With the right amount and combination of privilege, skin color, accent, and emotional connection, the bureaucracy's indifference to people's everyday struggles can be put aside for an instant, and the power of the face-to-face can draw empathy. Such are the beautiful moments that see uniforms melt away and hard rules set aside.

On September 11, 2001, almost twelve hours after the first plane crashed into the World Trade Center, the police officer could not connect with Sireen's olive-faced, Arabic-accented pleas.

🌿

On the other side of the world, in Palestine, Iyad was meeting with several of his comrades in the village of Arraba to convince the fighters in that village to leave. Two nights before, Israeli warplanes had been seen circling low over the village, and there was a growing sense that Saraya al-Quds fighters were not safe there anymore. Iyad spent the afternoon of September 11 with other leaders in the village trying to plan an escape. Among them was Mohammed Ardah, who, twenty years later almost to the day, on September 7, would break out of the high-security Gilboa Prison with four other members of the Islamic Jihad and a member of Fatah.

Mohammed noticed that Iyad was not himself that afternoon. "What's wrong?" he asked.

"My sister lives near New York, and my father is there now," Iyad told him. He had not heard their news, but he knew they were in the hospital. He was also caught up in worries about his father's pain. And he had a sneaking suspicion that the events in New York were not going to play out well in Palestine.

By nightfall, news in the US began to report that al-Qaeda was behind the attacks on the World Trade Center and the Pentagon. Iyad caught this on a small TV set with a broken antenna and bad reception. He also received word that there was new troop movement on the outskirts of the village. Israeli prime minister Ariel Sharon was going to use this moment to order a series of attacks on the Palestinian resistance, and one of those attacks was going to be against fighters in Arraba.

And so, before dawn on September 12, Israeli forces moved into the village, heavy-footed, with no element of surprise. They covered their forward movement with rounds of fire and artillery shells.

"Mohammed, it's time to go," Iyad said in a rush as he grabbed an M-16 stolen from the Israelis and swung a cheaper "Carlo" submachine gun over his back for backup. "I know a way out, but we need to distract the army so the others can escape. We just need to keep it up for a few minutes."

Iyad and Mohammed, their faces wrapped in black-and-white kaffiyehs so only their eyes were visible, left their safe house with machine guns and reserve ammunition and took cover behind a cement wall. Iyad gave Mohammed a signal to start shooting. Mohammed emerged from behind the wall and took several shots at soldiers at the very far end of the street. At the same time, Iyad hustled to the corner of another building to get closer to his target. He waited a moment as the soldiers responded with a volley of bullets, then he came out and fired a round of his own. They went back and forth this way several times.

But the military was approaching, and soldiers were taking cover behind a Merkava tank. Iyad came out one more time, and after that volley, there was silence from Mohammed.

Iyad looked back but could not see him. The Israelis increased the intensity of fire. It looked like the Merkava was ready to shoot high velocity munition at the wall from one of its guns. Iyad felt the moment expand as he waited, hoping Mohammed would show his face.

Just then, Mohammed let out a whistle. He had slipped away to a building nearby. He signaled to Iyad that he was out of ammunition.

Iyad exhaled. The Merkava let out a round of shots at the wall and pulverized a section of it. Iyad gave Mohammed a quick signal. They were to pull back, pivot right at the end of the street, run past some buildings, and dash for the hills. Iyad knew his way around those hills like he had known the cracks on the walls of his prison cell. From there they would head toward Fahme. After his signal, Iyad sprinted a few meters and pivoted right. He let out a round of shots while Mohammed scurried across to join him. They were out of view of the soldiers and in the clear from there on.

Whereas Iyad and Mohammed escaped shortly after dawn, three of their comrades, still holed up in the safe house where they had all met the previous evening, and now completely encircled, would perish from the gunfire of Israeli troops.

30

Early February 2002

Iyad climbed a small wall and scurried between a few trees in the garden of a three-story building in Kufr Ra'i. It was a clear night of a quarter moon, a cherished night of infinite constellations. The stars guided him now as they did all those years ago during the First Intifada, when he would run out of his house and into the dark hills to escape soldiers on his trail.

He came upon a green steel door and felt around for a keyhole in the pitch dark of a village without electricity. He opened the door with a key he had been given and snuck into an unfinished ground-floor apartment. It was one large, open space that resembled an underground garage.

Once inside, he walked to an unlocked wooden door at the other end of the empty space, hearing his light steps echo as he treaded carefully. Iyad opened it and slipped out into a stairwell, careful to make sure no one was there. He glided softly up two flights of stairs unnoticed. There, he unlocked a door to his relative's apartment. On many nights, he could enter without waking anyone in the house.

On this night, he was with a comrade, speaking in whispers, when the relative's seven-year-old son heard them. He was awake and knocked on their door. Iyad opened, looked down, and greeted the boy with a large, radiant smile. They had formed a bond over the span of a year. Iyad would joke and play with him. The young boy had become fond of the larger-than-life resistance fighter. Iyad gave him a big hug. He let him hold his gun. Then the boy's mother came, welcomed the men, and told her son to go to his room.

The two men slept on thin foam mattresses laid out for them on the ground. They had been on the run the last few days because the occupation forces had stepped up their search for the men behind the latest operation involving a man named Murad Abu al-Assal. So, when morning broke on this particular day, they remained indoors. They continued to hide for a few more nights.

Murad Abu al-Assal's story was a curious one. Muʿtasem had learned that Murad was turned into a collaborator during his time in prison. Murad was twenty-two and from a village near Kufr Raʿi named Anabta, the same village Muʿtasem was from. The Islamic Jihad narrative and Sireen's version conflict as to how Muʿtasem found out Murad was a collaborator. The party claims that Murad came forward, told Muʿtasem his story, and offered himself as a double agent. Sireen heard that Murad's collaborationist activities had been discovered and that his double agent work was a way to redeem himself.

When Muʿtasem learned about Murad, he informed Iyad. The two of them were of equal rank at the time, but more than that, they were inseparable friends and comrades who planned everything together. They discussed what to do with the information. Iyad then took this up the chain of command, and a plan was agreed on. The Saraya al-Quds in the area decided to allow Murad to continue sharing information with his Israeli handler to gain their trust, but the leadership chose what information he could share. This went on for several months.

On January 30, Murad left Anabta midmorning. He gave his mother a kiss on the forehead before calmly leaving the house dressed in a baggy navy tracksuit. He caught a taxi to the outskirts of Tulkarem and had the driver drop him off near a roadside café. He waited a few minutes, smoked a cigarette, then found another taxi to take him to the Taibe, الطيبة, checkpoint, a central Palestinian town not to be confused with Abu Yousef's village.

Some distance from the checkpoint, Murad exited the taxi and waited on the side of the road, smoking another cigarette. Several minutes later, a white Volkswagen appeared in the distance and drove to where Murad was waiting. It slowed to a stop. Murad looked around and over the top of the car for passersby, but there was no one in the vicinity. He threw his half-smoked cigarette on the floor and stepped on it. A man emerged from the car. They shook hands.

"How are you, Murad?" he asked.

"I'm good, man! How are you?" Murad responded cheerfully.

"Good, good," the man replied, somewhat distracted as he patted Murad down to search for weapons. "Get in."

"Thanks!" Murad climbed in. There was another man in the car. Both men were Shin Bet agents.

"Hi, Murad. Do you have anything for us today?" The driver said as he whizzed through the checkpoint and out of the West Bank toward the town of Taibe.

"Of course I do," Murad answered with a half-smile. As he said this, through the rearview mirror, the driver caught Murad pointing at his clothes.

"What's that?" he asked, slightly panicked.

"It's a gift for you!" Murad replied, still holding his half-smile. The other agent in the passenger seat turned around to see what his partner was asking about. Murad then took a deep breath. He made eye contact with them both. Then he announced in a calm, deep but loud voice, *"Allahu Akbar!"*

And with that, Murad, armed with half a kilo of undetected TNT strapped to his body, detonated the explosives in the car, killing himself and the two agents.

The night before, Murad had recorded himself reading off a script with machine gun in hand, a bandana with the words Saraya al-Quds wrapped around his forehead, and a black flag hoisted up beside him with "There is no god but God" written on it in Arabic. He looked subdued. At one point, he read incorrectly and corrected himself.

Murad had recorded his speech and lived his last night in the presence of Muʻtasem. Iyad may have been there too. Sireen watched the video on YouTube years later, trying hard to decipher who else was in the room through the reflection in Murad's eyes. Perhaps it was Iyad who held up the shaky camera and whose perspective of Murad could be observed through the camera lens. Perhaps it was a third person, and Iyad was off to one side. Sireen watched and tried to imagine looking through her brother's eyes. Then the video cuts out. And how banal the moment after the recording must have been! Did they joke around? Did they dine together? Did they go over the operation one last time, or did they just talk about the world? Or maybe they simply left Murad to himself in prayer before he headed home to his mother? Today, in Anabta, there is a roundabout bearing Murad Abu al-Assal's name, erected almost twenty years later.

Iyad used his relative's place as a safe house one last time after the Abu al-Assal operation. After that, his movements became even more clandestine, and Kufr Ra'i became too risky a place for him to hide. Although the wanted have a way of disappearing and of walking among people unnoticed, it was easier to disappear in the cities, like in Jenin, Nablus, or Tulkarem. There, a larger network of safe houses existed, and the occupation forces did not regularly patrol the streets because those areas remained under PA control. In Kufr Ra'i, it was far easier to be caught by a collaborator because everyone knew everyone and Iyad could not be sure who might sabotage him as revenge for what he had done during his years in the Fahd al-Aswad. Still, he did pop up at his home irregularly, but he never stayed more than a few minutes.

We used to speak more often the first year of the Second Intifada. I was as excited as a little girl every time—smiling from ear to ear, trying to catch up with him as fast as I could before he had to hang up. I remember I called him once after a huge demonstration in DC. He told me he was going crazy trying to see if he could locate me in the crowd. I had given interviews to the media in past protests, so he thought he might catch sight of me. But by early 2002, it became very difficult for me to reach him.

My father, still in the US, expressed his disappointment in Iyad. I asked him why. "You don't know, but he is going to get our house demolished," my father used to say. I don't think he knew either, but he sounded sure of himself.

Even before my father had come to visit me, he had lost control of the situation with Iyad. He didn't want Iyad coming home with his male friends, who carried bags that probably had explosives. Iyad shared with me his sadness that his father didn't want him around. He understood where our father was coming from, though, but he was committed to fighting for our liberation.

The fights between Iyad and his father over the safety of the family were futile. "We can't just pray and wish for the occupation to end!" Iyad said with a raised voice. In embracing the Islamic Jihad, Iyad subscribed to a different worldview. He believed, with Fathi Yakan, a prominent Muslim thinker, that "the tyranny of the principle of seeking safety and exaggerating this principle . . . will only result in the permanent killing of the spirit of sacrifice in individuals."

My father struggled to keep up with events in Palestine and lost track of Iyad's whereabouts in the first few months after his amputation. He was focused on physical therapy. Once his wound healed, they gave him prosthetics, and he spent three months learning to walk until he could do so without crutches.

Abu Yousef stayed with Sireen for another seven months after his surgery, until the spring of 2002. He loved being with his daughter, but he was determined to leave. There wasn't anything in particular that drew him back to Kufr Ra'i; it was simply the life he knew, and he could not stomach the world of Kingston, New Jersey. He also hoped that his presence would give pause to whatever Iyad was up to and make his son think twice before putting his family in danger.

When Iyad learned of Abu Yousef's plans to return, he called Sireen in a desperate attempt to change their father's mind. The intifada was at its height, and the Israelis were performing nightly raids into villages. What did the old man want from such a life?

"Allah yikhrub shitanek, Sireen!" he yelled. "Don't let him come back, Sireen! If he discovers what I am doing, he will lose his mind and he won't be able to handle it!"

Iyad begged me not to let my father return to Palestine. But he wouldn't say why. I felt caught in between them. I began to lose sleep, to have body aches.

What could my father not handle? Why would he lose his mind? I could sense Iyad was getting more deeply involved, but how? I had no clue and was unable to convince my father to stay much longer.

31

Late February 2002

The winter months of 2002 were mild in Princeton. They were some of the driest on record. But the little house on Laurel Avenue, with its land of two-thirds of an acre, was nevertheless chilly. Sireen wasn't used to this cold. Her apartment in New York had always been warm, and a T-shirt had been enough in the winter.

One night in late February, Sireen stood at her bathroom mirror, close enough that her breath fogged up her face. She often felt the mirror staring at her. It would watch her as she scuttled back and forth between her room and Salma's. It would wait to catch her reflection when she came up the stairs after a long day tending to her family without thanks, without appreciation. The bathroom mirror saw through her, could reach in, and elicited a sad loneliness that Sireen thought she could hide from others.

It was not unusual for her to stand at the wall-to-wall mirror, to stare at the real world, to decode her infinity. It was so usual that she began to think nothing of it.

On this particular night, she wanted to escape the present—and the future. And so she fogged up the mirror, making it hard to see her eyes and allowing herself, momentarily, to evade the mirror's gaze. She tilted her head back and waited for the heat of her breath to evaporate. The mirror cleared and gazed back at her. She leaned forward again, exhaled, and disappeared into the fog. She did this over and over until she could no longer escape.

She looked down at her black velvet pajamas, then stared back at them through the mirror. They were hideous—too thick to ever wear in her New

York City apartment, but serving her well now in the icy night of her new house. She looked up, and then down again at her black pajamas.

She looked up once more. A vision flashed in the space between her and the mirror. She was weeping. Iyad was lying beneath her. He was wrapped in a white shroud. The Palestinian flag lay across his legs.

Crowds were there. She couldn't understand why.

He was smiling, peaceful, and she stood there weeping.

The mirror pulled desperately at her hair, like a hand from the future forcing her out of time. A sinking feeling overcame her. The scent of funeral flowers was everywhere in the bathroom, and she could feel tears welling in her eyes. The tug at her hair grew stronger and heavier; her head was pounding. She swung her head back, grabbed her pajama top, and snapped it off her body. She looked at herself again, free of the black velvet top, and she could breathe once again. This was not real. It would never be real.

She collected herself. Opened the bathroom door. Walked into her daughter's room and crawled into bed beside her.

32

March 2002

Iyad was hiding in the hills somewhere between Nablus and Tulkarem. Muʿtasem was hunkered down in a wooden shack in a field on the outskirts of the village of Balʿa, بلعة, with another comrade, Maher al-Balbisi. It was a particularly sweet Mediterranean spring day, the kind you never want to see end because the warmth of the sun mixed with a soft, cool breeze feels perfect on the skin. In the field, Muʿtasem could see all around him the blossoming short-lived flower of martyrs—the red anemone, the poppy—with its tender petals, stained, as they say, by the blood of Adonis. From his position in the hills, Iyad could see the flowers as well. One could spot them everywhere in March, and the two men took note of their beauty, knowing they would wither soon, until future springs.

Tensions in the West Bank were high. The occupation forces were sweeping into villages and stepping up efforts to capture or kill resistance fighters. Near Ramallah, there were major troop deployments despite US statements of wanting to see a full withdrawal from Area A. All in all, there were around twenty thousand troops engaged in military offensives in the Gaza Strip and the West Bank. Iyad and Muʿtasem knew they were hunted.

By now, Muʿtasem had risen high on the army's wanted list for preparing roadside bombs and explosive belts, training others on how to use firearms, and, alongside Iyad, getting caught up in a number of firefights with Israelis. Ultimately, the Israelis wanted him in connection with Murad Abu al-Assal's death and an operation he had planned in Beit Lid, بيت ليد—a Palestinian town a few kilometers south of Tulkarem in the West Bank.

Muʿtasem, like Iyad, knew how creative the Israelis had gotten with their killing. A year earlier, members of Unit 504 had assassinated a comrade, Iyad Hardan, when they rigged a payphone they knew he used and it exploded in his face. Mu'tasem and Iyad also knew about how mobile phones could be turned into weapons. On the one hand, fighters could use them to communicate more clearly and across greater distances than with walkie-talkies, and these devices allowed them to circumvent the occupation forces. Yet the phones could be turned into remote detonators or used by the Israeli military to locate fighters and assassinate them. If militants got separated from their phones, they could even be booby trapped. If they hung on to the same number for too long, the Israelis could pinpoint their location and fire rockets at them. The mobile phone worked as a technology of resistance just as much as one of surveillance that strengthened the hand of Israeli power.

Iyad and Mu'tasem were on the phone. Iyad had called to update Mu'tasem on troop movement. Less than a minute into the call, they both heard the chopping of Apache helicopters rising over the hills. Iyad was probably not too far from Mu'tasem in Bal'a or perhaps near Kufr Ra'i. He warned his friend to be cautious, that the helicopter might be for one of them.

"Ya ilak, ya illee." That's what Iyad told me he said to Mu'tasem when we spoke about the incident. "It's either for you or me."

As Iyad finished the sentence, there was a deafening noise. BOOM! The line cut.

In the distance, a farmhouse exploded. Iyad wasn't sure if he experienced the line cutting or the explosion first. He was close enough to hear the impact from the hills above. He squeezed his eyes shut. His heart momentarily hollowed, as if a spirit had been sucked out.

Mu'tasem and Maher didn't stand a chance. They died on impact from the helicopter's missile. At least, this is the story the Islamic Jihad tells. But Mu'tasem's family clings to a slightly different version. In it, only Maher was killed on impact. Mu'tasem was praying and escaped the blast. He managed to fight ground troops. The firefight was long and intense. It lasted over an hour, until soldiers had him in their sight and shot him dead.

One by one, Iyad's comrades continued to be picked out.

Alone, he cried at the loss of his friends. And he promised revenge. After Mu'tasem's assassination, he printed his comrade's face on a white T-shirt.

Above the photo were written the words *Wa'dan wa 'ahdan*. A promise and a pledge. And below it, *Lan ansak*. I won't forget you.

Today, in Anabta, there is a football team named in Mu'tasem's honor.

I recall that around the time he was killed, my maternal grandmother died. My mother left the condolences gathering and went to his mother's home. It was the first time the two women met. Mu'tasem's mother hugged my mother tightly and wailed when she found out she was Iyad's mother.

33

April 2002

A few weeks after Mu'tasem was assassinated, and while Iyad was hiding in a village near Tulkarem, hundreds of troops encircled the Jenin refugee camp in preparation for the battle of Jenin, which was to begin on April 3. This move was part of a larger Israeli military offensive, launched five days earlier, which saw a takeover of the main Palestinian cities in Area A—Ramallah, Bethlehem, Tulkarem, Qalqilya, Jenin, and Nablus. The stated goal of this offensive was to put an end to Palestinian militant actions across the Green Line in Israeli cities, but, in actuality, it served to reinforce the Israeli military administration's ultimate control over the entire West Bank.

The military believed that destroying the resistance in Jenin would deal a severe blow to the resistance's operations across the West Bank. In the Jenin refugee camp, the different military wings of the Palestinian factions were united in their resistance. They shared one headquarters to coordinate all their operations, making them effective and deadly.

By 2 a.m. on April 3, Merkava tanks began to systematically shell the refugee camp. Meanwhile, special forces penetrated the outskirts and positioned themselves on top of high buildings and mosques. They continued to do so into April 4, strategically locating themselves in units of twenty-five to thirty soldiers. The home of Ibrahim Amer, a resident of the camp, was one of the first to be occupied in the early days. His eldest son, Zeid, was shot in the head, his body left in the living room for the duration of the battle. Iyad was receiving this information live from the network of Islamic Jihad fighters bunkered in the camp and from others a short distance away in Jenin's city center. He felt restless. Helpless. Guilty for not being with his comrades.

In those first two days, the eastern access to the camp was open, and some residents were able to escape, but by April 5, the entire camp was besieged. Apache and Cobra helicopters began to fire missiles at the camp. On April 8, the advancing troops found an opening and were able to enter the camp from the eastern side toward the Hawashin neighborhood in the center.

The next day, the Palestinian resistance killed thirteen soldiers of the occupying army as they fought intensely in narrow alleyways that the resistance knew well. Iyad heard this report on the news. He was with other comrades in a safe house where no one could hide their excitement. Even though he knew the army would continue its onslaught, he felt pride. The resistance was able to hurt its oppressor. To strike fear in the soldiers. To deal a powerful blow. The Israeli army began demolishing homes, mostly without warning residents inside. Most of the Damaj and Hawashin neighborhoods were destroyed in this way.

As their neighborhoods were bombarded and houses demolished, thousands of residents fled to nearby villages, and others were arrested. Israeli soldiers forced hundreds at gunpoint to leave the camp. Many went to the town of Jenin for safety. Ultimately, there was a massacre.

The stories of many residents have been documented. Abu Jandal, a civilian resident of the camp, was blindfolded and executed at gunpoint. Abdelkarim Yusuf al-Sadi, another resident, was gunned down with his hands up and face to the wall. Hala, the wife of Attiyeh Irmilat, both parents and longtime residents of the camp, recounted her husband's last moments to a team of investigative journalists:

He came crawling into the living room and found it full of glass shards. He came back to put some shoes on and returned to the living room. Barely one minute later I heard one bullet. He was calling to me. He called to me three times, "Hala, Hala, Hala . . ." His voice was different. It was the voice of someone who was hurting. I knew he was shot. I was with the kids in the bedroom, and he was still in the living room. I came running, and the kids ran behind me. Once I stepped into the living room, I found him still standing. He looked at me, and he asked what happened; he gestured with his hands as if he still did not know what had happened. I asked him, "What happened to you?" Then I saw the blood gushing out of his head. He opened his mouth to

Top, the Jenin refugee camp before 2001 and, bottom, the camp in April 2002 after the battle of Jenin, showing the area destroyed during the battle. Source: The Applied Research Institute - Jerusalem Society (ARIJ).

answer me, but he couldn't muster one word. He tried to speak again, and blood gushed out of his mouth, from his nose, and more from his head. He fell down slowly. I gazed at him, and then looked to my frightened children. I wasn't sure where he was hit because blood was coming from everywhere. He looked upon me and upon our children, and then he shook. I knew that he had died.

Attiyeh's body remained in the house for seven days. His children continue to carry their father's pain.

By April 13, the bombing had stopped. Over the next few days, the military gave only limited access to the Red Cross to recover the dead and injured. The organization stopped its recovery efforts on April 15 in protest of the army's lack of cooperation. A few days later, Peter Hansen of the United Nations Relief Works Agency (UNRWA) stated, "I and my colleagues, working in crisis situations for decades, do not recall a situation where cooperation from the authorities has been less than what we have experienced from the Israeli government." In the days that followed, a UN fact-finding mission was assembled and then abandoned after Israeli objections and noncooperation. Human Rights Watch found prima facie evidence of war crimes committed by the Israeli army and called for a criminal investigation that never took place.

❦

A few weeks later, in early May, a meeting was held late at night by a Saraya al-Quds member in high command and Iyad, Saeed Tubasi, and several of their comrades. The operative, on orders from Nuʿman Tahayneh, was there to pick a new leader. During the Jenin battle, Mahmoud Tawalba, commander of the Saraya al-Quds in Jenin, was killed, and members of his cell were either killed or captured. A Saraya al-Quds cell needed to be reconstituted in Jenin, one of the strongholds of Palestinian resistance, and to do that the Islamic Jihad needed a new leader in the city. This person would be responsible for being the main line of communication with the command outside and taking charge of reestablishing the cell.

Iyad sat cross-legged in a circle with four others, listening to the operative give an assessment of the full situation in Jenin and what had to be done. He had his shoes off. He was dressed in white crew socks, khaki cargo pants, and the T-shirt with Muʻtasem's face on it. Iyad's hazel green eyes glistened under a dim light as he focused on every word being said while fiddling with the edge of the rug they congregated on. Saeed sat with one leg crossed and the other extended out in front of him. He was in khaki pants as well and a green long-sleeved crew top. Saeed was light skinned with big, dark, intense eyes and thick, dark-brown eyebrows. For an eighteen-year-old, he had a well-formed beard. Near Iyad, he sat small but confident, looking up to his mentor.

After a full summary, the operative explained that it was up to them to choose their next leader. Iyad, Saeed, and their other comrades looked at each other uncomfortably. No one wanted to assume this responsibility. Saeed nudged Iyad. Iyad shook his head. *"Insa, ya zalameh.* Forget it, man," he said as he stared at the ground. He knew where this was going and understood it was partly performative. He had been directing a small crew already, he was much older than them, and he was the most experienced person in the room. But Iyad was humble in his dealings with people. He never cared for credit or compliments and often didn't know how to accept them. After Iyad's words, there were a few moments of silence. Iyad's head was pointed at the floor and his hands fiddled faster. When he looked up, he saw everyone in the room staring in his direction, and he knew it was decided.

And so, it was in this way that he assumed command of the Saraya al-Quds in Jenin. It was the greatest responsibility of his life thus far. From now on, he would be the point of contact, responsible for communicating messages between Jenin and the Saraya's West Bank leadership.

And in the midst of all this—with a massacre unveiling and a battle ongoing, and as he assumed command of resistance operations—life trudged on, and Iyad was trying to get married again.

34

April–May 2002

Almost a year after my brother's fiancée Mariam left, and not long after the battle and massacre in Jenin, Iyad met someone else. She had gone to college with my sisters, and her brothers were in the Islamic Jihad. They introduced her to my brother. At first, Iyad did not want to meet her father. He believed him to be a collaborator. He could not be too careful about anyone, not even the father of Islamic Jihad members whose mother was from Kufr Raʿi.

Iyad spent a full week getting reassurances about her father from trusted sources. When he was finally satisfied, he showed up at her father's house unannounced to seek his approval. The visit did not last longer than fifteen minutes, and he got her father's approval.

Now he was ready to marry, but first he wanted to officially divorce Mariam. He spoke to my father, who was still in the US and who refused to pay the *muʾakhar* to Mariam's family in order for the divorce to go through. He wanted her family to first pay the money owed for the marriage ceremony before he dished out this second deferred payment, which is often paid upon divorce. Iyad was furious and argued with my father over the phone. "I don't want anything to do with her anymore. It's over! Let me just be free of her! I don't want their money!" But my father refused, and Iyad was not willing to take the new woman as a second wife. He asked me and Yousef to help with the *muʾakhar*—around 1,500 Jordanian dinars or 2,000 US dollars.

After much argument and back and forth with our father, Yousef and I each contributed an amount and sent it to Iyad. He had a relative represent him as a lawyer for the divorce. Iyad would be able to marry soon after the divorce was official.

*

As Iyad was going through these divorce procedures, his family went to ask for the new woman's hand. They explained to her father that they would make it more official once Abu Yousef returned from the US. Sireen went to Macy's to buy the woman a dress and her brother a suit for the *katb el-ktab* ceremony. She felt light and happy, as if it were her life that was looking up. Iyad was moving on, and they were putting the scandal with Mariam behind them.

In May, Abu Yousef returned to Palestine and was ready to attend Iyad's marriage ceremony. He was elated that things might just turn around for his son. Iyad made an appearance at the family home shortly thereafter. Father and son embraced. Iyad kissed his father's hand and forehead in a sign of respect. Abu Yousef looked older now. His health was not what it used to be, but he was happy. A happiness that was but a fleeting moment in his long life. And as his son left, he was consumed by the uncertainty of whether or not he would see him again.

Signing the divorce papers was not easy. Iyad was already on a wanted list, and his movements were unpredictable. He never kept appointments. Arselene explained this to the judge. She was worried that if they set a time, it would turn into a trap. The judge told her to just have Iyad pass by anytime to sign the papers. She relayed this to her brother, who told her to let the judge know he would come in about a week. The next day, she called the judge to let him know, and he informed her that Iyad had already signed the papers. Arselene was left relieved but perplexed at her brother's clandestine movements.

In the meantime, in the Jenin refugee camp, as residents were still trying to recollect themselves after the April massacre, and with a lot of activity in and out as part of the cleanup and humanitarian operation to restore people's lives, Iyad relocated to the house of one of his comrades in the camp. There, he set up a place to manufacture bombs along with three other comrades. One comrade, Saeed Tubasi, had become his closest confidant, even inviting him into his family home, which Iyad thought of as a second home and where he sometimes had meals with Saeed's parents. Iyad and Saeed believed it was harder for the Israeli forces to discover them there because of the density of the camp. Together, they cleared rubble from the road to allow themselves easy access and fixed up a new explosives depot without the knowledge of residents.

As commander of the Saraya al-Quds in Jenin, in addition to setting up a cell to prepare explosives, Iyad organized a group to recruit new fighters and acquire machine guns and ammunition. Even though members of the Saraya al-Quds were hunted, new recruits were always available. The youth wanted any means to resist Zionist colonization, and the reputation of the Islamic Jihad as an effective fighting force meant that if one was from the northern West Bank, especially from Tulkarem or Jenin, then the Islamic Jihad was the movement of choice. The organization didn't require one to be strictly religiously observant to carry arms.

Iyad allowed the young and adventurous to join his ranks because he needed the recruits and understood people's frustrations with living under occupation. He understood their need to find dignity through resistance. The Islamic Jihad was accepting of those whose religious positions were still in the process of becoming and who were still, as teens, trying to find themselves in this world. Iyad saw himself in the youthful excitement and adventuresomeness of these young recruits. He remembered how, not so long ago, he too had roamed aimlessly without God. The Islamic Jihad tried to find a middle ground between nationalism and religion and so allowed such people to fight among its ranks. It was about Palestine—not Muslim Palestine or revolutionary Palestine—but Palestine. At least this was the way it was meant to be at its conception and based on its founding ideas. It was committed to showing people there was a revolutionary Islam. Teens who were discovering themselves, the leadership hoped, would be swayed by these positions.

In a couple of months, the Saraya al-Quds had armed and trained several hundred fighters of various ages. In Jenin, especially around the market, men dressed in khaki uniforms could be seen openly carrying their weapons. These foot soldiers walked in groups of two or three, owning every step they took, and lingered in the streets all day. They were boys and men of various ages who grew up in Jenin and were ready to defend it at all costs. They were often found chatting and joking with residents strolling the streets. The people of Jenin could see in their presence that the battle of Jenin had only strengthened the resolve of the Islamic Jihad and that the Saraya al-

Quds had been reconstituted and was ready to engage the enemy again. In parallel, Iyad's unit had developed a sophisticated explosives facility able to smuggle explosives out of the district of Jenin to anywhere in the West Bank and over the Green Line.

Soon they would put this to use.

35

January–May 2002

In Kufr Ra'i, Israeli military incursions into the village increased, and the torment of Iyad's family intensified. The army's raids reminded Um Yousef of the First Intifada, but they were more aggressive, more determined, now.

They came to the village—and the Sawalha house—over twenty times between January and May. They would come in a convoy of jeeps at various times of the day, zooming through the village, driving recklessly, and raising dust. One time, they put the village under curfew, went from home to home in search of different activists, arrested more than ten men, confiscated tractors, and dug up backyards searching for weapons. Then they set up checkpoints at the entrances of the village and dug up the roads to make it difficult for anyone to escape while they searched homes.

In one of their visits to the Sawalha home, more than a dozen soldiers occupied the street that led to their gate. Most lingered outside while four soldiers forced their way in, ruffling the jasmine tree at the entrance. The first to walk in had his eyes focused on locating his target, his lips pressed into a thin line, his head held high with disregard for the family. "Move out of the way," he shouted, and then commanded the family to huddle in one room. "When was the last time you saw Iyad?" another asked. The family remained silent. The commanding officer ordered the soldiers to ransack the house and locate the family's photo albums. They searched through the house, opened drawers, pulled clothes out of closets, upturned their furniture, and found albums here and there until they had accumulated a large stash that could fit into four garbage bags. It was almost all the photos the family owned. "We'll be taking these," the commander said.

"Hasbi Allah 'aleykom!" Um Yousef screamed. God would avenge her.

She tried to grab the bags from them, but they pushed her back. "You can come to the station to collect them," the commander told her. She knew this was futile. They would just give her the runaround, and in the meantime, people would begin to suspect her of being a collaborator. She tried to snatch the bags one last time. The commanding officer pushed her back again; this time her white veil came slightly undone. She shot her eyes at him, chin up, lips tight, shoulders rolling toward him. They could arrest her past, try to erase it, but she would not be broken. *"Itla'!* Get out of here. *Allah yikhrub baytak,"* she said with scorn.

These invading soldiers were often Palestinians of Druze faith with Israeli citizenship; they were not Jewish. The Druze leadership, prior to 1948, had collaborated with the Zionist movement in order to protect itself. Later, in 1956, this leadership signed an agreement with the Israeli government that mandated the Druze community to join the Israeli army. Despite the community's allegiance to the Israeli state, however, the Druze faced much of the same institutional discrimination that other non-Jewish communities experienced, and as second-class citizens, they tended to be poorer than their Jewish counterparts. During this period, they served primarily in a Druze-only unit. The army used Druze soldiers, who were Arab and spoke Arabic, in the West Bank to enter Palestinian homes and deal directly with Palestinian civilians.

These guys are so much tougher and meaner than the Israeli Jewish soldiers. I think they feel they have something to prove; they have to show to their Jewish colleagues that they are as patriotic as them, that they are as Israeli, and any sign of weakness could be interpreted to mean they were a fifth column.

In one incident, after my father returned from the US in May, the soldiers busted our outdoor front gate, marched to our front door, and barged into our house. They were rude and aggressive with my family. Imagine—my father couldn't say or do anything, completely at their mercy, humiliated in a village where a man is meant to protect his family. My father, dressed in a gray blazer, blue-gray pants, and sneakers, and using a cane to stand with his prosthetic leg, was pushed aside and was unable to put up a fight. My siblings were ordered out of the house. Arselene walked out reluctantly, screaming at them, with Baha holding her back and trying to calm her, not daring to say a word. Only my mother stood in front of the soldiers.

They looked at her and smiled. One asked nicely if she would tell him where Iyad was and spare everyone the trouble. He knew this question was futile. My mother did not dignify him with a response.

Um Yousef stood composed and proud in silence, but deep inside, she was afraid. The truth was, she had no idea of her son's whereabouts, and she knew what these soldiers were capable of. She had seen families experience immeasurable loss from the mere act of silence. But silence was the only option.

After a few seconds, one of the soldiers looked around the house and noticed a large collection of plants and flowers. My mother loved to bring home all kinds of plants, sometimes from our land and other times from neighbors. She had an assortment of *khunshar, sijaddeh, um mahmoud, bakhur mariam,* and *chamaa*—fern, coleus, hunter's robe, primrose, and the wax plant. She had flowers and plants in vases and pots. The terrace was completely lined with them. The soldier went up to the primrose, took a deep breath, and inhaled its sweet scent. He then picked up his machine gun and, along with the other soldier, began to shoot at the plants around the house.

They first shot up all the plants outside on the veranda, mud splattering everywhere. Then they turned to a large glass table with plants and sprayed it with dozens of bullets. The glass shattered into a thousand pieces, and all that was left of the plants were petals at my mother's feet. Our living room floor was bullet ridden, as was one of the walls. During all this, my mother said nothing. I don't know what the soldiers were thinking as they turned our house upside down. What pleasure were they deriving from this? The soldiers tried one last time to get information from my family, but it was useless. No one knew anything. Iyad had made sure of this to protect them. Before they left, they went to the kitchen and there, dumped out all our flour, rice, sugar, and oil.

The next day, my mother packed some of her valuables—paintings, a china set with British designs of Romeo and Juliet, and other belongings—and sent them to members of our extended family so that if the soldiers returned, they wouldn't destroy them.

I, on the other hand, could not imagine—or refused to believe—what my brother was up to. I believed in resistance as the only way to free ourselves, but my brother was my brother, above all. I suppose I preferred others to do the armed resisting if anyone was to do it. My brother was mine. He remained mine, not the nation's.

*

In Jenin, Iyad was preparing a response to the April massacre in the camp. With Saeed Tubasi and others, their cell had divided the work of bomb-making between those who delivered materials such as nitrate, those who built the bombs, and those who were in charge of hiding the bombs. Saeed had become quite close with Iyad and was instrumental in providing him with different types of protection. His family took care of Iyad in Jenin, and Saeed found him secret locations in which to hide and build bombs and made sure it was easy for Iyad to get around.

When Iyad wasn't engaging in street battles, sitting in meetings, or preparing explosives, he was thinking of the next operation, the next encounter with soldiers, the next escape route. Being on the run had become his life, and he no longer thought much of it.

By May, Iyad's cell in Jenin was already active. In their workshop, Saeed and Iyad were working quickly with clarity and focus. But sometimes, when they took breaks, or late at night, they would discuss the future and their strategies. "Where do you think this is going, Iyad?" Saeed wondered out loud once.

"I have a good feeling. We're building something here. We need to shut out the critics and focus. We're building something."

"Yes, I know. I hope we'll see the results," Saeed said.

"We may. We may not. But we lay the seeds for others in any case."

Saeed went back to arranging some wires. "It's amazing how the world rejects our bombing operations and calls us cowards."

"They'll reject any act of resistance so long as it comes from us. It's as if we are not human. But let's see what they would do in our situation." Iyad was dismissive as he lay on his side on a sponge mattress, his head cradled in his hand and supported by his elbow. After a moment of silence, he lifted his head up and spoke with a raised voice. "They can't shame us into surrender. They can't force us to fight with their rules when we have no weapons." Then he lay back down again, cupped his cheek, and cursed his enemies.

Saeed laughed. He hadn't meant to get Iyad worked up. "God will make us victorious," he said to calm his friend. Every Jewish Israeli was working to erase them off their land, trying to exterminate them. This was their reality. There was no question about what had to be done. They just did their work, determined and motivated by the principle that no occupier was ever expelled without armed resistance.

The next day, they sent a bomber to the town of Afula, العفولة. The man strapped an explosive belt under his sweater and made it to a bus stop a few kilometers over the Green Line on the outskirts of that town. There, a passerby alerted authorities that there was a man standing at a bus stop who looked suspicious. A military vehicle arrived before he boarded the bus. It slowed down so the officers could question him. As it got closer, he detonated his explosive belt, killing himself instantly and sending shrapnel at the military vehicle. No Israelis were injured.

Iyad regrouped with Saeed and his comrades and reflected on what had happened. They met over several weeks in an apartment near the central bus station in Jenin, where their comings and goings could go unnoticed in the crowds. There, they spent long hours discussing developments in the Saraya al-Quds, planning military operations, and meeting with rank-and-file fighters and supporters from the city and its surrounding areas to provide military advice and direction. Iyad operated under a pseudonym in these meetings, and the fighters only knew him as Ahmad. It was at one such gathering that Iyad would meet Hamza Samudi, a shy boy that Iyad would go on to recruit for a special mission.

36

June 2002

Hamza Samudi was born in al-Yamun, اليامون, a town west of Jenin, and later moved with his family to Jenin, where his father worked as a smalltime businessman. Hamza was the youngest of eleven children, coddled and babied by his tight-knit family and best friends with his older sister. His father struggled to find work, and by the time Hamza made it to high school, his father was too old to work. So, Hamza left school to take care of his parents and worked as a cart seller in Nazareth. Later, he worked in a stonemasonry in the village of Salem, سالم, on lands taken by the Zionists in 1948.

Hamza was not known to be a member of any political party. His mother did not even think he was much into politics. Like most seventeen- or eighteen-year-olds, he threw stones at the occupation forces a few times, but as the Second Intifada grew into an armed confrontation, he mostly stuck to work and caring for his family. But after the battle of Jenin, curfews made life harder, movement became more difficult, and he was unable to get to work most days. For a long time, he had been collecting posters of martyrs, admiring their commitment and sacrifice. He connected with Saraya al-Quds fighters in the aftermath of that battle, and it was through them that he found himself in an apartment one night, face-to-face with Iyad.

In those meetings during the last weeks of May, Iyad and his close comrades decided they needed a new strategy for inflicting harm on their enemy. Ultimately, they resolved to prepare a car bomb that they would send over the Green Line. Hamza volunteered to carry out this mission.

He met Iyad one night in that apartment by the central bus station. There, Hamza committed to the job, and Iyad planned and prepared the operation. His comrades had to smuggle explosive raw materials, prepare the car, and choose a target.

On June 4, Hamza returned to the apartment. It was the second time he met Iyad, whose real name he still did not know. There, Iyad took his photo for the martyr posters that are usually posted on walls, and he videotaped Hamza's last testimony, as was customary before every martyr operation. Hamza posed with a grin, carrying an M-16 in his hands that was strapped around his shoulder and wearing a black Saraya al-Quds bandana on his forehead and his favorite blue T-shirt with a few red and white stripes. He had chubby cheeks, a baby face with some stubble on his chin. His hazel eyes hung heavy as he casually stared at the camera with indifference. Iyad gave him a glass of water after they videotaped the testimony. Hamza was slightly nervous in this unfamiliar place and knowing what was to come. Iyad put his arm around Hamza's shoulder to comfort him. "God will acknowledge your martyrdom. God will care for you. Have faith my brother. You will go first, and we will follow," Iyad whispered in a peaceful, comforting voice. Hamza smiled.

Afterward, Hamza went home and had dinner with his family. A friend stopped by, and they chatted and joked over watermelon. He stayed up late into the night talking about religion with his mother. When her eyes grew heavy, he let her go to bed and went to his room. He did not fall asleep. He waited for the sun to rise, performed his prayers, and was out of the house before anyone woke up.

He met Iyad on the outskirts of the city of Jenin. They shook hands, exchanged pleasantries, and then Iyad began to discuss with him the details of the operation, which, up until then, Hamza had not been privy to. Iyad handed Hamza the keys to a Renault with yellow license plates. He would take it in the direction of Meggido and should have no trouble crossing over into '48 Palestine, Iyad reassured him. They prayed briefly together. Iyad gave him a kiss on his forehead and asked him to put his trust in God: "*Tawakal 'alla-llah.*" Up until a few days ago, Hamza had not known how to drive and had needed to learn and practice. But even now, he was surprised to learn that he was not going to be strapped with an explosive belt. He had not imagined that the car would be the vessel; it had not been done this way in Palestine before.

And so, Hamza, with stubble on his chin that could hardly hide his tanned baby face, stepped into the driver's seat and drove off. Iyad walked off the road at a gentle pace and then, moments later, disappeared.

*

Hamza's mother woke at dawn and noticed he was not in his bed. She found it odd. She looked around and saw cash on a side table. If he had gone to work, he would have taken it. She checked his bed and saw a folded paper. She grabbed it. It was a will. In it, he told her and all his siblings to forgive him, to work hard, and to live by God's teachings.

Her arms began to shake. Even decades later, when she retells these events, they will shake. Her head spun. She felt heavy. She could feel the weight of her tongue.

She ran to her other son, Akram, woke him, and asked if he knew anything. But he was half-asleep and dismissed her, saying Hamza was probably out or at work.

Her heart began to drum faster. A cold sensation took over her palms and fingertips. She imagined soldiers catching him and torturing him. That was as far as her imagination took her. She returned to Akram two more times before she told him about the will. Each time he told her not to worry, that Hamza was probably playing his usual pranks.

Relenting to his mother's pleas to do something, he promised to find his brother, dressed, and left the house. He returned a short while later from the market having learned nothing of Hamza's whereabouts but told his mother he would continue searching.

At around 7:14 a.m., Egged bus no. 830 had picked up many of its passengers and was driving along Highway 66 when Hamza pulled onto the highway a short distance from it. Behind the bus was a man driving to work at a casual pace, windows down and enjoying the morning breeze. The man was sandwiched between the bus and a pickup truck trudging along lazily behind him, neither bothering to overtake the bus. Hamza gathered speed. The man saw him zoom past. The Egged bus driver saw him as well from his sideview mirror. Meggido Prison was closing in, a few hundred meters away. No one had time to suspect what might happen. They might have imagined Hamza was in a rush.

The distance to the prison closed in.

500 meters.

400 meters.

300 meters.

Hamza began a brief prayer. He was up near the bus's fuel tank now. He let out an *"Allahu Akbar"* that only he could hear, and . . .

At the Meggido Junction, located at the entrance of the Wadi ʿAra, وادي عارة, mountain pass, adjacent to Meggido Prison where Iyad had done time, and a few kilometers from Jenin, lay a bus, angry flames engulfing it and thick black smoke billowing into the sky. The Renault van Hamza had been driving detonated near the fuel tank of the Egged bus no. 830 traveling from Tel Aviv to Tabariyya, طبريا, Tiberias, sending the bus rolling in multiple flips to crash on a grassy embankment outside the barbed-wire fence of the prison. The Renault was ripped apart and charred, its driver, Hamza, unrecognizable. Inside the bus, survivors panicked. A few seconds later, there was a second explosion as flames encircled the fuel tank. Some of those who had been ejected from the bus by the initial blast were lucky not to burn alive. The bus driver and one soldier were able to rush out before the bus was scorched and consumed by flames. Thirteen soldiers and four civilians were killed that day. Another forty-three passengers were injured, most of them soldiers as well. All the dead had families that would miss them and whose wounds would reopen each year of remembrance.

Inside Meggido Prison, a structure that was used by the British forces during the Mandate period, approximately 1,200 Palestinian political prisoners heard the sound of the blast as if it had happened in their cells. They could see glimpses of a burning vehicle and smell the smoke. Later, they could also pick out the scent of seared flesh. In Section 7 of the prison, the section closest to the site of the blast, there was a series of *takbir* from the Palestinian prisoners. *"Allahu Akbar! Allahu Akbar!"*

Many prisoners could not contain themselves, and some tried to climb the prison walls to get a glimpse of the operation. They smiled and cheered. They did so despite the possibility of retaliation from prison guards. They could not help but feel the blast as a burst of fresh dignity from the daily humiliation of imprisonment. Prison guards perched on top of watchtowers stood helpless in the face of the carnage.

It is likely that targeting the bus at the Meggido Junction was intentional, because Hamza had been following the bus for a few minutes and could have detonated sooner. Indeed, the narrative presented by the Saraya al-Quds was that the Israeli military itself confirmed the site of the blast was meant as a message to the prisoners that they are not forgotten and that their struggle continues. For Iyad, having masterminded the operation, there was a more personal sentimental dimension: A message to his one-time captors that resistance cannot be caged. A gift to former inmates—lifelong brothers—that he had their back.

The explosion reverberated far into the alleyways of towns in the surrounding area. The village of al-Lajjun was one such place that experienced the tremors. There was a time when some of its Palestinian residents would have been waking up, drinking their early morning tea or coffee, their kids on their way to school. On this day, the Palestinians of al-Lajjun were not present. They had been driven out long ago in 1948, mostly resettling in Um el-Fahm, أم الفحم. Al-Lajjun was now partly settled by Jewish residents of Kibbutz Meggido, and in some parts, its remaining land had been planted over with wheat, barley, and almond trees. There were some animal sheds, a fodder plant, and a pump that had been installed on the spring of ʿAyn al-Hajja, عين الحجة. In other parts, it was deserted, tightly fenced off and its entry blocked. It was the Jewish residents who heard the boom of Hamza's operation and felt the ground beneath them shake on that day of June 5. A few remaining village buildings also trembled from the explosive sound, as did the white stone mosque built in 1943 now used as a carpentry shop and a few partially destroyed Palestinian homes, a deserted health center and grain mill, and the neglected cemetery, with only the souls of ancestors left as witnesses.

Hamza's brother, Akram, was on his way home when a friend stopped him, excited about a beautiful operation that had just been conducted against the occupier. But he noticed Akram was down and that he became even more dejected when he heard the news. Akram explained his worries, but the friend assured him they were impossible and that Hamza was not into such things. "I was with Hamza last night. We were enjoying watermelon and chatting. Hamza has nothing to do with this," he remarked.

But soon, word was out. People were already holding photos of Hamza in the Jenin refugee camp. Outside his house, his mother began to hear a commotion. She heard someone call for God to give happiness to a mother. *"Allah yisʿed al-batn ilee hamalu!"* And again, people chanted, "May God give joy to the one who bore him!"

And she knew in her heart that she was that mother.

*

Iyad was at the apartment near the central bus station in Jenin when he received news that Hamza had completed the operation and inflicted heavy casualties. He greeted it with a smile and a *takbir* in a hushed voice followed by a short prayer. Shortly after, his comrades came over, and they hugged and rejoiced at their success. Only a few people knew that he had planned this operation, from preparing the bomb to meeting with the volunteer, from selecting the target to choosing a date that coincided with the anniversary of the 1967 defeat. Later, the Israeli military recognized that this attack had created a material shift. It was the first time Palestinians detonated a moving car alongside a bus rather than dispatching a bomber to physically board a targeted vehicle. It also suggested the sophistication of Palestinian intelligence: in order to be able to attack outside the borders of the West Bank, they had coordinated with people over the Green Line. The infiltration beyond the '67 borders showed that the Israeli offensive that began in April had failed despite the fact that the military took control across the West Bank. Iyad had shifted the dynamics on the ground, and as a result, his capture would become a top priority.

Almost two decades later, Hamza's mother recalls that the Israelis did not demolish her house the next day. "There are hundreds of examples like ours, where the family home of a martyr is demolished immediately. But they didn't come for our house that day. They didn't enter our home until two months minus a day. I think they were still trying to gather all the information about the operation, until they learned that Hamza was driving a stolen car from Tel Aviv. That Iyad was the one who took his last picture. And maybe Saeed Tubasi placed the 100 kg explosives in the car. I didn't even know these details until a year later as people talked here and there."

Um Hamza does not blame her son. She is not angry. She is not sad about what he did. But one thing brings her to tears, will always bring her to tears. It is the fact that Hamza never said goodbye to her. She does blame him for that. The thought breaks her every time she confronts it.

And she has nowhere to turn to ease the pain, no grave to visit at which to say her goodbyes or feel near to him again. The Israeli authorities took his body, and she was never able to recover it from them.

"*Yuma!*" she often hears his voice calling. "Mom!" She'll be washing the dishes and she'll feel him. "I'll hear his voice ring inside me and turn around to look for him. There isn't a day that goes by that I don't think of my Hamza," she says. And she slips into *byut 'ataba*, poetic lines lamenting lost love,

ميلي يا شجرة الزيتون
ميلي ع حمزة المزيون
ميلي ومية صمله عليه
رشي المخدة يام أدهم بالحنة

Lean, O olive tree
Lean on Hamza the balanced one
Lean and a hundred bismillahs upon him
Sprinkle the pillow with Henna O mother of Adham

"And then you live," she says, her voice trailing off with melancholia. "What can you do? God gives you patience."

37

I am standing on the balcony of my family home in Palestine. Iyad comes from the field in the distance. He is wearing a black leather jacket and a headscarf, the Palestinian *hatta*. He is holding a baby, a newborn baby boy wrapped in a white shroud. I see the boy. "*Ya Allah!* Oh my God!" I say with excitement. "Is this your son?"

"Yes. Is he cute?" he replies.

He hands me a photograph. In it, I see him as he is in front of me. A man in a black leather jacket, holding a newborn baby wrapped in a white blanket.

I ask him to come in.

He refuses.

"The one inside with my mother is a collaborator," he says, before disappearing.

38

June–July 2002

It was not long after Iyad divorced Mariam—it could not have been more than a month—that she was back in Palestine, after having disappeared for a year. Sireen believed she must have learned from her grandparents that Iyad was divorcing her.

Baha, now Iyad's only brother still in Palestine, was curious and wanted to know what happened. In one of his meetings with Iyad, he pressed him, "Don't you want to know? How did she leave the village? Who smuggled her out?"

"Who cares!" Iyad shot back, "I don't want anything to do with her."

Mariam's return came after Israeli soldiers visited the Sawalha home and blew out their front gate. For a while, Um Yousef had deferred fixing the gate, expecting more damage to come, but Baha had finally taken the initiative to get it done. The only one in town who could fix it was *joz 'amet* Mariam, her paternal aunt's husband, who was a blacksmith. Baha went to see him. There, he ran into Mariam.

"Baha, how are you? Please, please, please let me speak to Iyad, even if for a moment," she pleaded.

Baha hesitated. But Mariam kept pushing, and he didn't know how to refuse. He called Iyad from his cellphone, and Iyad picked up. As soon as Baha said hello and before he could explain, Mariam snatched the phone to talk to him.

They spoke briefly. She said very little. He agreed to see her, but not because of anything she said in particular or the way she spoke; sometimes the heart is inexplicably captured, hypnotized, intoxicated.

Two days later, they met in Jenin.

They met in the *hisbah* around the old city. The market was bustling again, enough time having passed since the battle in the refugee camp a few kilometers away. The *hisbah* is a spectacle of colors. Vendors sell all sorts of things: fruits, clothes, furniture, toys, and produce. On paths through the market, blood and water from butcher stalls mix and trickle down. The *hisbah* has little patience for paved streets and almost consumes them entirely. A four-lane road is reduced to two lanes and cars must ask permission from shoppers to pass. Parts of the market are covered by large tarps to protect people from the summer sun, but in other areas, people walk in the heat and vendors wait under umbrellas for the day to end.

Iyad and Mariam met among the shadows cast by a late afternoon sun and strolled through the *hisbah* accompanied by a mild summer breeze. No one in the city knew Iyad's face, so he walked with little disguise. They spoke for a long time and whispered back and forth while Mariam's tears streaked her cheeks, invisible except to him. In whispers he would never repeat, he learned what she had been through, how miserable she had been, and how she had returned when she learned he was moving on. In those moments, she exposed her insecurities and begged him to forgive her.

Afterward, my brother was a different person. He told our parents the next day that he wanted to call off his marriage to the other woman.

"*Keef?* How can you do this?" my father said calmly but angrily. "*Ruhna nitlub eedha. 'Ayb!*"

"I no longer want her. I want to remarry Mariam," Iyad said with confidence.

My father was visibly upset. "Are you crazy? We went to ask her family for her hand, this is shameful! When did you see Mariam? What did she tell you?" he asked. But Iyad said it was none of anyone's business.

My father pressed him in disbelief. "What are you saying? This is insane!"

"What does it matter to you? I want to return to her and take her back." Iyad was convinced.

"But *habibi*, she left you from the first days of your marriage for a whole year. This is disgraceful," my father said.

When I heard the news, I felt like someone had punched me in the stomach. I couldn't sleep and found myself pacing around the house barefoot. I needed to talk to him, and when I did, we argued. I don't know what Mariam could have told him that day in Jenin. He told us that she got scared and ran. After they got married, her aunts and uncles began to tell her that Iyad was a killer, that he killed collaborators, that he committed many crimes. She was apparently confused and afraid. She told him that she loved him so much and that it would be impossible to do this to him again and to live without him.

"But Iyad, you kept calling me and telling me how much you hated her and that you would never let her into your house. And you're a sheikh. How could you let her in now?" I clamored on the phone with him one day.

"She had her issues. *Khalas*, I've decided." That was his final word.

In the midst of a summer of great pain and heavy resistance, with Iyad deeply undercover heading operations in the Northern West Bank and preparing explosives for others to detonate, his relationship with Mariam remained a point of contention in the family.

The problem was that my brother was running out of time. In Islam, according to our laws, if a couple wants to nullify a divorce, they must do so within ninety days of when the divorce was first granted. This period during which a divorce can be annulled is called the ‘*idda*. Should ninety days pass, the only way for a divorced couple to remarry is for the woman to first marry and divorce another man, called the *muhalel*. Only then can the original couple remarry.

If Iyad had just taken the other girl as his second wife without trying to divorce Mariam, maybe she wouldn't have known and wouldn't have returned. But Iyad insisted on the divorce. He did not want to take a second wife. Nothing made sense.

Nothing would ever make sense.

Is this what they call love?

Love? Maybe.

Arselene felt Iyad had a kind heart. That maybe he was naively seeking affection because he lacked it as a prisoner. Others believed he wanted to show his wife the right path of Islam. That this was a true test of his piety.

My father was livid. If Iyad were to annul the divorce and go through with the marriage, he would disown his son. He swore on it. He said he would do it legally through the courts.

Yousef called me to ask me to convince Iyad. If he remarried her, I was to tell Iyad that the family would disown him.

I spoke to Iyad for about thirty-five minutes. "Aren't we an educated family?" he lectured. "It's so sad that this is what you all learned in your travels and with your degrees," he continued. "If Yousef wants to disown me, then I don't want anything to do with him anyway, and he can throw his degree in the garbage."

I asked him what he would do if she left him again. He said that it didn't matter, that he could marry a second or third time. He was angry and lashed out. "She told me the reason why she left, and I am completely convinced by it," he said.

"So what is the reason? Tell us so we support you."

"There is no need to tell you. It is enough that I am convinced and know the reason."

"This is unbelievable! *Habibi*, this isn't right."

I remember so vividly asking, "What if the Mossad knew about your activities already? What if Mariam had never left the country and was in Tel Aviv the entire time? What if the Mossad trained her?" He didn't listen. He thought we were foolish.

And maybe they were foolish. Maybe Iyad was not wrong.

I tried to offer him more advice, I tried to lecture him without angering him, but it was useless. He was determined. And I had nothing more to say.

"*Allah yikhaleek,* Iyad. Think about this rationally," I pleaded. I wanted to pull out my hair!

"*Allah yisamehkom.* I've made my decision. I'm happy."

"*Allah yihmeek, dir ballak.* Take care of yourself," I said.

"*Tawakali 'alla-llah,*" he responded.

I gripped the phone, then looked up at the ceiling and exhaled. We said our goodbyes and hung up.

I rubbed my face several times and then looked around, surrounded by silence. I couldn't understand what was going on. Everything was spiraling out of control.

Cities were besieged, and villages were being cut off from their sustenance. Israeli forces that were meant to act as a kind of policing force under occupation had turned into an unabashed war machine managing people's fates from the sky. And here was the Sawalha family, having to deal with a marriage crisis.

I couldn't believe it. Did Islamic Jihad members have time to deal with matters of the heart?

This man who could outmaneuver the Israelis, who could bypass the tightest security—how could he get into this type of relationship?

And what was Mariam's father thinking? Iyad was a person the Israelis wanted dead or alive. Rumor had it that he was responsible for a lot of martyr operations and other operations around Jenin. There were also rumors that he was the head of the Islamic Jihad in the north of the West Bank. How do you hand your daughter to such a person… again?

It is also said that the wife of a resistance fighter, the wife of a high-ranking Islamic Jihad fighter, brings respect and status to the father of the bride.

After we fought with Iyad—it must have been late July-—we didn't hear much from him, and certainly nothing about Mariam. We held out hope that he would listen. Then, in early August, her grandfather made a huge announcement that shocked us!

39

August 2002

The Sawalha family was looking forward to late summer. They were planning a family reunion in Jordan. Abu Yousef and Um Yousef, along with all
their kids in Kufr Ra'i, were set to travel to Amman to meet with Suzanne,
who was flying in from Dubai; Maysoun, who was coming from Jeddah; and
Yousef, who was traveling all the way from Ohio. But in early August, the
mood dampened. Mariam's grandfather announced that Iyad and Mariam
had annulled their divorce and remarried in secret and that she had moved
to be with him.

Abu Yousef received the news in his wheelchair. His giant shoulders
slouched. His large eyes shrank to a crescent moon, and he fell silent. The
moment was yet another level in the scaffold of loss on which his life was
built. Um Yousef was seated near him on a sofa that devoured her small
figure. She remained stiff except for a moment to adjust her veil. Anger was
visible in the narrowing of her eyes. For several days, barely a word was said
by anyone in the house.

But their children convinced them to go to Amman anyway. The reunion
would be good for them.

In Princeton, Sireen was trying to make plans of her own to meet up with
her family and then return to Palestine. But it was not looking likely; her
husband was refusing to let her go. Thinking of how to convince him kept
her awake at night. During the days, she was hardly able to eat, her stomach
in knots, her body experiencing mild aches.

214

We were quite broke that year. We had been working on our new house in Princeton all summer and had spent a lot of money on it, and I had to feed three kids. I pleaded with my husband.

"Mohammed, I have a favor to ask of you," I said. "In the last eight years, I have only seen Iyad twice, behind bars. I have not seen him since he was freed. Please. *Haram ʿaleyk.* Everyone talks about him, speaks highly of him, thinks he's a hero. But all I do is speak to him over the phone, and I can't even picture him. How has he grown? Who has he become? Is he thin? Does he have a beard? How does he look when he eats or drinks? How does it feel to laugh with him? These are the things I want to remember."

We fought throughout the day and into the evening.

He finally told me that if I could find a cheap enough ticket, then I could go. I found one and booked it. I called my mother and told her that I was going to come. She was so excited. "Yee, everyone is waiting for you. They will be so happy, especially your sister's kids."

I told her that if I went, I was going to leave the kids with her and go to the *Daffeh*—the West Bank—for two days to see Iyad.

"Are you crazy! So they use you to catch him?" she shot out. My mother went on yelling. "He tells everyone that he has no problems being a martyr, but all he asks is to let God give him the time to see you. The Israelis know this! *Ouʿek!* Don't you dare! *Rah tibleena.* You'll ruin our family and create so many problems. If you go, the Israelis will catch you at the border so they can get to Iyad. And you are the only person Iyad will give himself up for so you can return to your kids and husband."

When she said this, I told her that I wouldn't meet with him. I would just see him from afar, let him see me, and part ways.

She said I was crazy. "What are you talking about, from afar? If you are coming for this reason, then don't come!"

But what was I going to go do otherwise? Go to Amman to sit in an apartment and see my mother and father? I had just seen my father in the US, and I wasn't interested in going through all the trouble to see my parents and the rest of my family. I wasn't afraid for them.

I canceled the trip.

On August 13, Um Yousef made the trip to Amman with her youngest, Esraa. She had spent the days before finally repairing and repainting the living room after it had been sprayed with bullets in a recent Israeli incursion into their home. She was glad for the break, but in the back of her mind, questions surrounding Iyad's marriage loomed heavily as she tried to make sense of his decisions. At the bridge, the Israeli border police let her through with no issues. In hindsight, Sireen thinks it is because her last name was not Sawalha. The next day, her father, with Arselene, Suha, Sawsan, Baha, and Salam, tried to cross, but they were denied passage. They were told that as the family of Iyad Sawalha, they were forbidden from traveling.

That day in August, I remember, my heart began to pound, and my stomach was tied up in knots again as I became so nervous.

40

August 16, 2002

The air was dead, the night mute when Israeli military vehicles rumbled into Kufr Ra'i and came to a halt at the Sawalha family home. The soldiers disembarked from their vehicles, and one of them thundered to the front gate and slammed against it with great force, upsetting the leaves of the jasmine tree that leaned on it.

"We want Iyad!" soldiers yelled from outside, breaking the 2 a.m. silence.

"Iyad is not here," Abu Yousef replied from his bedroom. He was, by now, used to the intimidation and the soldiers' frequent visits, though they usually came at more reasonable hours. The whole family was up even before the pounding. Barking dogs had alerted them to the approaching convoy, and they had heard the aggressive sound of vehicles before the soldiers arrived at their doorstep. Arselene was already near her father when he shouted back at them.

"Then get out. Get out now!" the same soldier demanded.

Arselene looked at her father; he returned her gaze. They were confused. The army usually just barged in, did what they liked, interrogated them at will, and left. She thought for a moment and had a sickening feeling. Then she yelled back at them, wanting answers, "Are you going to destroy our house?"

"No, we're just going to search it."

"If you're going to destroy the house, tell us! If you are going to do that, please let me have my father's medication and prosthetic leg!"

"No, we're not!" A soldier retorted.

Arselene held on to the promise in his words—hope was all she had.

The soldiers shuffled her out along with her father and three sisters. Baha

217

was there too. He had no time to escape, and the soldiers cuffed him. It was enough that he was Iyad's brother. They placed him in a military jeep and, later, took him away to be questioned and released a day later.

The family filed into the street in their pajamas. It wasn't their first house search, nor was it their first ransacking. But it was the first time their father was forced out barefoot, limping on his prosthetic leg, held up by Arselene.

Arselene had been distraught when they first took Baha. She begged them to stop. But when she saw her father upset, she tried to hold herself together. A neighbor had brought a chair for Abu Yousef to sit on, and Arselene sat on the ground beside him, holding his hand, telling him everything would be okay, that he needed to remain strong now that Baha and Um Yousef were not around.

More soldiers entered the house. They were from the Yahalom unit. Demolition experts. There were more than a dozen of them, carrying explosive material and other gear. Some proceeded to extend wires through the rooms while others waited and watched the perimeter. They put explosives in the closets and piled the furniture on top of them in key places to ensure the explosion would burn the furniture and the rest of the house.

I think the Israelis wanted to make sure there could be nothing to return to, nothing for us to save. They believed that belonging and memory perish together, that we lose it all.

As the soldiers were placing the bombs, Arselene reentered the house and saw them. She recognized what they were doing and began to scream.

"You're going to blow up the house!"

"Yes, of course. Wasn't Iyad Sawalha born in this house? Then we will wipe this house off the face of this earth."

"But my mother gave birth to twelve other kids in this house! It is not only Iyad's house. It is not only his house. There are twelve others! Please!"

"This is the house where Iyad opened his eyes for the first time. It will be destroyed," one soldier taunted.

We all learned to walk in that house and had our first meals in that house. All thirteen of us fell on the stairs of that house and have scars from that house. I carry Arselene's words of anger with me as if they were my own. They keep me going.

Arselene, usually able to sweet-talk people and get her way, approached the soldiers, but this time with little effect. When they wouldn't let her in, she began to ask for only a few things. They refused. She persisted, in tears. She got up close, in a soldier's face, and pulled on his arm until he finally allowed her to take her father's diabetes medicine. His walking stick and wheelchair remained behind, as did the dentures that he kept by his bed.

The whole family stood there on the street. Alone.

Arselene felt lost. She tried to appeal to the soldier keeping guard near them while his comrades set up the house for demolition. She pleaded for him to see her as a fellow human in need of a place to call home, as a woman in need of shelter. There was no one else who could help her, no villagers who could come to her aid, and Iyad, gone underground, was not ready to surrender.

At around 4 a.m., the soldiers walked out of the green two-story house. It stood there, empty, alone, in those final moments. Its red-framed windows looked out into the valley of cherries, and its green steel gate, always seeming taller than the house, creaked one last time, as if weeping in submission, while the jasmine, usually independent and wild, clutched the gate in panic. Floral curtains on the second floor, caught by a gust of wind, called out to Abu Yousef through an open window.

Abu Yousef looked up. It was Um Yousef who should have been there. Not him. It was she who had sacrificed her life for this house. Who in 1967 returned to raise her family on this plot of land. Who poured her sweat into building every room while he lived abroad. But now, as the house took its final stand, she was nowhere in sight.

He looked up past the house and searched beyond the stars, hoping for an answer, for mercy.

A tear. A lonely tear slid down his cheek, as if to confront the Israelis one last time—to plead, to connect, to resist. A tear that carried the memories of an entire life for them to see, if only they could see.

And then, in an instant—before he could look down, before he could say goodbye, before his tears had a chance to plead—his life, their memories, their past, came crashing down to the discordant staccato of dynamite.

In the days and years to come, they would collect their lives, rebuild, and carry their past with them. Pasts have a resilient way of escaping erasure even when threatened with dynamite. But in that moment, as the dust sprang up into the night sky of Kufr Ra'i and the neighbors stood at their windows to weep for their collective fate, the few present members of Dar Abu Shqara—Arselene, Suha, Salam, Sawsan, and their father—felt their present torn and shattered, dismembered from an annihilated past without which they were unable to make sense of what the future held. Baha, handcuffed in the back of a military jeep, squeezed his eyes shut to trap his tears.

Moments after the explosion, any remaining villagers still asleep had woken up, and many households had turned on their lights. The army, sensing the possibility of resistance, announced a curfew on their loudspeaker. No one was to leave their homes. Any hope that neighbors would console the family was dashed.

The soldiers waited until they were sure the house was completely demolished. The family remained on the street. Arselene passed out from all her yelling and crying. Nearby, Um Yousef's sister, Fasayil, had heard all the screaming before the explosion. Then, silence. She thought part of the family had been wiped out. She began to wail. Her cries increased in crescendo, and her arms beat her head as her body swung like a pendulum marking time. Her husband, himself in shock, could not console her. Neither knew the fate of their relatives. Not till news traveled from house to house.

For over two hours, no one dared to come out to shelter the family. Sireen's father, Arselene, and the three sisters sat there, on the side of the road, in the warm August night, waiting for the soldiers to leave and watching as the dawn slowly revealed their own humiliation.

When the dust finally cleared and they could see, only one wall and the door of a destroyed beige wardrobe remained. On the wall was a picture of Iyad and another of Bassel, Sireen's son. And on the wardrobe door, inscribed over the years, were the dates of birth of all thirteen children of the Sawlha family.

Hours later, as morning settled on the eastern bank of the parched Jordan River, Um Yousef stood in front of a TV in a relative's apartment watching news of Palestine and the world. At the bottom of the screen a ticker scrolled by: "Breaking News: Israeli forces demolish the family home of Iyad Sawalha, a member of the Islamic Jihad."

She read it and felt nothing. She did not experience the news as her life. The shock took some moments to settle, and she needed to make some calls to confirm.

Later, she would grieve when she returned and saw the rubble, the shreds of curtain, the burned pictures, and the mangled jasmine tree still clinging to life by its roots. But now, she was silent in disbelief. In 1967, they had tried to take her land, but she had walked back under the cover of night. Now, as if to get back at her for challenging the forces that tried to erase her, they took her house of almost four decades as she watched from Amman.

As she regained herself, she found some solace in the thought that if they had destroyed the house, it meant they would at least leave her son alone. She could accept this sacrifice and whispered as much to him, "*Fidak al-bayt, al-mohem inta.*"

The phone rang at 2 a.m., which was 9 a.m. Palestine time. It startled me. I had spent the last two days in the hospital in Rutgers because my son, Zeid, had had a severe asthma attack. I was totally out of it, and Mohammed told me it was one of Diaa's friends and to go back to sleep. My brother was staying with us, and they sometimes called at odd hours from Palestine.

I fell back asleep, but Mohammed could not. He went down and sat at the TV the rest of the night. At 8 a.m., I heard the phone ring around seven times. But I was so exhausted, it felt like part of my dream. I didn't wake up. I finally got out of bed about half an hour later.

I went downstairs, and Mohammed said that Zeid hadn't eaten a good breakfast in days and told me to make breakfast. I complied, though I found his concern for breakfast unusual and wondered why he was so insistent.

Moments later, the phone rang again. Mohammed picked it up and spoke in Arabic. All I heard was him saying "No, she doesn't know." I asked him what it was about, and he said it was nothing. Again, I didn't give it too much thought.

A few minutes later, the phone rang one more time, and it was my brother Baha, though I didn't know it at the time. He gave my husband a number that he wrote on a piece of paper, and I overheard parts of it. By then, I had already made eggs, a plate of za'atar with olive oil, and another with *labneh*, and I had laid them out with olives on the counter in the kitchen. When I heard the number, I told him, "Oh my God, they got me Iyad's new number, didn't they?" I had not spoken to my brother in some time, so I was excited.

Mohammed said yes. But he told me to have breakfast first and then call. I couldn't. I didn't have the patience to. I took the number and dialed. It was busy. I tried again. It was busy and busy, again and again. As I was dialing yet again, in the background, Al Jazeera Arabic was playing, and I caught the news ticker that read, "Israeli forces demolish the family home of Iyad Sawalha, a member of the Islamic Jihad."

The ticker scroll hit me like a thousand daggers in my heart: "Israeli forces demolish the family home of Iyad Sawalha," my own reality presented back to me in third person.

The number Mohammed had given me was the phone number of the place where my family was staying temporarily. I was meant to call them after I found out. I spent the rest of the day in tears, surrounded by friends from Jersey who came as soon as they heard.

That day, talking to my mother and sisters in Amman and to my brother in Moscow, my emotions were mixed. In between the tears, I told myself the house had been sacrificed for Iyad. *"Fida Iyad!"* I kept repeating. The Israelis had gotten what they wanted in the house, they had gotten their revenge, so I was hoping they would now leave Iyad alone. I eventually spoke to Iyad, and he made it sound like it was no big deal. He said, "It's nothing. God will build you a palace in heaven."

But my father was furious. His rage was audible when he spoke to me. "See! See, *yaba!* See what Iyad has done! He's turned me into a beggar! He's turned me into a beggar! Me, who has never asked for anything from anyone. He's made us poor!"

"It's ok, *fida Iyad,*" I replied. What could I say?

"We're living at Abu Jassir's house directly across the street. Seven of us in one room now, *yaba.* We have nothing. And Iyad hasn't even called."

After the dust cleared that morning, we learned there were two pieces of unexploded ordnance left over. The house was gone. Our belongings too. But we still had to remove the rubble to start over. People tried to pick at the shattered bricks, but they couldn't get too close.

Neighbors called the Israelis to remove them, but the Israelis refused.

Eventually, that day, people in the village managed to remove one piece of unexploded ordnance. The next day, they came for the second, but it was gone.

Later, I learned that Iyad had returned to the house, dismantled it, and taken it with him. Our neighbor told us. She had heard rummaging in the rubble and looked out and saw my brother.

Their eyes met. She smiled.

*

Three days later, Iyad was finally able to reach my family by phone. He apologized that because of him the house we were all born in was gone. My father did not speak to him. He did not speak to him again after the rubble.

But through several contacts in Jenin, Iyad helped my parents refurnish. We were able to get all kinds of things for free—a refrigerator, clothes, and new appliances. People came from all over to help: from Tulkarem, Jenin, and even further. Someone brought shoes, another clothes, another a robe, a brush, and on and on. Abu Jassir's place was a single room with a traditional Arabic toilet, and my father, being on a wheelchair, couldn't use it. So a plumber in town redid the plumbing, built a shower, and installed a toilet and a water tank with a boiler so my family didn't have to boil water. People also gave bed sheets, plates, a set of pots and other kitchen supplies. They fixed the kitchen, tiled the floor, and made the place livable, all in the span of a few days.

Neighbors tried to console us by saying, "It's fine. They destroyed the house, so they aren't going to go after Iyad." People kept repeating this, and it made me feel better. But I think my father remained tormented because he understood well that the hunt would not end here. '*Fida Iyad*' were words of comfort that did not provide him with the solace that it did for me and others.

41

Iyad sends me a message to meet him at the big mosque during the Friday prayer. I go with my sisters, Maysoun and Suzanne, and all our children, and we sit in the mosque waiting for him.

Two ladies come in. They are both wearing black abayas, and their faces are covered in black veils. They sit down next to me.

Moments later, they remove the veil and show their faces. It is Iyad and his wife.

In my euphoria, I start crying and crying while trying to talk to him. He tries to get me to come to my senses.

"*Ya habla!* Stop crying. Don't be an idiot, and use this time carefully and speak to me. I miss you. You are wasting time crying. Look at Maysoun and Suzanne, they are not crying! Why are you?"

We speak for a bit, then he asks me to bring a pen and paper and to write down my phone number for his wife. He tells me he wants Mariam to call me so that I can take care of her if anything happens to him.

I get a pen and paper, but the pen won't work. I try another one, and another, but none of the pens will write. I finally find a red pen to write with. I write down my phone number in New York. I write it again and again. I can only remember that number. I try to write my number in Jersey, but I can't. I just can't! It won't come to me. I have forgotten it. I keep repeating the same New York number. Keep on repeating it over and over!

The Friday prayer ends. Everyone starts running. Iyad goes in one direction, and my sisters and I run in another. And we hear shouting and shots. And I have to keep my eyes on my sons. And we all run. And I lose my brother. He is gone, and I have not said goodbye.

42

October 2002

Ever since the Israelis demolished his home, Iyad had been busy planning several operations. On September 9, he sent twenty-three-year-old Abdel Fatah Rashed to Beit Lid, where the man detonated an explosive belt that resulted in a number of wounded but no deaths other than his own. Another mission Iyad organized later in the month was thwarted. By mid-October, he was preparing yet another.

Saeed Tubasi and other members of Iyad's cell found two young men to take part in a double-martyr operation. Ashraf al-Asmar and Mohammed al-Hasnein were members of the Saraya al-Quds. Mohammed was a *ka'ak* vendor, selling sesame bread rings from a cart. Ashraf had a small shop near his friend's home in Jenin. Iyad met Ashraf and Mohammed at the Jenin mosque near the main market. They knew neither who he was nor his name, just that he was someone who had instructions for them. Iyad explained to them the details of the operation. They were to be smuggled over the Green Line into '48 Palestine in a car rigged with explosives. There, Ashraf and Mohammed would split. One of them was to carry an explosive briefcase and walk to a target; the other would drive the car into a bus. After their meeting, Iyad, Saeed, and their comrades set to work on preparing the explosives.

On the day before the operation, Iyad met Ashraf and Mohammed to take their pictures and go over the plan. They still did not know Iyad's identity when they met in a makeshift photo studio in an apartment in downtown Jenin. Ashraf and Mohammed were slightly tense, but Iyad greeted them with hugs and smiles. He spoke to them about the importance of what they were doing, thanked them for their sacrifice, and together they performed the Maghreb prayer. After, they each recorded themselves reading their final testimony, calling on their mothers and fathers not to mourn but to celebrate them, and ended with placing their faith in God.

The operation was ready. The car had already been smuggled over the Green Line earlier that day. The briefcase was in the car, and both were loaded with explosives. Ashraf and Mohammed were to cross the Green Line themselves the afternoon of the next day, meet at the car, and continue toward their different targets.

On the afternoon of October 21, 2002, a twenty-three-year-old Palestinian from Taibe with Israeli citizenship by the name of Suad Jaber boarded Egged bus no. 841. The bus had come from the northern settlement of Kiryet Shmona, built in 1949 on the remains of the Palestinian town of al-Khalisa, الخالصة, and was headed to Tel Aviv—a three-hour ride. With her light brown hair and contagious smile, Suad was smart, talented, and full of life and initiative. She had just completed a degree in statistics and mathematics and was working part-time as the editorial board secretary of *Panorama*, one of the larger Arabic-language newspapers, which her uncle owned. She boarded near Um el-Fahm and walked to the first vacant seat on the bus. On her way, her eyes met those of a few soldiers. Suad acknowledged their presence with tightly pressed lips. She took her seat in the fourth row and got comfortable. She was going to transfer to another bus soon; she was on her way to Haifa University to collect her degree.

Some time later, Aiman Sharuf, a twenty-year-old Palestinian Druze with Israeli citizenship, boarded at the Border Police Memorial in Wadi Ara, وادي عارة. Aiman was a policeman who had served in al-Khalil for the last two years. He had been transferred to a posting at the memorial that week after being injured in an accident.

He noticed Suad as he walked past her and got a glimpse of her smile. She turned to the window and looked out, staring into the Palestinian sky, the Mediterranean haze reflecting an image of her future. Aiman sat across from her in the same row. The bus began to move.

They zoomed through Wadi Ara. About five minutes later, the bus, almost at full capacity, pulled up near Karkur, كركور, Junction and slowed down. There was a security vehicle trailing the bus. This had become common with increased security measures. But the security detail was useless, and as the bus slowed to a stop to pick up passengers, a car approached.

Ashraf al-Asmar and Mohammed al-Hasnein were silent as they drove. They were best friends, inseparable at all times except when working and sleeping. Even through the heavy days of the intifada and the Israeli incursions into Jenin, they found time to hang out, smoke arguilleh, and horse around with other boys in their neighborhood. They had crossed over the Green Line with no incident and made their way to the drop-off point in Baka al-Gharbieh to pick up the rigged car and briefcase. Ashraf was going to take the briefcase and catch another ride to his target, while Mohammed would drive the rigged car. But when Ashraf came to examine the briefcase, he found a problem with the detonator. Perhaps it was fitting, serendipitous, for the two friends had found it hard to go the final few kilometers alone. Ashraf threw the briefcase back into the trunk, and they decided to ride the fifteen minutes to Karkur Junction together, where Mohammed was meant to find his target.

As they drove, they felt like unarmed soldiers vulnerable on the battlefield. To pass the time, and the fear, they talked, rolled down the windows to feel the sweet October air, and made light of the moment. If they had any doubts, they kept them from each other. Palestine was greater than either of them in this moment, and they were ready to live and die for it.

At approximately 4 p.m., as the no. 841 bus finally came to a stop at Karkur Junction, Mohammed pulled the vehicle up next to the fuel tank. Ashraf put his hand on his friend's shoulder; they looked at each other and smiled. Then they both took comfort in God's presence and greatness. *"Allahu Akbar, la ilaha il-allah,"* they both repeated over and over . . .

It was over in a split second, before the flash.

The blast killed fourteen people, at least seven of them military personnel. Not all of them died instantly. Fifty others were wounded as steel and gasoline mixed with one hundred kilograms of explosives. A number of nearby cars were set ablaze. People lay lifeless, some completely blackened. The lucky were grabbing a partially severed leg or a wounded stomach in agony. Those who could stand were roaming around dazed. Ammunition carried by soldiers on the bus set off a further chain reaction, leaving rescuers unable to reach the injured.

Suad and Aiman were not identifiable at first. It took some hours before their families were informed. In addition to their parents, Suad left a brother and sister, and Aiman four brothers. They were both reported as Israeli fatalities in the total death count.

When Iyad heard the news, he recited the *Fatiha* from the Quran for the two brave men that had given their lives for the cause. In the moment, he felt a whiff of victory and great pride that the operation was successful.

Later, he'd learn of Suad and Aiman's deaths, two Palestinians. He cared less about Aiman, a policeman. He'd feel a tinge of pain about Suad and recite the *Fatiha* for her, though he then forced the news out of his mind. It wasn't about her or him.

Four days after the bombing at Karkur Junction, the Israeli military launched another major offensive. The mission objectives were clear. The army was to encircle the old town center and refugee camp in Jenin and demolish the homes of the men who had blown themselves up at Karkur. Intelligence gathering had also led the Israeli authorities to believe that the planners of the martyr operation were operating out of Jenin. The Israelis were to capture or kill this vanguard.

The army deployed hundreds of troops on October 25. Among them were ninety snipers. "We need to split up," Iyad suggested to his close circle. "Saeed, take a group of men and leave the city."

"And what will you do?" Saeed Tubasi asked in return.

"I will stay behind for a few more days and follow."

Saeed Tubasi and others left the city for a safe house in the nearby village of 'Arqa, عرقة. Iyad was to lead the counterattack. The army had already forced its way into some fifty buildings on that first day, conducting house-to-house searches and making some arrests. There was some resistance to the approaching army, and six Fatah members were seriously wounded.

The next day, as the offensive continued, the Israeli forces made dozens of arrests and demolished a house. Days later, they killed two people, fatally shooting a man checking the water tank on his roof during the curfew and a young boy standing outside his home in the refugee camp. They also raided a school and dug trenches around the city to prevent people from entering or exiting except through three checkpoints.

On November 1, the army raided the village of 'Arqa, discovered Saeed

Tubasi's safe house, and arrested him. They wanted him for plotting the Meggido and Karkur bombings alongside Iyad. Saeed was tortured to extract information about Iyad.

From his hideout, Iyad could hear the screams of people whose homes were being converted into sniper positions, and he could recognize when houses in the vicinity were demolished. He could hear footsteps as soldiers entered homes nearby and arrested boys, sometimes with their fathers.

The thought of leaving crossed his mind on several occasions, but it was too risky. When trenches were dug around the city, he settled in for the long haul. Mariam was with him. They had stored enough food for several weeks, and Mariam was able to leave and return in disguise during the few daytime hours that curfew was lifted. The neighbors did not suspect anything; they just saw a poor woman trying to get by.

As the Israelis raided house after house, terrorizing the population day in, day out, the city of Jenin turned into a no-man's zone over the week. At night, even if one wanted to defy the curfew, there were barely any lights on. Stray dogs descended into the city streets. During the day, most shops remained shuttered, and the usually colorful stalls in the market were no-where to be found. In the casbah, the alleyways were littered with puddles from broken pipes, and bricks from damaged homes lay strewn around. Cobblestone paths had been dug up by the military and checkpoints and barriers erected in their place.

And all around the West Bank and the Gaza Strip, assassinations and house demolitions continued. In Bayt Hanun, بيت حانون, and Rafah, رفح; in Nablus, نابلس, and Tulkarem, طولكرم; in al-Khalil, الخليل, and Qalandia, قلنديا; in Khan Yunis, خان يونس, and Gaza City, غزة; the resistance was being hunted down.

In Kufr Ra'i, just twenty minutes away from Jenin, three military vehicles zoomed up the main village road late in the morning on November 8, kicking up dust in their wake. They pulled up in front of the temporary house sheltering the Sawalha family.

There must have been at least two dozen soldiers in all. Four got out of their vehicles and made their way to the house; the others stood guard. All stared ahead coldly. All were tense.

In the house, Um Yousef had barely woken, having stayed up until dawn to have her *suhur*, the predawn Ramadan meal before beginning the day's fast. Abu Yousef was not at home. Despite the house demolition in August, despite the constant raids, there was a way in which the family's life had adopted some normalcy. Um Yousef cooked, she found time to go out to the field—when there was no curfew—she called on her kids to perform tasks to keep the house in order, and she waited. Waited for the call to prayer. For the sun to set. For this intifada to end. For the soldiers to return.

She waited for Iyad.

Moments later, soldiers knocked on their door, and Arselene opened. They demanded that she and her sister leave with them. "Leave us alone," Arselene screamed. "We don't know where he is. We don't know what he's done!"

They grabbed her and insisted she come with them. Her other sisters jumped in their way. Her mother too. The soldier holding onto Arselene strengthened his grip.

They had reason to believe that my sister knew of Iyad's whereabouts. On the first day of Ramadan, whether they knew this or not, Iyad had sent her a message. "God Bless you. Ramadan Mubarak. Don't be angry at me. Forgive me. *Inshallah* we will spend the next Ramadan together."

The two had also continued to meet in Jenin almost weekly until recently. But for Arselene, this meant nothing. My brother dropped by unexpectedly, always catching her in the street on her way home, and she knew nothing of where he was living. Often, they did not even walk side by side, but separately, with him at a distance behind her. He said very little, mostly pleasantries and expressions of care and concern for our family. She did most of the talking, filling him in on how everyone was doing. The encounters were essentially food deliveries. She handed him everything. His favorite chocolate and biscuits, or my mother's homemade meals. But Arselene never knew when he was coming. Sometimes, she kept things in her office for days. Sometimes the fresh food rotted before he stopped by. But even these fleeting meetings had mostly ceased back in early August, when Iyad remarried Mariam and Arselene sided with our parents.

"You have no reason to take me," Arselene protested to the soldiers. "I have nothing to do with Iyad. You destroyed our house. What more do you want?"

Arselene's sisters tried to pry the soldier off her again. This time they succeeded. She pulled back and tried to reason with him: "You give us an

ID when we turn sixteen. At that point we are responsible for ourselves. I am not responsible for Iyad anymore. Go look for him yourself. He is not my responsibility." It didn't work. The standoff continued for about an hour as the soldiers tried to arrest Arselene and one sister without escalating the situation.

Finally, Abu Yousef returned. He said it was not possible to take anyone without taking the whole family. The soldiers agreed. They told Arselene and her sister to get in one jeep and the rest in another. Um Yousef protested and forced herself in a jeep with Arselene. The rest were put in another jeep. But once Arselene and her mother were in, they told the others to get out of the other jeep and drove her and her mother to a military camp in Arraba.

There, she and her mother sat in an office waiting until a soldier walked in and passed her the phone. An officer, who was known to people as Captain Ashraf, was on the other end. He questioned Arselene about her brother, and she questioned him about arresting her. "What do you want from me? Why did you arrest me?" she screamed. Captain Ashraf responded that she knew where Iyad was. "We know you meet with him in Jenin!"

"Yes, it's true. But he always came to me. Did you ever see me look for him? You think I know where he is or anything about him? He's the wanted one, so go search for him. What do my mother and I have to do with it?" She followed with attacks of how the Israelis deserve everything they get.

"Your brother is a terrorist," the captain charged.

"You are the terrorists! You are the ones that came to us, that occupied us, not the other way around."

"Your brother killed my people!"

"He killed your people because you killed our people. And how many did you kill!" The argument went on for a bit longer until he hung up. Arselene was combative with every soldier she encountered. She cursed at them and threatened to hunt them down if they did not release her. After this initial phone call, Um Yousef and Arselene remained there, in a bare office, until after 5 p.m., when they were released. The soldiers demanded to see Baha, but his mother said he was in Nablus and had nothing to do with Iyad.

Hundreds of miles away, Sireen, at home tidying her living room, wearing a loose pink T-shirt over white cotton trousers, received the news of the arrest as she often did, through the breaking news ticker on Al Jazeera: "The mother and sister of Saraya al-Quds leader Iyad Sawalha have been arrested by the occupying forces."

I remember my jaw dropped, and I squeezed my eyes shut, then smacked my hands on my temples before I began to cry.

The arrests were meant to trigger Iyad—part of a playbook. He had heard the screams of women in prison. He knew about the humiliation female prisoners endured. And about the woman whose father was forced to attempt to rape her, or the one who was held down as objects violently penetrated her. These tales put doubt in his whole project of community before family. When his mother and sister were captured, it caused him great pain and panic.

He messaged Baha to find out what had happened. Three messages in total.

The last one Baha received was at 12:30 a.m. on November 9.

Baha, who was in Nablus, sent one last text to let our brother know Arselene and my mother were released and unharmed.

43

Jenin's Old Town Center, after Midnight on November 9, 2002

The late October siege of Jenin made the olive harvest impossible that year. For the Sawalha family, who were still picking up the pieces of their past, the harvest was the furthest thing from their minds.

The Israelis hoped that whatever the outcome, a siege would at least prevent resistance from originating from the city. If the Islamic Jihad leadership was underground, it could not meet, organize, or prepare activists to blow up Israeli targets. The Israeli Golani Brigade had already caught some fighters but were not ready to end the siege until they had found the head of the Jenin cell. They waited, terrorizing the civilian population in the meantime. They had been waiting for two weeks, ever since the Shin Bet had received word that the leadership was still in the city.

In the first hours of November 9, the fourth day of Ramadan, a unit of the Golani Brigade received new intelligence and zeroed in on a few streets in Jenin's old town. Rather than moving randomly from house to house this time, they were intent on simultaneously storming a group of houses to maintain an element of surprise. From whom did they receive this intelligence?

In a small apartment tucked away between other homes in the old town, Iyad had been eating *freekeh* with chicken, his favorite. He loved the smoky flavor of green wheat. He scooped the dish with bread held firmly between three fingers, chewed slowly, and inhaled with appreciation. His hands were clean, but one could read the long story of resistance and his life on the run by glancing at the hardened tips of his fingers and the roughness of his palms.

Mariam sat across from him, dressed in a long white gown with *tatreez* patterns embroidered along the bottom. She stared at her half-empty plate, her face besieged by exhaustion. They were sitting in silence in one of two domed rooms that had a cave-like feel to them and were sparsely furnished with little more than two sponge mattresses and a few of their belongings. Scattered around the rooms were several washbasins, some of their neatly folded clothes, a prayer rug, a few books, notebooks and pens, and a bunch of loose batteries and wires. It was shortly before 4 a.m., and they were having *suhur* under a dim light that could not be detected from outside, as there were no windows. Soon they were meant to begin their fast for the day.

Iyad knew the soldiers were out there, but he also knew he was well hidden. To get to his hideout, one had to discover the secret passageway behind a sink attached to a ceramic wall in an otherwise vacant apartment. The soldiers had unsuspectingly passed this hideout and the empty apartment several times during the week. Thus, despite the military vehicles lingering in the vicinity, he was feeling reassured.

Khaled Kamil, who worked for the local municipality and lived in the same alleyway where Iyad was holed up, had just been nudged awake by his wife, who, with a look of terror, told him that the army was in their alley. He did not have to strain much to hear the Hebrew whispers in the still night. He insisted she prepare tea and a meal for *suhur* while he sat in silence trying to understand where the voices were coming from.

Minutes later, there was a small explosion outside, and shrapnel flew through the kitchen window. The kettle of water, which had almost come to a boil, fell to the ground and just barely missed him and his wife. "*Wladi! Wladi!*" he shouted, in search of his three young children. The soldiers pushed open the door and around fifteen men rushed into the house, yelling, "Get inside! Get inside the house!" They confined them to the bedroom, and then searched the house: the closets, kitchen, guest room, bathroom, under the beds—everywhere.

When they were done, they told Khaled to come with them. They asked him if he knew why the army was in the area. He said he didn't. They asked again. His response was the same. Then the commander asked about the man living opposite him. Khaled knew it had been rented but he did not know the neighbors—just a man and his wife, he remarked.

"What do they look like?" the commander shouted.

"They look like everyone else."

"You know who lives there! You're a liar! You know who lives there! Do you want your house destroyed?"

The two argued, and Khaled insisted he had no idea who his neighbors were. Then the commander grabbed Khaled by the arm, and a soldier pushed him into the neighbor's house. They had hammered through the wall between the houses and created a gaping hole. They used Khaled as cover, making sure he went through first.

"You say a man and his wife live here. I see nothing but a computer. The house is empty," the commander said. He asked again about what they looked like, but Khaled could not give specifics. "The people who came in and out were veiled. Leave me alone!"

The commander barked at him, "*Kathab!* Liar!" And then he threatened again, "Do you want to have your house destroyed? Do you want to live in a tent? We'll demolish your house."

The commander pulled out a newspaper photo and went on, "Who's the man in the picture?" Khaled had no idea.

Eight soldiers searched the house. They looked through papers. Then they came to a wall with ceramic tiles. They asked Khaled what it was, but all he saw was a sink. They told him to move aside.

By now, Iyad had heard the soldiers make their way up into the short alleyway that led to his house. Their military boots thudded against the jagged cobblestone road as they approached, and their movements caused military gear to shuffle and fear to run through the last vestiges of the night.

He also heard them blast open his neighbor's door, and he could make out the sound of hammer on stone, but not where it was coming from. He heard two men speak in Arabic, one yelling, the other—Khaled, the neighbor he had never met—responding meekly. Iyad discerned the word "liar" from their conversation, but the voices were muffled, and he could not gather much more. Then, finally, came the word he hoped not to hear: "Iyad!"

If only his mother had given him a different name.

"Iyad Abu Shqara! *Itla'!* Come out! Come out with your arms in the air!" A soldier of the Golani Brigade called out in his hebraized Arabic accent, using Iyad's family nickname.

"Abu Shqara! Come out, and we will not harm you!" The officer repeated these hollow words several times.

Iyad looked up into Mariam's eyes, wanting to find shelter in her, but there was no time for vulnerability. He smiled and calmly told her to change out of her nightgown. She undressed, put on green pants and a green shirt, and wore a long robe, a *jilbab*, over them to protect her from the chilly night. He changed too—into khaki trousers and his trademark white T-shirt that he often wore in combat displaying Mu'tasem's printed face and the words "A Promise and a Pledge."

"Abu Shqara! We know you are inside. *Itla'! Itla'!* You are surrounded. You cannot escape. Don't do anything stupid!"

Outside, the night was giving way to twilight as Iyad faced his darkest moment. Would Mariam and he live to see the new day? Would they smell the sweet scent of their village again? Did they even ponder these things, or was living in the moment—their life, now—all that mattered?

Iyad looked up at the concave ceiling, its raw cement cracked. He raised his hands to his face, took a deep breath, and exhaled as he brushed his palms down along his trimmed beard. In this moment, testifying to the oneness of God, and Mohammed as His prophet, gave him solace and strength. And so, with his fists drawn and his index finger to the air, in his mind, he recited, "*La ilaha ila allah, la ilaha ila allah, wa Muhammadun rasul allah,*" before considering how to get Mariam out safely and escape.

The old town, like any casbah, is an intricate maze of layers of streets and homes. As soldiers were assaulting Khaled and his family and blasting into Iyad's apartment through a wall from a lower level, other soldiers approached from the street above. There, they took Abdel Hameed Mobayd, a forty-eight-year-old repairman, and pushed him ahead of them across the street toward the section of apartments where they believed Iyad to be. Abdel Hameed did not know the couple across from him either. The soldiers asked him if there was a cave under the house. No, came the response. They yelled the question back at him, threatening to demolish his house, and because they could, they made Abdel Hameed stand on one foot for some time to humiliate him for his answers. Then they began to move in. They approached the door to the apartment across the street. It was locked. They blew it open.

They pushed Abdel Hameed into the apartment first, with a soldier following right behind with his gun over Abdel Hameed's shoulder. They saw mattresses and panicked. They could be booby trapped, or this could be an ambush. They threw stun grenades. Then they made Abdel Hameed turn the mattresses over to make sure the coast was clear.

Far below, Iyad and Mariam heard the powerful booms and bangs. The walls shook and dust fell from the ceiling as large cracks emerged. Soldiers smashed a part of the ceramic wall from the lower entrance after moving Khaled aside, and dust shot into Iyad's hideout.

He went over to Mariam, who was trying to hide her fear but was unable to do so through a flood of tears. He told her to come over with him to the main entrance.

"*Habibti*, I want you to get out of here. I'm going to tell them that I'm sending you out. You have to go."

"No, Iyad. No! I'm staying here with you. Whatever you decide to do, I'm staying with you till the end."

"Don't be afraid, *habibti*. You need to leave, to tell my parents not to cry, to tell them of these moments. Don't worry. I will find you again."

Mariam tried to put up a fight, she tried to resist, but he was more stubborn, and he did not let her have her way.

It is unclear how Mariam emerged, how the soldiers seized her rather than shot her on sight. Perhaps Iyad yelled out to them to let her out. She was terrified. And when she was finally in their custody, they searched her, removed her veil and *jilbab*, and left her in her green shirt and pants.

Khaled was told to look inside past the hole in the ceramic wall. He found an alcove but could not make out anything in the total darkness. Khaled also saw some mattresses. He told the commander.

"Liar!" he screamed. Then he pulled Khaled aside and told him he wanted him to go inside. "Call Iyad, and tell him that he's better off coming out, because if he doesn't, we'll destroy his house and the houses nearby."

Khaled went in, terrified for his life. It was all dark, dark enough that Iyad could mistake him for a soldier. He felt his knees weaken and his pulse beat against his bones. There was a silence as still as the end of the world, broken only by Iyad's name leaving Khaled's tongue: "Iyad! Iyad, they are going to destroy your house. Turn yourself in." Iyad found the threat ironic.

Khaled was met again with silence, silence from the end of the world. And then, as his eyes briefly adjusted, he saw Iyad, and their eyes met in that silence, and for a moment, they connected through the dark, hallowed space separating them, and the two men felt a power between them emanating from an undying resistance, as if Khaled were signaling that though this battle was lost, they would not lose forever.

Mariam stood behind Khaled and cried out to Iyad. "Iyad, come out, otherwise they'll hurt me. Don't let them do anything to me. Don't let them kill you."

Silence.

She cried out to him again and again.

Silence.

The soldiers moved her and Khaled to a house nearby. Then a unit went in to confront Iyad. Explosions and gunfire ensued, and Israeli soldiers were heard screaming and cursing in Arabic: "*Kiss Imak*" and "*Ya 'ars*," mixed with loud moans and groans as a result of their injuries. Two Belgian Shepherds from the Oketz unit were sent in to attack and subdue Iyad. He shot them both. One died on the spot and the other whimpered from its injuries until he shot it again.

Above the battle site, Abdel Hameed was forced to stand in a room and wait. Between blasts and bursts of gunfire, a zinc roof collapsed close to him. If Iyad decided to blow up the structure, Abdel Hameed would come crashing down with it. Gunfire ensued.

Iyad had enough ammunition to hold them off for some time and was determined to take down as many soldiers as he could. He fired at them, and they fired back.

He could not feel it, but he was injured. He fired another round of ammunition. As the gun battle grew fiercer, fear raced back and forth between Iyad and the soldiers, as if it were being tossed between them with each bullet fired. He had intended to escape through the tunnels, but the military had been tipped off and had sealed the exit with some type of toxin. He was left with two options: surrender or die.

Gunfire rained into his cave. He had lived in these small enclosures half his life, between hideouts in the foothills of Palestine and solitary confinement in Israeli prisons. The isolation was familiar. His eyes panned around the room, then looked down at his hands. He had fought for the world, but it looked like he would die alone. He was content with this. We all die alone.

But he was alive in God's hands. He felt this so viscerally in the moment, carried by his faith like the Prophet on the *buraq*.

Gunfire rained down once again.

He was ready for this moment, and not ready. He let out a *takbir*: *"Allahu Akbar!"* He shot back. And again, with a louder voice, *"Allahu Akbar! Allahu Akbar!"*

The sounds of gunfire continued to pierce the air, but they didn't need to anymore. Iyad had exhaled his final *takbir*.

In total, my brother took fifteen bullets to the body, and a grenade, because cowards cannot take their chances.

Part IV

"HOLD ON TO ME"

44

A phone rings near the living room. It is an old phone with a finger dial hanging on the wall. The wall has an opening with no door. It is a big closet with white shelves that extend into the bathroom.

I answer the phone, leaning on the shelves.

It is Iyad. He is talking to me on the phone and simultaneously entering through the sliding door from my garden. He is wearing white sportswear and is barefoot. His feet are covered in blood. Dark blood, and a lot of it.

As he is entering, I tell him that his feet are covered in dirt and the carpet is brand new. He tells me to wake Bassel up to help him wash. He wants to wash for ablution so he can pray in my house.

I tell him I can help with ablution because Bassel is asleep. But he refuses. He wants Bassel. He wants him to bring an old earthenware pot for ablution and wants him to hold it for him while he washes before prayer.

Now he is standing in front of me. I tell him, before he leaves, that our mother is asking if his wife is pregnant. He is about to leave, but he turns back, laughs, and says, "No, my wife is not pregnant."

Then he adds, "Don't leave Mariam in prison just like you left me for seven years. You need to get her a lawyer and get her out of prison." As he says these words, he grabs me. His right hand is bleeding heavily. I let out a loud gasp. Then I run to the bathroom to find a bandage to stop the bleeding.

He laughs. I ask him why they aren't treating his injury in prison.

"You really still are the crazy, naive girl, aren't you! You think they help those they want to execute?"

I try to treat the wound, now a missing hand. But he insists that I need to help Mariam.

And he wants me to write something down about a letter and a pressure cooker and to look under the covers for Mariam's white dress. I ask him why. He tells me to hurry.

Then he insists that I wake Bassel up because he has to pray. And before I can say anything, he is gone, and the phone's dial tone is left tooting.

45

Morning of November 9, 2002

The morning after Iyad's last battle was cold and overcast, and as dawn turned to day, a crowd formed around the Red Cross ambulance where his body had been placed. Soldiers had started to withdraw from the town but remained in the vicinity. Shopkeepers could be seen mopping the street in front of their stores. A few taxi drivers lingered at the central station. Some kids bicycled around the streets and alleys as calm and quiet returned to Jenin's casbah after the end of the two-week siege.

Earlier, soldiers had sent in Abdel Hameed, one of the neighbors, to retrieve Iyad's body because they were afraid the place was boobytrapped. Abdel Hameed stepped into the darkness through unsettled dust, trying to navigate the rubble. Soldiers followed. When they reached Iyad, they picked him up from his legs and began to drag him outside. Abdel Hameed held his hand and tried his best to keep Iyad's head off the ground. But it was not easy, given the uneven surface. When they emerged, Mariam was pulled outside to identify him. She wailed.

She was taken to an Israeli prison where deportation procedures against her soon began. The court charged her with being an illegal alien after charges of being an accomplice were dropped by the military judge. The process was sped up by Lea Tsemel, a lawyer well known for her defense of Palestinians, who the Sawalha family had retained for her. The family was never thanked for their help, and they never saw Mariam again.

A short distance away in Kufr Ra'i, clouds had rolled in from Jenin, covering the morning sun and casting a shadow over the village. Um Yousef and

Abu Yousef had already had their breakfast. Um Yousef was in the kitchen cleaning up, dressed in a light blue gown and a sweater to keep her warm. She looked noticeably angry, agitated from the previous day's interrogation, fed up with worry and anticipation. But despite her hard life and the fifty-eight years behind her, her still-smooth skin made her appear young, only a few wrinkles visible at the edges of her kohl-rimmed eyes. Abu Yousef was sitting on his wheelchair outside on the veranda, looking out over the village. One of his pant legs was sitting loosely and covered his stump. His good leg rested on the foot of his chair. He wore a black-and-white kaffiyeh on his head that flowed down the sides of his face, partly obscuring his age.

Both Um Yousef and Abu Yousef had been following news of the Jenin siege over the last two weeks but assumed Iyad was out of the city by now.

Abu Yousef turned on the radio to listen to the news. He caught a commercial and some regional news, then the latest updates from Palestine at the top of the hour. The news presenter broadcasted that the curfew on Jenin had been lifted because the Israelis had succeeded in killing the Islamic Jihad's Saraya al-Quds leader, Iyad Sawalha. The news was piercing.

"No, no, no! They killed Iyad! They killed Iyad!" My father began to scream.

Abu Yousef bent his head and threw his hands to his face, slapping them over and over as he rocked in his wheelchair. His kaffiyeh came undone and was sliding onto his lap. Tears streamed down his cheeks as his face crinkled from the agony in his heart.

My mother heard his yells and thought he had fallen. She rushed over, but when she learned of what happened, she started screaming.

Um Yousef's arms swung to her face. "*La!* No! What are you talking about!" But she saw the way Abu Yousef was, in distress. And she knew. And she raised her head to face the clouds above, and she let out her voice in one burst, expunging all the air in her lungs. The entire village heard it. Birds startled and dogs barked in the distance, and over her, it was as if the clouds shuddered and let through the sun. She let out another scream while smacking her cheeks. And another.

Eventually, my mother passed out from the shock. She didn't wake up till Iyad's body was in the square outside our house. The ambulance brought him to the house still bloodied.

I think of this image a lot. Of how my parents were practically alone in the house and my father was handicapped in his wheelchair unable to do anything. They brought Iyad and just put him in front of them. Esraa was the only one at home with my parents. Arselene, with Suha and Sawsan, had left earlier that morning for Nablus to find Baha. And Esraa was just twelve years old!

Minutes later, people from the village hurried over and crowded our house.

After waking and seeing her son, Um Yousef rushed to him and fell to her knees. She swung back and forth, her arms flailing, and clapped her cheeks over and over. Then, as before, she released an anguished cry. Before her, Iyad lay with his slightly blackened face marked with freshly dried blood. He was not cleaned, for Muslim tradition holds that the martyr shall not be washed before he mixes with the earth.

From the house, Iyad was taken to the mosque in a procession that grew slowly as news traveled through the village and people began pouring into the streets. Many boys from his old Fahd al-Aswad gang during the First Intifada were absent. Abu Yousef had prevented them from attending and called them out for being traitors.

In Islam, the dead should normally be buried within twenty-four hours. But the sheikh who was going to pray over his body said that it was *haram* to keep a martyr's body for that long. Iyad should be buried within an hour or two, he insisted. Esraa rushed to her sister Salam's school to break the news. Family and friends tried to reach Arselene by phone to see how much longer she would be. She did not pick up.

The sheikh was growing more aggravated as time passed, but Um Yousef was being her fierce and stubborn self, waiting for her girls to return with Baha. In the streets, people were chanting resistance slogans. "*Ya Iyad, irtah, irtah, ihna nuwasel il-kifah,*" and "*Ya Sharon, ya haqir, dam il-shuhada ghali ktir.*"

The sheikh finally put his foot down. Iyad needed to be buried. "May God give patience to his sisters."

Early that morning, at 8:30 a.m., Arselene had woken to a phone call from Yousef's friend Abed. He was checking to see if she and her mother had returned from Israeli custody. After she woke, she called a taxi to go see Baha in Nablus. Her interrogator had been asking about him during her arrest, and it was safer to warn him in person. She took Sawsan and Suha with her to buy them winter clothes, as they had lost everything with the house.

An hour after they left, Esraa called to tell Arselene that Iyad had been martyred. Arselene didn't believe the news. "You're falling for the Israeli media trick, trying to get someone to reveal Iyad's hideout," she told her youngest sister.

When she arrived in Nablus and met Baha, he confirmed the news. But even then, Arselene refused to believe it. She felt that Iyad knew they were looking for him. There was no way he had stayed in Jenin while it was under siege for two weeks.

Instead of warning Baha that the army was searching for him, they took the same taxi and headed back immediately to Kufr Ra'i.

"*Mush ma'koul!* It's not possible. There's no way they got him. No! No! No!" Arselene screamed through tears.

"*Khalas!* Shut up! Cool down!" Baha shouted back. "We'll see soon enough. Just let the driver drive." Suha and Sawsan were also in tears, and with Arselene, they all tried to hold it in.

Earlier, they had gotten in and out of Nablus through back roads, skirting checkpoints, but on the way back to Kufr Ra'i, they came upon an improvised flying checkpoint. "Get yourselves together," the driver warned. He drove up to the soldier and gave him all their identification papers. It's all the soldier needed. There was not a soldier that day who did not know the name Iyad Sawalha or Iyad Abu Shqara.

He told the passengers at gunpoint to get out of the car and had them sit on the side of the road in the dirt. And so, the three sisters, Baha, and the driver sat there, somewhere on a deserted hill on the outskirts of Nablus.

The air was chilly. The sky gloomy, as if it were about to rain. They sat surrounded by rocks and green shrubs. They stared at the ground, into their palms, up at the sky, and finally into the eyes of their captives. They remained in disbelief that their brother had been killed, but in this moment, it was not tears but anger that consumed them, and thoughts of how to escape. This scene did not last long. Soon, two soldiers walked over to Baha, slapped him with handcuffs, and without saying a word, despite his sisters putting up some resistance, took him over to their jeep, threw him in the back, and left. Arselene, Suha, and Sawsan, guarded by troops, were told to stay put until given further instructions. Baha was not released until a few days later.

Relatives finally got through to Arselene on her cellphone and tried to rush her. Arselene begged them not to let them bury her brother, insisted that she was coming home soon. She cried and screamed. She begged the soldiers to let her and her sisters go. "We'll go on foot. Keep the car. Please!" she cried.

But they refused.

She continued to cry and beg, stuck on those desolate hills of Nablus.

At that moment, a car approached. The soldiers shot in its direction to halt it at a distance. There was a commotion, another car approached, and the line at the checkpoint grew. In the distraction, Arselene, her sisters, and the driver got in their taxi and drove off. The soldiers fired several bullets in the direction of their car but missed. Perhaps they did not think the matter worth pursuing, perhaps they calculated that targeting the sisters of a martyr on the same day was not in the army's strategic interest, or perhaps it was enough that they had Baha. Whatever it was, the sisters drove off into rugged hills, escaping the sound of bullets.

Minutes before the burial, Arselene, Suha, and Sawsan arrived, screaming. The prayer stopped, and the sisters scuttled over, showering Iyad with kisses before letting him go for the last time. Suha kneeled down, held by her fiancé. Sawsan took out tissues and wiped her brother's face as she wailed. Arselene hugged him hard. She screamed for him to return. She kissed him. "This is from Sireen, this is from Diaa," she cried, and she recited the names of her absent siblings, a kiss from each. "From Yousef, from Ihab, from Baha." She begged everyone to allow her more time with him. She thought she saw his eyes open. She thought she saw him stare at her as they raised him on his stretcher in his final move to the grave. After that, darkness. And the next moment, Arselene was home.

In addition to the religious need for a quick burial, the crowd and the sheikh were also afraid that the Israelis would come back for his body. This Israeli practice of keeping a corpse has become even more common in recent years.

It was so quick that my mother didn't have time to pray over him, and they had to pull my sisters off his body, so my sisters barely saw him for more than a few seconds.

At least they saw him. With Baha under arrest, no son of the family was present at Iyad's burial. Yousef, in the US, was lucky to have seen Iyad some years ago when his brother was first released from prison, and Diaa, also in the US, had left Palestine around two years earlier. Ihab, in Russia, had never seen Iyad again since the day he left for Amman all those years ago in 1989.

Ihab lives with this absence. The regret can be seen in his reddened eyes whenever he recalls his brother. It can be heard in his cracking voice even a decade later when he talks about Iyad's death. Regret for not going to see Iyad in 1999, after his little brother's release. Regret for not suggesting to his little brother, who stood up for him all those years ago, who was his childhood best friend, that he visit Russia instead of returning to Palestine. Regret for all the years that are impossible to rewrite.

His only consolation, Iyad's dignity. That he died fighting for what he believed in.

Iyad was wrapped in two flags, one black with the logo of his political party, the other green, symbolizing Islam, both emblazoned with holy verses. His face was visible, with white tape covering a wound under his bottom lip. His hair was covered with another shroud that attempted, not so successfully, to conceal the blood. As he was raised, and as though it were his wedding, some of his female relatives in the streets and neighbors atop roofs undulated to welcome him as a groom and sang him a common wedding song: "*Sabbal 'ayouno wa mad eedo wa hanulo.*"

Iyad—with his eyes shut, his three-day stubble, his body lifted above the crowds, and hundreds of people walking in his procession—appeared prophetic. And as the people marched through the village, they chanted, "With our blood, with our souls, we sacrifice for you, oh martyr."

Sireen was convinced that martyrs usually left behind letters, but none were found in Iyad's case. His wife told Sireen that he didn't think he was going to be killed. He was ambushed. Sireen is unsatisfied by such answers.

His life was at risk, he was one of the most wanted men in Palestine. How could he not be prepared with a letter for us? What did that letter say? So many people saw his body before us. People entered his cave afterward and took things, and no one was willing to tell us. His will went missing. Something was in it. Something that someone didn't want others to find out about. But what? Had he written about who had turned him in? Was the collaborator afraid, and did they get to his body first?

Two days later, presumably from Syria, Ramadan Shallah, the leader of the Islamic Jihad, gave a eulogy for Iyad via telephone at a gathering in the American University of Jenin. In it, he called Iyad Sawalha "a nation in a man."

He continued, "Brothers, O youth of Palestine . . . O generation of revolution and redemption . . . O heroic men of jihad and resistance . . . Our people of Jenin of al-Qassam . . . Jenin of Mahmoud Tawalba, Iyad Sawalha, and Iyad Hardan . . . as we say goodbye to the great leader Iyad Sawalha, we do not lower the curtains on the end of a hero . . . because his blood, today, nurtures the land for new beginnings. It grows new heroes, leaders, fighters, and martyrs. People who will carry the flag after him to prove to the entire world that we will not break, we will not submit, and we will not back down."

🌿

Less than a year after Iyad's final battle, Sireen visited his hideout. The deeper parts were still accessible at that point. Walls outside were not painted over, and one could see rudimentary drawings, most likely made by soldiers, that mapped Iyad's location, including the sink that revealed a secret passage to the caves. Sireen recorded her visit on video. In it, she ventured that a collaborator had drawn the map to lead the soldiers to Iyad. When she walked deep into the caves, everything was buried under rubble. She searched frantically for clues, for a letter and a pressure cooker she was determined to find. All she found was burned film, a torn prayer rug, Iyad's slippers, unexploded ordnance, and undecipherable remains of burned words in an obliterated journal. She believed anything else of value had fallen into the hands of the army, either directly or through collaborators who got there first.

Three years later, when she returned, it was clear that the old neighborhood had recently been rebuilt, although there continued to be marks from the November siege. There was a Star of David on a doorway here, and a few bullet holes on a brick wall over there. But mostly, the cobblestone pathways of the casbah had been retiled, the facade of homes renovated with new sandstone brick, and doors that lined the road fixed and repainted white.

Khaled Kamil and Abdel Hameed were not present any of the times Sireen or her family visited the hideout. She only encountered two women who talked about their fear on Iyad's last night and how they had no idea what was going on outside.

Sireen took steps toward Iyad's hideout. Above her, the wooden green shutters of a window had been left open. Eleven years later, when she would retrace these steps, Sireen would see the same wooden shutters, still open, their green paint browned by occupation's arrested time.

46

I am walking to Iyad's grave. I am visiting to adjust the flowers and clean up his resting place. I have planted tulips and lilies and want to check on them. It is their season to bloom.

While I am cleaning around the grave, my foot brushes against Iyad's hand. He moves, and I startle.

He begins to speak, "It took me a long time for my wounds to heal so I could come back."

He steps out of his grave and laments, "I'm so hungry and exhausted."

As he stands, I can see bullet wounds around his waist where the Israelis have shot him. "Let me tell everyone you're alive," I say excitedly.

He refuses, "Everyone will talk about me. The media will call this a miracle. They will call me a prophet. They will begin to make up stories. I don't want any of this. I don't want anyone to know I am alive. I am hungry. Just give me something to eat."

"What do you want to eat?" I ask.

"I want to eat fried eggplant. The way Hajjeh used to prepare it, with a sprinkle of sumac and a splash of lemon."

But it is midnight, and I say it is too late to prepare fried eggplant. I tell him I will cook it for him the next day. For now, I can prepare three fried eggs, *labneh*, and a plate of *zeit ou za'atar*. He agrees. I make the eggs. He eats and eats, as if he has never seen food before.

The next morning, I looked around the room as if he were really there. It felt so real. I could feel his breath in the room. I swear, if I were in Palestine, I would have rushed to the cemetery to check if he was there. His presence felt so real, so true.

In those first days of mourning, Sireen regularly encountered her brother at dawn, his soul's memory expressed in a dream. And so it was that often that year, Sireen found herself in the time-space of the *barzakh*, where the searching souls of dreamers meet the dead.

47

Summer 2003

Half a year had passed since Iyad was martyred. Spring had not been enough to wash away the loss when Sireen left Princeton for Palestine, anxious, as the Second Intifada was still in full force and the situation was not safe.

She had not been back since 1999. Her husband had not let her, and she had complied. She was like a prisoner in his home, in their marriage, trapped in the role of the good wife. She had stayed when her family's house was demolished, and when Iyad married, and when he was killed. Though she did not accept her fate in silence and complained every chance she got, her anger was always followed by inaction. She remained in the marriage despite it all, seeing it as the sacrifice she needed to make for her family in the intensely tragic times they faced.

Yet now, even as her husband and everyone around her advised her not to return—she was the sister of a martyr after all—her return was nonnegotiable. Her father was sick. He had injured his foot with a nail when visiting the site of the new house they were building, and it had become infected. Doctors in Jenin recommended amputation, but he had refused, and Sireen was determined to save his other leg.

She traveled with her three children at the beginning of June.

When I arrived in Kufr Raʿi after the long journey from JFK to Amman and then over the bridge into the West Bank, the kids were asleep in the taxi, so I asked the driver to go directly to Iyad's grave. Reluctantly, he drove me there and waited. It was my first time visiting him. I stood there, in front of his gravestone, and I panicked. I did not know what to do! What do you do? Do you shed tears? Do you read the Quran? I just stood there. I couldn't believe what was before my eyes.

Sireen was then taken to the apartment that the family was renting. It was up on a hill with a view of the valley and the graveyard. She walked in like a stranger in a strange place seeing familiar faces. She could not feel at home here. She'd never feel at home again.

Our old house stood out with its red-framed windows. It was weird looking, but when I came back to the village, I could always spot it from far away, and I knew I was home. Even if the color of paint changed, or the balcony was shut by glass curtains to make more room... still, I knew the house.

The new house is the color of stone. Off-white. It has no character. I cannot see it when I close my eyes under the Princeton sun. I cannot dream of it when I sleep.

Abu Yousef needed immediate attention for his injured foot. In Jenin, doctors recommended amputation. He refused despite Um Yousef's protests to listen to the medical experts.

The day after I arrived, I went to Jenin to coordinate with the Red Cross to move him to a hospital in Nablus. Jenin was easier for all of us given the checkpoint situation, but we couldn't accept the fate of doctors there.

Without the Red Cross, it might have taken them a whole day to get to Nablus, and even if they were allowed to cross all the checkpoints, they would still have had to travel by foot through the Huwara checkpoint at the entrance of the hermetically sealed city—the Israelis had tightened control of Nablus during the Second Intifada and especially after their military offensive in April 2002.

An ambulance was secured. Sireen kept her children at her mother's house with her remaining younger siblings. Her plan was to spend a few days in Nablus at her mother-in-law's house and return for the kids once her father was stable.

In Nablus, they got the same advice. Abu Yousef met this with resignation, his head slightly lowered, his eyes staring into space. The next day, they amputated his leg below the knee. This time, Abu Yousef experienced the defeat less through the dysphoria from his phantom leg and more in his knotted throat and the whirling of his gut.

They told me there was no other solution. The alternative was to suffer multiple amputations, and then end up with the same result.

Abu Yousef was going to be bedridden in Nablus for weeks, far longer than Sireen had initially anticipated. She had to return to Kufr Ra'i to get her children as well as her sister Maysoun and Maysoun's kids. They would stay in an apartment in Nablus's old town owned by Mohammed's family.

I was unable to leave through any of the usual arteries out of Nablus. In those days, the city was shut to everyone. The Huwara checkpoint was closed off except for emergencies like my father's, if one was lucky. Even then, when we entered, they searched our ambulance with some type of metal detector and asked us all sorts of questions. I remember my frustration. I couldn't comprehend how the emergency workers could do this day in, day out.

If one wanted to enter or exit the city, one had to pay ambulance workers and fake an illness. A woman might lie in the back with an oxygen mask over her face in order to get through. The ambulance was like a business in those days, like a taxi when no other transportation was allowed and mobility was impossible. I remember a woman . . . she was being transported and using the oxygen mask trick, but the oxygen wasn't working. The Israelis realized, and they sent her back. But so many people got through that way, and then there were the real cases where it was obvious to anyone with a mind that the case was an emergency. A woman in labor, for example, and they did not let her through, and she had to give birth at the checkpoint, and sometimes the baby had no chance of survival in those conditions.

The World Health Organization reported sixty-one checkpoint births between 2000–2004, of which thirty-six were stillborn. One such case is that of a woman named Tarab. She woke up in the middle of the night bleeding heavily but was denied access to crossing a checkpoint where an ambulance was waiting on the other side. Her husband tried to take another route and again was denied access. As a pool of blood began to collect under her, soldiers finally gave them a permit to cross, but only on foot. Tarab's husband carried her onto a cart, which lost balance, and she fell to the ground. The journey took them eight hours. By the time they reached a hospital, they were informed that the baby had died in her womb.

Since leaving Nablus through the Hawara checkpoint was impossible, I found a smuggling route with a driver who took a group of us up and down dirt roads through a mountainous area to 'Assira al-Shamaliya, عصيرة الشمالية, a village between Nablus and Jenin. From there, we were to switch cars and be off to Kufr Ra'i.

Even in the heart of night, 'Assira al-Shamaliya was full of life, as though it were a night during Ramadan. Women and children filled the streets to sell to those in transit anything from water, tea, and coffee to hummus, corn, *tirmus*—lupin beans—and all kinds of homemade food. Just as the area around a checkpoint often develops its own economy, so too was the village booming after becoming the new transit hub for people leaving or trying to enter Nablus. The specific routes could change once discovered by the military, but 'Assira remained a constant hub for travelers regardless. Sireen found the bustling town a funny sight to see.

The area was lit up and crowded with people awake at night. They played music and hung out before traveling on in the dark hours of morning, so as not to be detected. People were making the commute regardless of all the strains and closures. It was as if the Israeli checkpoints and the hermetic sealing of Nablus were not meant to provide Israelis with more security so much as they were meant to suffocate our lives.

When I was crossing to get the kids, the Israelis spotted us. Our driver let us out, and we began running. We tried to hide behind boulders and bushes, but a helicopter above us located our position. I was filming the entire journey on my video camera.

In the video, a helicopter is heard from above, and there is the sound of gunshots nearby. Sireen is with a group of a dozen other people. There are terrified college students with backpacks, middle-aged men in short-sleeved dress shirts and pants trying to get to work, people trying to visit their families, and others who are seeking treatment in Nablus and are slow moving. Everyone scatters and begins to run for their lives. Sireen lowers the camera but lets the film roll. It captures stones, shrubs, and her feet fumbling as she hastens to escape.

She is heard breathing heavily. "Huff-huff-huff." Occasionally, a person appears for an instant, running. "Yalla, yalla, *imshu*. Move it!" someone screams. Others try to give directions and rush those unable to keep up. Above, they can hear the chuff-chuff of helicopter blades.

There is also excitement. Hesitant, anxious laughter about the absurdity of the moment. And fear.

Then she finds herself alone momentarily and sees Israeli soldiers coming her way. Recognizing she is not going to outrun them, Sireen stops in her tracks.

I left my camera behind when I was surrendering to the soldiers. I did not want them to confiscate it. I was taken by two soldiers who were around seventeen or eighteen years old. They asked me where I was going. Stupidly, I told them I was heading to Jenin. No one told me the protocol. I was supposed to lie and tell them Nablus, because they often sent you in the opposite direction of where you wanted to go.

When I got caught, I was alone and thought I was the only one who had been caught. I pulled out my American passport and showed them my children's passports as well. I thought I could appeal to them by showing them that I had kids I needed to return to.

The soldier said, "Isn't it dangerous for you to be here? Don't you watch TV? Didn't you see the shootings and killings?" I told him that yes, I saw that, but I also saw that there would be peace.

"How could there be peace when there was an explosion the other day in Jerusalem?" he asked.

"If you stop killing people in Gaza and the West Bank, we would stop the explosions," I responded.

"Are you coming to talk politics here or are you trying to pass?" he said, shutting me up. Of course, all this was in English because, from his accent, I gathered he was from Brooklyn.

He took me behind a big rock, and I saw more than two dozen people who had been caught as part of a bigger raid on this route. I laughed and asked everyone what they were all doing there. They explained to me that the soldiers were catching people and holding them until sunset. Some would be imprisoned, but the majority would be released. In the meantime, the soldiers taunted a man, hurled sexual comments at a woman, made jokes at our expense, and sung joyfully as if we were not miserable. I even heard that they sometimes let dogs off a leash to send people sprinting in different directions.

Everyone who was continuing to Jenin did so except for me. I was forced back in the direction of Nablus with those who were actually headed in that direction. I picked up my camera on the way and caught a ride back to 'Assira with the same driver that had abandoned us earlier. The next day, I took another route to Kufr Ra'i, successfully.

Sireen spent two days with her family in Kufr Ra'i, and then, with Maysoun and all their children, she returned to Nablus through 'Assira al-Shamaliya. They spent several weeks in Nablus until Abu Yousef's leg healed. They then made the same terror-filled journey back to Kufr Ra'i through the hills while Abu Yousef returned in an ambulance on empty roads.

By the time he returned, Abu Yousef was mostly a shadow of the man he had been. In Kufr Ra'i, he could be found sitting in his wheelchair on the balcony, glassy-eyed and staring into the village graveyard. He remained quiet unless spoken to, lost in memories of a time before heartbreak and despair became normal.

48

My brother Diaa appears in my room with his friend by his side.

I am asleep. They hover over my bed until I see them. They are both crying.

It is my father. Something is wrong.

I enter a room. There, I see my father with old men just like him, on wheelchairs. They are all just sitting there in a silence broken by the echo of tears.

49

2004

Abu Yousef traveled to the US again in mid-November to get a full medical checkup and see his kids—Sireen, Yousef, and Diaa. He also needed to keep his Green Card valid and so had to visit the US as often as possible. By now, every line on his face, every contour, seemed to whirl together, sketching a portrait of loss. Wheelchair-bound, he needed an airline escort to get him through the airports.

As on his previous visits, when he arrived, he stayed with Sireen in New Jersey. He enjoyed being with her. She filled his silence with stories and made him smile. And despite all the loss in his life, or because of it, his heart grew tender, as it did in 1948.

"*Akh*, Sireen! Help! *Akh*," Abu Yousef cried out just three nights after his arrival.

Sireen heard the screams as if part of a nightmare.

I opened my eyes and heard him yelling for me again, my father. Startled, I pounced out of bed, almost catching my foot in the sheets. From the top of the stairs, I could see my father at the bottom, on the floor, holding his chest in agony. He was breathing heavily when I finally put my arms around him.

"Baba, what's wrong? What's going on?"

"Akh, Sireen! Akh . . . akh . . . albi!" My father screamed. It was something about his heart.

"Baba, hold on to me! We have to carry you out to the car." I tried to talk to him as we struggled to move. Legless and practically unconscious at this point, I had to carry his full weight, drag him out of the house and down the makeshift ramp we had built for him, and then up into our Ford SUV.

I sped along dark roads, finally arriving to the emergency entrance of Princeton Hospital. I stepped out of the car screaming for help. The emergency medical staff rushed to my father. Someone took me aside as I stood in panic with tears gushing. Others quickly worked to stabilize him. It was a long night, but it ended well, and my father was safe for the time being.

He was released a few days later, on a Friday, and told to return the next Monday for open-heart surgery at Columbia Presbyterian Hospital. That Sunday, my father had another, more severe, heart attack. We rushed him to the hospital, but this time he slipped away to the point of needing resuscitation. Once he was stable enough, doctors transferred him to Columbia University for the heart operation.

At that point, my husband told my eldest brother, Yousef. Yousef said that if my father died and he didn't get to see him, he would never forgive me.

I did not want Yousef to know. I knew what he would do. And, like clockwork, Yousef was there the next day, and three days after the surgery, he wanted to take my father to Ohio, where he lived.

My father initially refused and began to scream at Yousef. He did not want to go. He begged Yousef not to take him.

I stood up to Yousef. He said that if he didn't take my father, he would never talk to me again. At that point, my father couldn't bear the fighting anymore. He preferred to go with Yousef than for us to ruin our relationship. "This is your brother; you will need him all your life. If anything happens to you, if anything happens with you and Mohammed, he will be there," he advised me.

In late December, I told Mohammed that I hated my dreams and couldn't deal with them. I wanted to go to Ohio and get my father. "Are you crazy? No way! It's too far to drive there with the kids," he shouted.

I didn't care. The next morning, I took the kids, stopped at ShopRite, bought snacks, and drove the eight hours to my brother Yousef's house.

When I got to Yousef's house, I was shocked at the state of my father's health. He looked so skinny and weak. I wanted to take him back with me. Yousef was furious at the thought. "In our country, the father stays with his son, not with his daughter. Who is Mohammed, this stranger, to take care of your father?" he said.

I was so angry and upset, I almost wanted to plot how to take my father back to Princeton.

That first night, I couldn't sleep because my legs were swollen from all the driving. My father spent the night in and out of sleep, talking to me—or maybe to the wind. What he said didn't always make sense.

The next morning, my father felt his health deteriorating and asked me to take him to the hospital. As I was leaving, Yousef stopped me and told me he would take him. "Yousef, I came to see my father and to take care of him. I don't want us to fight here and in front of him. I drove all this way. Please, just let me take him," I protested.

"No, I told my friends that you're coming and you're going to make us *msakhan* and *knafeh*. Go to my store and get all the ingredients. I already put aside the bread, chicken, and onions. I'll take the Haj to the hospital and call you, and in the afternoon, you'll have everything ready."

I was upset. I went to my father to let him make his case to Yousef. He was too tired. "*Yaba*, just let me die, *birtah minkum*," he said, wanting to be left in peace and fed up with our arguments.

They went to the hospital. Four o'clock came around. I had prepared most of the food, but Yousef hadn't called. So I called all his friends and told them not to come because my father was sick. Yousef's wife took me to the hospital.

When I got there, Yousef asked what I was doing there. "You never called, Yousef!" I said.

"I couldn't call from here. Go, go home! Go take care of the kids."

I told him I wasn't leaving and that I had come to stay with our father. He relented and left me alone for two hours. Then he returned when visitation hours were over and didn't let me stay the night.

The next morning, I took off to the hospital before anyone woke up. I had written down directions the day before because I didn't want to depend on anyone. *Yi-hillu 'an rabi! Ma kan bidi jmeelet-hom.* I just wanted them to get off my case.

When I saw my father that morning, he started screaming, "You've starved me. It's been four days, and I haven't eaten. What have you done to me!" He screamed and screamed, went into hysterics. The doctors said he hadn't slept all night. "You and Yousef left me. For four days..."

"Baba, *walla*, I didn't leave," I interrupted. "I left last night, and here I am today, as soon as we could visit."

"No, they've been taking away my blood for four days, and I've had no food," he said with anguish.

I asked the nurses what was going on. They said his kidneys were failing him, and he had gone through dialysis at night. He woke up during the procedure in a panic.

I showed him a calendar and let him know the date. He didn't seem to understand, and his head shook in ways that didn't make sense to me. I stayed with him that night, and he ate. They gave him a drug to allow him to sleep well. Then, when it was late, I went home to be with the kids.

I was not sleeping well the last few nights. I was running on a lot of coffee and very little food. That night, around 4 a.m., I woke up after a dream. I had been searching between the dead. I was opening drawers upon drawers in a morgue, looking for my father.

I couldn't go back to sleep and went to the hospital in the middle of the night. When I arrived, the hospital was quiet. I got to his floor and learned that they were washing out his kidneys. They told me the process would take four hours. They said I could stay and wait, so I waited. I put the Quran in front of me and read for him the whole time.

When he was done, they moved him out of the dialysis ward to his room and said he was doing better. His kidneys were clean, and he could be let out in two days. I sat by his side and continued to read the Quran.

Later in the day, I put bags of ice on his forehead to cool him down. He was weak. In the late evening, I came to him and saw that he was different. His face was white. They took him down for a CT scan. When they returned, they told us that he must have had a stroke while sleeping.

I spent the next week, maybe more, in the hospital watching my father, day and night. He needed a feeding tube and a respirator because he couldn't breathe, and he was unable to move. I spent much of that time reading to him sourat Yassin and sourat al-Rahman from the Quran.

After all this time, I finally took a break from the hospital one night because I had a severe toothache and needed some rest. Before leaving, I read the Fatiha to my father. Then I whispered in his ear, "Baba, my mother is coming soon. Here she is, close. She's left to Amman. She'll be here in a few hours. See, *subhan Allah*, you've lasted this long so she comes to stay by your side. You'll see her again. You wanted to see her so much, you waited all week for her. Baba, you're going to go to Iyad, he loves you, he'll take good care of you, better care than we could. Forgive me, Baba."

As I spoke to him and read him the Quran, I could swear he moved. He moved three times.

Yousef thought I was delusional. He said I hadn't gotten good sleep and was imagining things, and he insisted that I had a tooth infection and was hallucinating from the medication. I believed him, went home, and he took over to be with our father.

At home, I couldn't sleep. I decided to cook *maqloubeh* to pass the night away. At 2 a.m., Yousef's wife came out and saw me awake. She said she had just spoken to Yousef, who was feeling bad that I was not at the hospital. I decided to return since I couldn't sleep anyway. I called Yousef before heading out to ask if he wanted the *maqloubeh*. He said he would just grab a late-night snack from the cafeteria. I told him I would leave soon but wanted to wait in case our relatives called from Amman with an update about our mother's trip.

Shortly after we hung up, at 2:30, Yousef called me back. He had gone to the cafeteria very briefly to pick something up. When he returned, it was all over.

On January 13, at the age of seventy-six, my father, Haj Abu Yousef, passed away.

No one was in the room when he left us. I was not there for him in his last moments. No one was present to hold his hand in the moment he transcended this life.

My father had thirteen kids. All his life, people around him thought he was crazy. "What are you doing? How are you going to raise them and care for them?" they asked. And his response was that he wanted us so we would be around him when he died. And all for what? Where were we? And on top of this, he was buried in a foreign land. Yousef wanted to respect the dead by burying him immediately. Now, none of us can visit him. We have to go to Ohio to do that. But I hate Ohio; I hate everything about Ohio.

Father was the only man in the village who had no legs, whose son was martyred, and who worked all his life to build his house, which was demolished. And then he died like this? Is there a man so downtrodden? A miserable life; a lonely death.

He had such a kind heart. He never raised his voice at us; he let us live. And with all his hardships, despite the tragedies, people respected him. I think Iyad gave him that. He gave him hardship, but with it came recognition and respect.

RETURN

It is no longer February 2005. Sireen is no longer wearing black to mourn her father, and I am no longer recording in her sunroom drinking tea with *miramiya*. I left that place, and New Jersey, a long time ago. No story spanning decades can be told in a singular time or place.

It is 2014, the months cycle on . . . and on . . . and on. The years turn—2019, 2020, 2021. Meanwhile, meanwhile, the Gaza Strip has experienced three official wars and several more that history is unwilling to name; the siege of the Gaza Strip continues; thousands of Palestinians have been captured under a policy of administrative detention; hundreds were shot dead by snipers in Gaza's Great March of Return; the US embassy moved to Jerusalem; the apartheid wall around the West Bank was completed; thousands of olive trees continue to be uprooted by Jewish settlers; settlement construction continues the expropriation of Palestinian land; and Mahmud Abbas maintains his hold on the presidency, exposing the Palestinian Authority as primarily an Israeli security apparatus. Through this, Palestinians continue to resist by whatever means they can—with knives, with rocks, with primitive rockets, with limited weapons, with art and music, through the law, and, quite powerfully, by building a movement for boycott, divestment, and sanctions.

Through all these seasons of life and death, Sireen has remained in Kingston. She finds it a depressing place, despite the sun that shines into her home and the land around it that she's cultivated to remind her of Palestine. She is divorced now. Her husband abandoned her and their kids one day in

2007, leaving Bassel with his sister at home while Sireen was away taking
Zeid to soccer practice. He skipped town, making his way to his brother in
Sweden. He didn't let her know till he was on the flight, and he wouldn't see
his children for a few years. Sireen was happier to be rid of him, but life was
difficult. No longer at the UN, she was a history teacher, and he had left her
with loans and fighting hard to get him to pay alimony.

In Kufr Raʻi, Iyad's name continues to echo. New generations of fighters
name their groups after him. A decade and a half later, they reveal names of
collaborators that they claim Iyad shared with them in his last will—that
same will Sireen says she dreamed of. The lives of the Sawalha family continue as well, interrupted and marked by the enduring violence of Israeli
settler colonialism. In the years since Iyad was killed, Baha was imprisoned
for three years, then released. Arselene was imprisoned for seven months,
then released. Their stories and the stories of their siblings, of Um Yousef,
and of her grandchildren, will trail off these pages, perhaps for others to
retell.

My meetings with Sireen are less frequent now, but never does an encounter
pass without her telling me that she remains haunted by a thousand suspicions surrounding Iyad's death. She continues to question Mariam's motives
for marrying him. Mariam's father has a straightforward explanation. He
says his daughter was young and looking for adventure. That she knew Iyad
was politically active but not the extent of his involvement. Being with Iyad
fulfilled her need for youthful excitement.

Sireen's suspicions don't help her let go, and she often relives Iyad's last
weeks.

We all lost contact with him back then. My father and mother threatened to
disown him publicly and stopped seeing him and Mariam after they got married.
The last time I spoke to him was in August, and in that call, we fought about his
marriage and never spoke again. I also stopped mentioning him to my parents. If
I did, my father would start shouting. And he had diabetes, so we didn't want to
aggravate him.

Iyad fought for all of us and died alone. The guilt pains me. How could I have
never called him back? He always let me know how much he missed me, how much
he longed to hear my voice and listen to my stories. We used to speak so often,

maybe once a week. And then, in his hour of need, in his last days under siege, I was not only absent and away from him but angry with him as well.

Sireen looks up at me, chin low, brows drooped. Her eyes look glazed, like the surface of a calm lake. In her voice there is the realization that it would have cost her nothing to be more loving.

I used to send birthday cards to my parents and all twelve of my siblings. I used to send my mother a Mother's Day card and birthday cards to my nieces and nephews. But then death strikes, and you don't feel like doing anything anymore. It strikes and breaks your spirit, your family's spirit, and there is no more meaning in cards. You become reserved, somehow overnight, or slowly, I don't know.

So I don't do that anymore. I remember their birthdays and special events, but I don't share it anymore. Perhaps I should. Perhaps death should not break our spirits but bring them closer, as if a little part of the world died to make the remaining spirits stronger. I wish it were that easy to pick up, though. Somehow, life today, when I look back, all starts with the sadness and hopelessness of death.

🌿

I return to Palestine with Sireen. On this latest visit, she and I walk down a sloped road passing some old homes close to the center of Kufr Ra'i. Once we have walked halfway down, we approach a pale-greenish steel gate struggling to hold onto its hinges and rusted by time. Over the gate sits a lone jasmine tree on a concrete street. Beyond it, a broken sink on the floor, some concrete blocks, and memories of where her story begins.

I stand before the green gate in the summer's heat. With my eyes closed, I see lives return, children laughing, a man running out the back gate down into the valley.

Then, my mind drifts. I hear the smashing sound of brick on brick, my lungs filling with dust.

Sireen is standing next to me, face-to-face with the remains of her house. Her story is not over.

"*Kadarna el-muqawama.* We are destined to resist," I tell her. She nods.

I recall Gilo Pontecorvo learning lessons from Algeria's liberation struggle: Once a war of national liberation has begun, despite setbacks, it is an unstoppable force. Like a river that goes underground and seems to disappear, sooner or later it will emerge again and arrive at the sea.

And today, like the river, the resistance in Jenin, the site of Iyad's last stand, emerges again and again, unable to be subdued. Yet the pain of losing a brother, a son, is worth a moment of pause beyond this defiance.

There is no parent who wants their child to be martyred. And if time could be turned back and my parents could know the extent of his involvement, they would probably go back and break his hands. That's how much they were hurt by all this.

Sireen and I return to her family's new home after our walk. We sit down with Arselene. She explains how tragedies do not lie atop one another but sit side by side as a grotesque panorama, intensifying a wound. She speaks of the loss of her brother and her house passionately in the same breath. They are entangled. "It is true that, *Allah yirhamo*, we lost Iyad. But the loss of our house was hard too. We grew up in that house. We lived for it. We poured everything into it," she says.

"The house contained all our possessions, all our past," she continues. Arselene was communicating to me how, in a world that was intent on stealing their land and erasing their history, the house, with its modest foundations, was more than a home. It was part of the structure of defiance. "When I dream, I still dream that we are living in our old house," she imparts to me as Sireen listens and nods, "and I often dream we are going back to it and that it is still as it was."

The next day, Sireen and I visit Iyad at his resting place. He remains as dust, bound with the land. It is the closest I've ever been to him.

We walk to the cemetery, descending the steep road from her family's new home to the main road that leads into the village. From there, we cross between a pink house and newly fenced-off land with recently planted cherry and olive trees.

The houses around us are all new. We are at the edge of the village. She remembers a time during the years when Iyad was wanted, when none of the houses here existed. It was all wild land, unconstructed, unfenced. Now, the two of us lose count of the homes in the sprawl of the village-turned-town.

We cross another road. It is one of several that have been paved in the last few years. These roads widen the entrances to the town, change its landscape. We arrive at the cemetery of the northern neighborhood of Kufr Ra'i. There is a partially burned tree, overgrown shrubs, and scattered cement blocks lying around with no purpose. I look around to see if I can spot the blood-red *shaqa'iq al-numan*, the poppy flower, but it is summer, and the flowers have already mixed with the earth.

At the entrance, she says words from a prayer: "*Intum al-sabiqun wa-nahnu al-lahiqun.*" You have gone before us, and we shall follow. The cemetery has a fence that did not exist years ago, when it just blended into the land around it, with no borders for the departed. Now, we have to go around the fence to get to Iyad's resting place, and the martyr section is separated from the rest of the deceased. On one tombstone, there is a wreath of roses that someone must have placed not long ago. The roses have withered, though the wreath remains intact. We stand in front of Iyad's two tombstones. One marks him as a martyr of the Islamic Jihad, an engineer of car bombs, a legend of martyr operations, and a leader of the Saraya al-Quds. Martyred on November 9, 2002. The inscription on the other tombstone is shorter and more classic, naming him as the heroic martyr: "*Al-shaheed al-batal* Iyad Aḥmad Yousef Sawalha, martyred on the date of Ramadan 4, 1423."

I stay still as Sireen gets closer to Iyad's tomb. His rectangular boxlike grave protrudes from the ground. The sides are encased with marble slabs inscribed with Quranic verses. On top rests a concrete slab where mother nature has lain dust and twigs.

Sireen kneels down, places her phone next to her, gently brushes one hand over the dust, rubs both hands, and extends them upward, palms open to the sky, to pray. She recites the *Fatiha* and wipes her dusty palms on her face when she is done. I look on as she goes through these ritual motions, her dark shaded glasses concealing a decade of loss.

After she is done praying, she caresses the marble slabs. Then she grabs dirt and rubs it between her palms again, this time more aggressively, as if trying to bind with the dust. I get the sense that she is trying to communicate with her brother. She gently and deliberately caresses the twigs, and when she notices how many of them there are, she begins to brush them off with her hand.

She stands up and moves away from his grave. I experience the moment as silence; she, as an orchestra of pain. I wait for her mind and heart to gather words and interrupt the wind.

There used to be a bench here by my brother, and the top of the grave was full of tulips, rosemary, and other flowers. But my brother Yousef has become very conservative and asked for all of it to be removed. It was wrong to treat him differently from all the other martyrs, he said. And as the number of martyrs increased, the space around him became needed.

Now, it is difficult to know where one grave ends and the next begins, like the homes in the casbah of Jenin, or Jerusalem, or Nablus. There is company in the closeness and the blurring of lines. I look around me and am left with the feeling that the martyrs are one.

A few graves over, I see the resting places of Fouad al-Ashgar, Jalal al-Aris, and Mohammed Kamel Yahya, some of the first martyrs of the village after 1967, who the Israelis killed in 1988.

We are standing under the shade of an olive tree planted some decades ago. I am holding my phone up to record this episode, and so I partly experience it through the filter of the screen. There is an immensity to the loss around me that I experience through the silence in the cemetery, intermittently broken by ruffling leaves and the gentle crackling of twigs under our shoes.

Sireen looks around and points at the grave of Mohammed Bassam Abu Amshi.

His mother was in my class. He was shot and left to bleed to death for three or four hours.

There are at least fifteen other martyrs in the village besides Iyad Sawalha and those I have just mentioned. Let us say their names:

Yousef Sbeih
Salameh Sbeih
Ayman Sbeih
Mohammed Abdullah Yahya
Ziyad Sbeih
Jamila Melhem
Yasser Sawalha
Yusra Sawalha
Ahmad Yahya
Imad al-Sheikh Ibrahim
Shadi Melhem
Tariq Abu al-Shawareb

Mohammed Thiyab
Mohammed Jawabra
Nabil Tafesh

Sireen is overcome with silence. Many memories of her youth are now entangled with loss, remembered in this moment under an olive tree in Kufr Ra'i's northern cemetery.

She takes a last look at her brother. I stand in a moment of silence for a man I've come to know and not know.

🌿

Hajjeh Um Yousef looks out at the village from her new home atop the hill. She has just prayed the morning prayer and, soon, will tend to the garden behind her house. The land Hajjeh Um Yousef used to farm, the *wad* and the *hawacheer*, the land that Sireen spent her childhood tilling and running through, the land that drives the spirit of this book, is unkept, dry, forgotten. The trees that bore the family fruit continue to stand under the summer sun. Sometimes you can spot a white butterfly or hear the woodpecker's calls and drums, but the trees are in need of care. Um Yousef is unable to give of herself anymore. She moves slowly and finds little reason to tend to the land.

My mother spends much of her time between Jeddah and Dubai now; it's where my two elder sisters live. Sometimes she'll fly to Russia to visit Ihab, or to the US to be with Yousef, Diaa, and me. On the anniversary of Iyad's death, though, she likes to be back in Palestine to visit his grave and to be there for the olive harvest.

With her family scattered, nothing is as it used to be, but Hajjeh Um Yousef always has summer to look forward to. It is the season of return.

🌿

And me. What about me? Sometimes I feel I go through life with a lump in my throat. A heartache. It stretches to my gut, and there it sits, entangled.

I don't know if telling this story will help. All I've said, and I haven't told you the half of it. I still feel unsatisfied.

2021. Source: Family collection.

ACKNOWLEDGMENTS

First and foremost, I want to thank Um Yousef and the Sawalha family. They opened up their home, took great care of me when I was in Palestine, and bore with Sireen and me as we asked for their testimonies. I hope, in their eyes, I have done them justice in the way I have told their story and represented them. Sireen would also like to thank her children, Bassel, Zeid, and Salma, who were sources of encouragement for her through all the difficult moments in her life and who supported her and discussed this project endlessly as if they were raising a fourth child.

At Princeton, I want to thank Rena Lederman, whose research methods co-seminar planted the seed for this project almost twenty-years ago; Asli Bali and Nisreen Salti, who introduced me to the Palestinian community in Princeton; Abdellah Hammoudi, who encouraged me to pursue this project; Rima Qassem, who first introduced me to Sireen; and Hilal Taha, dear Hilal, who welcomed me into his home and whose face and spirit I'll always remember and who passed a few years after we met.

Esraa Al-Muftah, Rana Barakat, Steve Caton, Ebony Coletu, Cynthia Franklin, Laleh Khalili, Sherene Seikaly, and Lisa Taraki read various drafts of this book, provided invaluable feedback, filled me with confidence, and encouraged me to continue writing. Malek Al-Manaa and Zeena Ojjeh, former students at Northwestern University in Qatar, worked as research assistants, doing the painstaking job of transcribing interviews. Without them, I don't know if I could have begun writing. Wesal did fieldwork in Palestine locating mothers of martyrs and other people. Sahar Francis helped me track down documents and understand legal procedures related to prisoners. Sara Saad translated prison notes in my possession. Nada Dalloul designed the family tree. Abdullah Al-Arian, Khaled Al-Hroub, Hala Alyan, Debbora Battaglia, Sabine El Chamaa, Omar Dahi, Ghassan Hage, Amaney Jamal, Anjali Kamat,

Darryl Li, Ismail Nashef, and Nadya Sbaiti supported and encouraged me in various ways on this journey. My writing accountability group—Mona Damluji, Jia-Ching Chen, Alda Benjamen, Arbella Bet-Shlimon, Hilary Falb Kalisman, Bridget Guarasci, Jennifer Tucker, and Shawna Yang Ryan—performed magic to set me on the course of daily sustained writing. Emma Borges-Scott and Jay Blotcher edited early drafts. Adriana Smith did a remarkable job copyediting. Lori Allen brought this manuscript to completion through her close read, great care, and marvelous professional editing—hire her if you're looking for an editor! And of course, Kate Wahl at Stanford University Press believed in this project and gave it so much of her time, and without her, this book would still be on my laptop. To all of you, I cannot thank you enough for being there for me.

I especially want to express my love and deep gratitude to my parents, Samir and Velma, for supporting me at every turn through the years. I also want to apologize to them for the great worry I caused them whenever I went on my trips to Palestine.

Finally, this book would be impossible without Diala Hawi. She has lived and breathed this text with me—thinking with me, engaging my scattered thoughts, providing line-by-line editing, shaping the book, and, in the end, coming up with the title. Words of gratitude will not do justice to your time and contribution, but I hope my love will make up some fraction of them.

NOTES

represented the amount of land a team of oxen could plow in a day. One dunam roughly equals 1,000 square meters). The biggest change and growth was in its diaspora. Details about Kufr Raʿi's size and population in the 1940s can be found in Mustapha Murad al-Dabagh, *Biladna falastine*, part 1 (Kufr Kare', Palestine: al-Huda Press, 1991). Details are also available at "Welcome to Kafr Ra'i," Palestine Remembered, accessed June 6, 2021, https://palestineremembered.com/GeoPoints/Kafr_Ra_i_1269/index.html#Statistics.

11 **ethnic cleansing of Palestine:** For various accounts of the Nakba and the process that led to the 1948 expulsion of Palestinians, as well as for accounts of the 1967 war, see Noura Erakat, *Justice for Some* (Stanford, CA: Stanford University Press, 2020); Rashid Khalidi, *The Hundred Years' War on Palestine* (New York: Metropolitan Books, 2020); Walid Khalidi, "Why Did the Palestinians Leave, Revisited," *Journal of Palestine Studies* 34, no. 2 (Winter 2005): 42–54; Ilan Pappe, *The Ethnic Cleansing of Palestine* (Oxford, UK: One World Publications, 2006); Edward Said, *The Question of Palestine* (1979; repr., New York: Vintage Books, 1992); Fayez Sayegh, "Zionist Colonialism in Palestine (1965)," *Settler Colonial Studies* 2, no. 1: 206–25; Sherene Seikaly, *Men of Capital: Scarcity and Economy in Mandate Palestine* (Stanford, CA: Stanford University Press, 2016).

14 **One of over two hundred such military orders:** Military orders nos. 58 and 59, for example, decreed that absentee land would be confiscated and appropriated by the Israeli state. The Israeli legislation and military orders in the West Bank and the Gaza Strip applied many of the same property laws already in effect in the lands taken in 1948, except in this case they would be continually renewed. For more on this, see Leila Farsakh, "The Political Economy of Israeli Occupation: What Is Colonial about It?" *Electronic Journal of Middle Eastern Studies*, no. 8 (Spring 2008): 41–58. On the population expelled, see Adam Hanieh, "Class and State in the West Bank," in *Lineages of Revolt: Issues of Contemporary Capitalism in the Middle East* (Chicago: Haymarket Books, 2013).

15 **In the census:** For details on the census, see Joel Perlmann, "The 1967 Census of the West Bank and Gaza Strip: A Digitized Version," Levy Economics Institute of Bard College, accessed May 26, 2021, http://www.levyinstitute.org/palestinian-census/. For the number of people expelled from Palestinian lands occupied in 1967, see BADIL, "From the 1948 Nakba to the 1967 Naksa," *BADIL Occasional Bulletin* 18, June 2004, http://www.badil.org/phocadownloadpap/Badil_docs/bulletins-and-briefs/Bulletin-18.pdf.

CHAPTER 2

18 **did not return to Taybeh for over two decades:** Sometimes the shock
    was too great to bear. Shafeeq Ghabra writes, "Many Palestinian exiles,
    seeing their former houses for the first time after thirty years or more,
    suffer heart attacks or physical collapse. The 'Abd al-Fattah family, for ex-
    ample, composed of father, mother, and five children, came to Kuwait in
    the 1950s. They decided to visit their house in Haifa in the summer of 1972.
    After being allowed a brief visit, the father, Khalil, experienced tremen-
    dous stress at the steps of his occupied house. That same day he had a heart
    attack and died." See Shafeeq Ghabra, "Palestinians in Kuwait: The Family
    and the Politics of Survival," *Journal of Palestine Studies* 17, no. 2 (1988): 79.

19 **over four hundred depopulated ones:** See Salman Abu Sitta, *The Pal-
    estinian Nakba 1948: The Register of Depopulated Localities in Palestine*
    (London, UK: Palestinian Return Centre, 2000); and Rochelle Davis, *Pal-
    estinian Village Histories: Geographies of the Displaced* (Stanford, CA: Stan-
    ford University Press, 2010).

19 **In the early 1950s:** For a sequence of events that took place in the 1950s
    and other times, see this wonderful digital resource: Camille Mansour,
    ed., "The Interactive Timeline of the Palestine Question," Institute of Pal-
    estine Studies, accessed April 10, 2023, https://www.palquest.org.

20 **he walked to Kuwait through the desert:** For an account of Palestinians
    in Kuwait and their journey from Palestine, see Shafeeq Ghabra, *Palestin-
    ians in Kuwait: The Family and the Politics of Survival* (Boulder, CO: West-
    view Press, 1987).

CHAPTER 3

25 **Israelis seize lands:** For more on Israeli policies of land expropriation,
    see Ghazi-Walid Falah, "War, Peace and Land Seizure in Palestine's
    Border Area," *Third World Quarterly* 25, no. 5 (2004): 955–75, http://www
    .jstor.org/stable/3993704. For information on land theft in the particular
    villages mentioned as well as others in the West Bank, see the village pro-
    file reports prepared by the Applied Research Institute-Jerusalem, "The
    Palestinian Locality Profiles," accessed April 12, 2023, http://vprofile.arij
    .org.

27 **the Allon Plan:** For details on the settlement project and how it oper-
    ates, see Eyal Weizman, *Hollow Land: Israel's Architecture of Occupation*
    (London, UK: Verso, 2007). For a chronology of events in this chapter, see
    Institute for Palestine Studies, "A Gaza Chronology, 1948–2008," *Journal
    of Palestine Studies* 38, no. 3 (2009): 98–121.

CHAPTER 4

29 **In August 1970:** In 1970, Palestinians suffered two major blows. The Israeli military launched a pacification campaign in Gaza that was a full onslaught, while in Jordan, King Hussein put an end to Palestinian resistance from within Jordan in what was later termed Black September. For reference to the pacification of Gaza, see Institute for Palestine Studies, "A Gaza Chronology, 1948–2008," *Journal of Palestine Studies* 38, no. 3 (2009): 98–121. For more on Jordanian politics, see my notes to chapter 8.

29 **methods for recruiting collaborators:** It is forbidden under international law for the occupying power to recruit collaborators. For more on this point, see "Harm to Palestinians Suspected of Collaborating with Israel," B'Tselem website, January 1, 2011, https://www.btselem.org /collaboration. For other readings on collaboration and collaborators, see Salim Tamari, "In League with Zion: Israel's Search for a Native Pillar," *Journal of Palestine Studies* 12, no. 4 (1983): 41–56; Salim Tamari, "Eyeless in Judea: Israel's Strategy of Collaborators and Forgeries," *Middle East Report* 164/165 (1990): 39–45; Human Rights Watch, *Justice Undermined: Balancing Security and Human Rights in the Palestinian Justice System* 13, no. 4 (2011). In all colonial contexts, the oppressor, or the more powerful side, is able to infiltrate or create conditions in the oppressed community, or the weaker group, to form a cadre of collaborators, spies, and traitors resulting in the natives turning on their own. See, for example, in novel form, Assia Djebar, *Children of the New World: A Novel of the Algerian War*, trans. Marjolijn De Jaber (New York: Feminist Press at the City University of New York, 2005).

29 **News of events:** For more on frictions between the Jordanian king and the Palestinian resistance, see Michael Hudson, "Developments and Setbacks in the Palestinian Resistance Movement 1967–1971," *Journal of Palestine Studies* 1, no. 3 (1972): 64–84. In general, the king of Jordan was more interested in creating his own fiefdom, or state, than in protecting Palestinian rights and limiting Zionist settlement and expansion.

CHAPTER 6

40 **new materials, new techniques:** For more on homes in Palestinian villages, see Suad Amiry and Vera Tamari, *The Palestinian Village Home* (London, UK: British Museum Publications, 1989). For life in Palestine, social organization, and kinship, see Lisa Taraki, ed., *Living Palestine: Family Survival, Resistance, and Mobility under Occupation* (Syracuse, NY: Syracuse University Press, 2006).

CHAPTER 7

44 **Jenin's economy:** See Roger Owen, ed., *Studies in the Economic and Social History of Palestine in the Nineteenth and Twentieth Centuries* (Oxford, UK: MacMillan Press, 1982); and Bill Dienst, "With the Palestine Medical Relief Society in Jenin," *Electronic Intifada*, December 14, 2006, https://electronicintifada.net/content/palestine-medical-relief-society-jenin/6601.

46 **not connected to the Israeli power grid:** Energy was one of the building blocks of the Zionist movement. It was through the building of an electric grid that the Zionists could realize the text of the Balfour Declaration long before 1948. Electricity drew the borders of Palestine, separating it from Lebanon and its other neighbors, and played a large role in turning an imaginary geography into a bounded national project. For more on electricity, see Fredrik Meiton, "The Radiance of the Jewish National Home: Technocapitalism, Electrification, and the Making of Modern Palestine," *Comparative Studies in Society and History* 57, no. 4 (2015): 975–1006.

46 **"give them something to lose":** For this policy, see Avram Bornstein, *Crossing the Green Line between the West Bank and Israel* (Philadelphia: University of Pennsylvania, 2002), 42.

CHAPTER 8

50 **The Jordanians had controlled the West Bank:** The Hashemite monarchy had played a key role in the foundation of the Zionist state, holding secret negotiations and agreements in the lead up to 1948. King Abdullah of Jordan, who ruled Jordan from 1921 until his assassination in Jerusalem in 1951, was supposed to be a friend to the Palestinians, but he had ambitions to control all of Palestine. When the British and Zionists made clear that this was not viable, he entered into secret pacts with the Zionists. King Abdullah saw an agreement with them as the only way to maintain territory on both sides of the Jordan River and increase the size of his kingdom, having already suffered blows to the east from al-Saud, who seized the Hejaz. In 1948, King Abdullah had instructed the Arab Legion, perhaps the strongest of all the Arab armies at the time, not to engage the Zionists should a war break out. The Jordanian-administered West Bank after the 1949 armistice agreement was formed based on how far the Arab Legion had advanced between the start of the war in May 1948 and the agreement in January 1949. In 1967, the Zionists took control of the entirety of Historic Palestine. In the aftermath, King Hussein, Abdullah's grandson, promised resistance but saw the Palestinian revolutionaries on

his territory as a threat to his rule and finally put a stop to them in September 1970. For a history of relations between King Abdullah and the Zionists, see Avi Shlaim, *Collusion across the Jordan: King Abdullah, the Zionist Movement, and the Partition of Palestine* (New York: Columbia University Press, 1988). For background on Black September in 1970, see Avi Shlaim, *Iron Wall: Israel and the Arab World* (2001; repr., London, UK: W.W. Norton & Company, 2014). King Hussein continued to administer the West Bank and lay claim to it until 1988. With the 1988 pronouncement, the development of the West Bank was canceled, 16,000 civil administration officials lost part of their salary support provided by Jordan, 5,400 were pensioned off, and all were told that they were now the responsibility of the PLO. This also meant that Arafat was the only one in a position to speak on behalf of the Palestinians and the Israelis had to negotiate with him directly rather than through King Hussein. For more on this, see Helena Cobban, "Roots of Resistance: The First Intifada in the Context of Palestinian History," *Mondoweiss*, December 17, 2012, http://mondoweiss.net/2012/12/roots-of -resistance-the-first-intifada-in-the-context-of-palestinian-history/. See also the text of King Hussein's pronouncement: King Hussein, *Address to the Nation*, July 31, 1988, http://www.kinghussein.gov.jo/88_july31.html.

CHAPTER 11

Details in this chapter about the start of the intifada are taken from Institute for Palestine Studies, "A Gaza Chronology, 1948–2008," *Journal of Palestine Studies* 38, no. 3 (2009): 98–121. See also Ann M. Lesch, "Prelude to the Uprising in the Gaza Strip," *Journal of Palestine Studies* 20, no. 1 (1990): 1–23.

67 **three thousand protests were recorded:** See Ziad Abu-Amr, *Islamic Fundamentalism in the West Bank and Gaza: The Muslim Brotherhood and Islamic Jihad* (Bloomington: Indiana University Press, 1994), 54.

68 **action to rein in other Palestinians:** See Helena Cobban, "Roots of Resistance: The First Intifada in the Context of Palestinian History," *Mondoweiss*, December 17, 2012, http://mondoweiss.net/2012/12/roots-of-resistance -the-first-intifada-in-the-context-of-palestinian-history/. For more on the Village Leagues, see Salim Tamari, "In League with Zion: Israel's Search for a Native Pillar," *Journal of Palestine Studies* 12, no. 4 (1983): 41–56.

CHAPTER 12

73 **The Fahd al-Aswad had just come into existence:** Fatah disseminated flyers that read, "If you are in a remote area, choose a dirty traitor . . . make

sure that he is a traitor, and attack him, burn him . . . he does not deserve to belong to our great people." As an organization under Fatah, the Fahd al-Aswad took up this task. For a fuller version of this flyer, see Ziad Abu-Amr, *Islamic Fundamentalism in the West Bank and Gaza: The Muslim Brotherhood and Islamic Jihad* (Bloomington: Indiana University Press, 1994), 55.

73 **The definition of a collaborator:** For a breakdown of types of collaborators, see Saleh Abdul Jawad, "The Classification and Recruitment of Collaborators," in *The Phenomenon of Collaborators in Palestine. Proceedings of Palestinian Academic Society for the Study of International Affairs (PASSIA)*, February 1, 2001, http://passia.org/publications/68. See also Mouin Rabbani, "In Honor of Titans," *Mondoweiss*, December 9, 2012, http://mondoweiss.net/2012/12/in-honor-of-titans/#sthash.QHHjwIAc.dpuf; and Joost R Hiltermann, "Israel's Strategy to Break the Uprising," *Journal of Palestine Studies* 19, no. 2 (1990): 87–98.

79 **"Much time has passed":** This is a translation of a WhatsApp text message sent by Haj Taha's son in August 2019. Haj Taha is a pseudonym, as are the names of anyone caught up in accusations of collaboration in this book.

CHAPTER 13

The events of this chapter and Iyad's character at this age were relayed to me by Ihab and others in the village. The latter story in the chapter also appears in M. Clement Hall, *Intifada* (Morrisville, NC: Lulu Press, 2009), 15–17.

CHAPTER 14

85 **"Palestine is Free":** The Arabic is usually translated into English as "Free Palestine," and this is the slogan usually used in protests. The English sense is more ambiguous, though. It could imply an assertion of "a free Palestine" or be a call by the unfree for freedom. I kept the less ambiguous literal meaning of the Arabic to communicate the defiance embedded in the slogan.

85 **Graffiti was used:** For a useful study of graffiti in Palestine, see (in Arabic) Ibrahim Muhammed and Tariq Muhammed, *Slogans of the Intifada* (London, UK: Muslim Palestine Publishers, 1994). For more on this publication, see al-Istiqlal Library, "Shiʿarat al-intifada: dirassah wa-tawtheeq," accessed April 8, 2023, https://library.alistiqlal.edu.ps/book-195-en.html.

CHAPTER 17

100 ***"Ma khirib baytna ila al-'umala":*** The Arabic translates to, "Nothing
has destroyed us more than the collaborators." On collaborators, see
Ruba Hasri, "Legends in the Nablus Intifada (*'Asateel fi intifadat Nablus*),"
Journal of Palestine Studies, vol. 2, accessed February 2, 2022, https://www
.palestine-studies.org/ar/node/34419.

101 **around 822 people were killed:** Cited in Human Rights Watch, *Justice
Undermined: Balancing Security and Human Rights in the Palestinian Justice
System* 13, no. 4 (November 2001), https://www.hrw.org/reports/2001/pa/
isrpa1101.pdf.

CHAPTER 18

The latter parts of the chapter in prison, as well as other prison chapters,
are taken from Kifah Nasraldine Tafesh, *Hawajis 'Aseer* [Obsessions of a
prisoner] (Jerusalem, Occupied Palestine: al-Jundi Press); Popular Front
for the Liberation of Palestine (PLFP), *Falsafat al-muwajaha wara' al-
qudban* [Philosophy of confrontation behind bars] (Palestine al-Raya Press,
n.d.); Esmael Nashif, *Palestinian Political Prisoners: Identity and Community*
(London, UK: Routledge, 2008); *Ghost Hunting* (film), directed by Raed
Andoni (France: ARTE, 2017); Lena Meari, "Sumud: A Palestinian Philosophy of Confrontation in Colonial Prisons," *South Atlantic Quarterly* 113, no.
3: 547–78; and *Shahed 'ala al-'aser: Abdelhakim Huneini* [Witness to an Era:
Abdelhakim Huneini] (film), 11 parts, *Al Jazeera Arabic*, 2014, https://www
.youtube.com/watch?v=_egmtdrn__E. I also interviewed former prisoner
Abdelhakim Huneini, from the *Al Jazeera* documentary, and others who
knew Iyad in prison. Some of what I have written is roughly translated and
adapted from the Arabic texts.

104 **Noor, on the other hand:** Over the years, there have been rumors from different quarters that Noor had been a collaborator all along. These rumors
came from Iyad's family, who has come to believe that he did indeed lay
the trap for Iyad's capture in 1992. The rumors also came from others in
the village who spoke of other incidents he seemed to be involved in. Decades later, a public statement called him out as a collaborator. Though
this is not proof, it suggests the sentiment is widespread. Despite this, the
last time I checked, Noor continues to live in the Jenin area, unharmed.

104 **came to pay their respects:** See Lena Meari, "Sumud: A Palestinian Philosophy of Confrontation in Colonial Prisons," *South Atlantic Quarterly*
113, no. 3 (2014): 547.

105 **ensure his *sumud*:** See Lena Meari, "Sumud: A Palestinian Philosophy

of Confrontation in Colonial Prisons," *South Atlantic Quarterly* 113, no. 3 (2014): 547–78.

105 **after Iyad's abduction:** For similar experiences, see Avram Bornstein, *Crossing the Green Line between the West Bank and Israel* (Philadelphia: University of Pennsylvania Press, 2002), 467.

107 **designated "security prisoners":** This is a designation not applied to Jewish Israelis and only reserved for Palestinians, whether Israeli citizens or not. Palestinians are not considered "political prisoners" by the Israelis. See Stephanie Latte Abdallah, "Denial of Borders: The Prison Web and the Management of Palestinian Political Prisoners after the Oslo Accords (1993–2013)," in *Palestinians and Israelis in the Shadows of the Wall: Spaces of Separation and Occupation*, ed. Stéphanie Latte Abdallah and Cédric Parizot (London, UK: Ashgate, 2015), 39–55.

108 **The other inmates greet him:** I refer to the prisoner in a gendered way as male because this story is about a male prisoner. There have been many female prisoners as well throughout the decades, although fewer of them. Their experiences in captivity and with terror are quite similar but also different. See Nahla Abdo, "Palestinian Women Political Prisoners and the Israeli State," in *Threat: Palestinian Political Prisoners in Israel*, ed. Abeer Baker and Anat Matar (London, UK: Pluto Press), 57–67. See also Ittaf Alian's essay in the same volume, *"Female Prisoners and the Struggle: A Personal Testimony,"* 183–87.

CHAPTER 19

111 **through sealed lips:** Adapted from the story of Osama Barham, who told his interrogators, "My name is Osama Barham; if you can get my name out of me again, I will confess to anything you want," see Osama Barham, "My Arrests, My Interrogations," in *Threat: Palestinian Political Prisoners in Israel*, ed. Abeer Baker and Anat Matar (London, UK: Pluto Press, 2011), 95.

111 **Iyad's first meeting:** Various descriptions in this chapter are based on rough translations and adapted from sections in Popular Front for the Liberation of Palestine (PLFP), *Falsafat al-muwajaha wara' al-qudban* [Philosophy of confrontation behind bars] (Palestine: al-Raya Press, n.d.).

113 **in a plain white room:** This description is adapted from *Ghost Hunting* (film), directed by Raed Andoni (France: ARTE, 2017).

113 **consumed rotten and cold food:** For details on what prisoners eat during interrogation, see Esmael Nashif, *Palestinian Political Prisoners: Identity and Community* (London, UK: Routledge, 2008), 48–49.

114 **the captive must maintain his focus:** See Popular Front for the Liber-
     ation of Palestine (PLFP), *Falsafat al-muwajaha wara' al-qudban* [Philoso-
     phy of confrontation behind bars] (Palestine: al-Raya Press, n.d.), 77.

114 **confessed to acts he allegedly committed:** For similar situations, see
     AFP, "Beware the 'Birds': Palestinians Decry Jailhouse Informers," *Al Ara-
     biya News*, May 16, 2013, https://english.alarabiya.net/perspective/features
     /2013/05/16/Beware-the-birds-Palestinians-decry-jailhouse-informers.

CHAPTER 20

116 **how to liberate Palestine:** See Ziad Abu-Amr, *Islamic Fundamentalism in
     the West Bank and Gaza: The Muslim Brotherhood and Islamic Jihad* (Bloom-
     ington: Indiana University Press, 1994), 114. For more on the history and
     beginnings of the Islamic Jihad in Palestine, see also Ghassan Charbel, *Fi
     'ayn al-'asifa* [In the eye of the storm: Interview with Ramadan Shallah,
     the general secretary of the Islamic Jihad in Palestine] (Beirut, Lebanon:
     Bisan Press, 2003). For other details on topics in this chapter, especially
     on al-Shiqaqi, see Erik Skare, *A History of Palestinian Islamic Jihad: Faith,
     Awareness, and Revolution in the Middle East* (Cambridge, UK: Cambridge
     University Press, 2021), 39–42, 52.

117 **traditionally attracted members of Fatah:** For a history of the re-
     lationship between Fatah and the different Islamic currents, see Saoud
     al-Mawla, *Min Fatah ila-hamas: Al-bidayat al-ikhwaniya wal-nihayat al-
     wattaniya* [From Fatah to Hamas: The Muslim Brotherhood beginnings
     and nationalist endings] (Beirut, Lebanon: Sa'er al-mashreq Press, 2018).

117 **the Islamic Jihad's vanguard and its resistance:** See Ziad Abu-Amr, *Is-
     lamic Fundamentalism in the West Bank and Gaza: The Muslim Brotherhood
     and Islamic Jihad* (Bloomington: Indiana University Press, 1994), 120.

118 **Like many Palestinians:** See Edward Said, "The Morning After," *London
     Review of Books* 15, no. 20 (October 1993), https://www.lrb.co.uk/the-paper
     /v15/n20/edward-said-the-morning-after.

118 **changed conditions in prison:** The Palestinians understood that the jail
     administrators could exploit interfactional divisions to the disadvantage
     of all the prisoners. They agreed that some written rules were needed. For
     more on how prisoners worked together, see Rebecca Granato, "Writing
     Palestinian Politics in Israel's Prisons Before Oslo," *Middle East Report* 275
     (Summer 2015), http://www.merip.org/mer/mer275/writing-palestinian
     -politics-israels-prisons-oslo.

119 **the signing ceremony:** The scene around the handshake was inspired

by an analysis in Mourid Barghouti, *I Saw Ramallah*, trans. Ahdaf Soueif (New York: Anchor Books, 2003).

120 **billed as an agreement:** The Oslo Accords were actually two agreements, the first signed in 1993 (Oslo I) and the second in 1995 (Oslo II), that set up a process commonly known as the Oslo peace process.

120 **they could invest:** For more on the permanence of Oslo's interim status and its relation to economic markets, see Noura Erakat, *Justice for Some: Law and the Question of Palestine* (Stanford, CA: Stanford University Press, 2019).

123 **The room was split down the middle:** For some descriptions of Jneid Prison, see Human Rights Watch, "Prison Conditions in Israel and the Occupied Territories," *Middle East Watch Report*, April 1991, https://www.hrw.org/reports/Israel914.pdf.

124 **Now, everyone wears the hijab:** Sireen was not suggesting that people were not veiled, but that there was a shift. While before it was ʿayb (shameful) to go out with short skirts or dress inappropriately, now it was *haram* (sinful). The social restrictions and taboos in the village had turned into religious injunctions and obligations.

CHAPTER 21

126 **formalizing a structure:** For details on closures, see United Nations, General Assembly, *Report of the Special Committee to Investigate Israeli Practices Affecting the Human Rights of the Palestinian People and Other Arabs of the Occupied Territories*, A/54/325 (September 8, 1999), undocs.org/en/A/54/325. On page 12, it reads, "During the six-year period from 1993 to 1998, there were 436 comprehensive closure days in total, and almost 20 per cent of potential working days were lost during those six years, with peaks of 29 and 33 per cent of working days lost in 1995 and 1996."

127 **roads that zigzagged:** For details on the "forbidden road" system, see B'Tselem, *Forbidden Roads: Israel's Discriminatory Road Regime in the West Bank*, information sheet, August 2004, https://www.btselem.org/sites/default/files/sites/default/files2/publication/200408_forbidden_roads_eng.pdf.

127 **around 795 km of roads:** See "The Israeli Bypass Road System in the Occupied Palestinian Territory," Applied Research Institute (ARIJ), POICA (website), August 22, 2008, http://poica.org/2008/08/the-israeli-bypass-road-system-in-the-occupied-palestinian-territory/.

CHAPTER 22

129 **should have been released:** To understand more of what was legally required of the Israeli government with respect to the prisoners after the signing of the Oslo Accords, see "Political Prisoners Detained Prior to the Oslo Agreements," Addameer: Prisoner Support and Human Rights Association, September 9, 2012, http://www.addameer.org/publications/political-prisoners-detained-prior-oslo-agreements.

129 **more difficult for family to visit:** For details about family visits, see Sigi Ben-Ari and Anat Barsella, "Family Visits to Palestinian Prisoners Held Inside Israel," in *Threat: Palestinian Political Prisoners Inside Israel*, ed. Abeer Baker and Anat Matar (London, UK: Pluto Press, 2011), 201–11; Lotte Buch Segal, *No Place for Grief: Martyrs, Prisoners, and Mourning in Contemporary Palestine* (Philadelphia: University of Pennsylvania Press, 2016); Inas Abbad, "Hours of Insult for Minutes with My Brother: My Monthly Trip to an Israeli Jail," *Middle East Eye*, May 18, 2017, https://www.middleeasteye.net/news/hours-insult-minutes-my-brother-my-monthly-trip-israeli-jail.

129 **he refused a plea bargain:** For more on the plea bargain, see Stephanie Latte Abdallah, "Denial of Borders: The Prison Web and the Management of Palestinian Political Prisoners after the Oslo Accords (1993–2013)," in *Palestinians and Israelis in the Shadows of the Wall: Spaces of Separation and Occupation*, ed. Stéphanie Latte Abdallah and Cédric Parizot (London, UK: Routledge, 2015), https://halshs.archives-ouvertes.fr/halshs-02190055/document. Abdallah writes, "The courts are constantly trying to increase the use of [the plea bargain] not only to save time and money but also to justify the involvement of the intelligence services in military courts and to give such military justice national and international legitimacy" (7).

130 **Iyad and the other prisoners:** See Mahmoud al-Saadi, "Al-Bosta . . . qabr mutanaqel yathkhin muʿanat al-ʾasra al-falastiniyeen," *Al-Araby al-Jadeed*, April 17, 2016, https://tinyurl.com/vxmck5hc; "The Bosta: A Journey of Endless Pain," The Palestinian Information Center, December 18, 2016, https://english.palinfo.com/news/2016/12/18/The-Bosta-a-journey-of-endless-pain; "Al-Bosta: Al-Qabr al-mutaharek," Alwatan Voice, October 9, 2014, https://www.alwatanvoice.com/arabic/news/2014/10/09/601662.html; *Al-Bosta: Rihlat al-Qabr al-mutaharek* [The Bosta: The Journey of the Mobile Grave] (film), *Al Jazeera Arabic*, 2014, https://tinyurl.com/47b9 4vu6.

133 **his only ticket out:** See Mounir Mansour, "Prisoner Exchange Deals: Between Figures and Emotions," in *Threat: Palestinian Political Prisoners in*

Israel, ed. Abeer Baker and Anat Matar (London, UK: Pluto Press), 177.

133 **veins of the prison community:** For a description of workers functioning as veins in the body, see Esmael Nashif, *Palestinian Political Prisoners: Identity and Community* (London, UK: Routledge, 2008), 55.

133 **he became calmer and more patient:** These details were taken from an interview with Iyad's prison mate.

CHAPTER 23

135 **leading to the Allenby Bridge:** Sireen calls it the bridge, as Mourid Barghouti writes: "Fayruz calls it the Bridge of Return. The Jordanians call it the King Hussein Bridge. The Palestinian Authority calls it al-Karama Crossing. The common people and the bus and taxi drivers call it the Allenby Bridge. My mother, and before her my grandmother and my father and my uncle's wife, Umm Talal, call it simply: the Bridge." (Mourid Barghouti, *I Saw Ramallah*, trans. Ahdaf Soueif (New York: Anchor Books, 2003), 10.

136 **as far as my eyes could see:** Israelis are not allowed to use this border crossing and most foreigners don't trouble themselves with crossing from here and thus do not have to deal with this congestion. Technically, foreigners are not supposed to claim they are visiting the West Bank; it makes entry more difficult. The Israelis claim this is for the foreigner's own security. Most will enter through Ben Gurion Airport, on the outskirts of the historic Palestinian city of Lyd, and most will do so without a thought about what happened to that city and how the Lyd airport was built before the Zionist state. Few will know that it was a mixed Christian-Muslim town, that Israeli soldiers came dressed like Arabs from the Jordanian Army, that they fought the people of Lyd, killed them, forced some residents to burn the remains of the slaughtered, and buried others in a mass grave. For more on Lyd, see Adam Horowitz, "The Ethnic Cleansing of Lyd, and How It Continues Today," *Mondoweiss*, June 24, 2011, https://mondoweiss.net/2011/06/the-ethnic-cleansing-of-lyd-and-how-it-continues-today/.

137 **her *tasreeh*:** A *tasreeh* is a travel permit that Palestinians use to enter and exit the occupied West Bank and Gaza Strip. Even though Sireen and her children have US passports, they are not allowed to use them to enter the country.

138 **straight to ʿAskalan:** Unlike Jneid Prison, ʿAskalan and Meggido were more difficult to visit because one needed a permit to enter the territory of the Israeli state from the West Bank. See Michael Sfard, "Devil's

Island: The Transfer of Palestinian Detainees into Prisons within Israel,"
in *Threat: Palestinian Political Prisoners in Israel*, ed. Abeer Baker and Anat
Matar (London, UK: Pluto Press, 2011), 188.

CHAPTER 24

The scene in this chapter is adapted from David Sharrock, "Israel Frees
Palestinian Prisoners," *Guardian*, September 9, 1999, https://www
.theguardian.com/world/1999/sep/10/israel. The *Guardian* article suggests
that people were chanting another version of the Palestinian anthem that
begins with "Biladi, Biladi" (my country, my country) not "Fida'i, Fida'i"
(warrior, warrior). The Palestinian Authority adopted "Fida'i, Fida'i,"
which was also the Fatah anthem and was adopted by the PLO, so it is also
possible that the prisoners would return to singing "Fida'i, Fida'i," and I
have gone with this version. For an explanation of the different versions
of the anthem, see Tamir Sorek, *Palestinian Commemoration in Israel: Cal-
endars, Monuments, and Martyrs* (Stanford, CA: Stanford University Press,
2015).

147   **"This morning, 9 September 1999":** See Palestinian Center for Human
Rights (PCHR), "Release of Palestinian Prisoners," press release ref: 90/99,
September 9, 1999, https://www.pchrgaza.org/en/release-of-palestinian
-prisoners/.

149   **among the angry prisoners:** Those who are released feel weak and powerless toward those left behind. The Palestinian prison negotiator takes
into account the opinions of the prisoners, which he then seeks to imple-
ment. The negotiator tries to take into consideration long sentences, but
Israeli authorities can refuse. For these sentiments and more on prisoner
releases, see Mounir Mansour, "Prisoner Exchange Deals: Between Figures and Emotions," in *Threat: Palestinian Political Prisoners in Israel*, ed.
Abeer Baker and Anat Matar (London, UK: Pluto Press, 2011), 176.

CHAPTER 26

157   **Shortly after his return:** "Khabar al-qiyadi qaʿdan: al-shaheed Tahayneh
kan al-shiqaqi fi Jenin wa-mughniyat al-jihad al-islami," *Palestine Today*,
July 13, 2017, https://tinyurl.com/3ahrw8ma.

157   **and Thabet Mardawi:** For more on Thabet Mardawi, see "Al-ʿaseer al-
qiyadi thabet mardawi yadkhul ʿamihi al-18 fi sujoun al-ihtilal," *Asra Media
Office*, April 11, 2019, https://tinyurl.com/mx4uf2df.

CHAPTER 27

162 **repairing their car:** See Mohamed Abu Tabeekh, *Darb al-Sadiqeen*, part 1 (Ramallah: Nomaan Tahayneh Press, 2008), 68–70.

163 **clandestine Unit 504:** See Eyal Weizman, *Hollow Land: Israel's Architecture of Occupation* (London, UK: Verso, 2007), 242.

163 **recognizing collaborators:** See Mohamed Abu Tabeekh, *Darb al-Sadiqeen*, part 1 (Ramallah: Nomaan Tahayneh Press, 2018), 38.

164 **Palestinian intelligence unit:** See Mohamed Abu Tabeekh, *Darb al-Sadiqeen*, part 1 (Ramallah: Nomaan Tahayneh Press, 2018), 69–70.

CHAPTER 28

167 **still living with them:** Although a marriage contract is signed at the *katb el-ktab*, it is traditionally more akin to an engagement and referred to as such. In other words, there is a difference between a marriage and a wedding. A woman and a man generally cannot live with each other until after the wedding, even though a marriage contract has already been signed. The plan was for Iyad to spend the next months or year fixing a place for him and Mariam, after which they would have a wedding and move in together. This distinction between the marriage and wedding is why Sireen later uses the word "fiancée" in reference to Mariam's relation to Iyad. Although technically married, in the eyes of the community, the two would be seen as engaged until the wedding. However, annulling this "engagement" would require a process similar to a divorce. I use the words "marriage" and "married" to indicate that the signing of the marriage contract has taken place, but keep in mind that there is one more step.

CHAPTER 29

172 **prep him for the surgery:** Details of the amputation procedure are based on a personal conversation with orthopedic surgeon Dr. Michel Diab (September 9, 2017).

175 **On the other side of the world:** This scene is adapted from Mohamed Abu Tabeekh, *Darb al-Sadiqeen*, part 1 (Ramallah: Nomaan Tahayneh Press, 2018), 135–36. The three comrades who were killed are Asad Daqqa, Sufian Ardah, and Wael Assaf.

CHAPTER 30

178 **Murad Abu al-Assal's story:** For details surrounding this event, see "Al-istish-hadi al-mujahed Murad Abu Assal mukhtareq al-shabak al-

sahyouni," Saraya al-Quds website, July 9, 2011, https://tinyurl.com/xy my33z3; and Saud Abu Ramadan, "Israel Blast Kills One, Wounds Two," *United Press International (UPI)*, January 30, 2002, https://www.upi.com/ Israel-blast-kills-one-wounds-two/20841012394776/.

179 **Murad had recorded himself:** The video link was available until sometime after 2019, when YouTube removed it for violating its policies, and likely as part of a broader issue involving censorship of Palestinian content online. On this censorship, see Ylenia Gostoli, "Palestinians Fight Facebook, YouTube Censorship," *Al-Jazeera Online*, January 20, 2018. The video had been on YouTube for over ten years, and it referred to an incident that took place almost eighteen years earlier.

180 **"the tyranny of the principle":** The Islamic Jihad relied on many of Fathi Yakan's writings and ideas. For more on him and for this quote, see Ziad Abu-Amr, *Islamic Fundamentalism in the West Bank and Gaza: The Muslim Brotherhood and Islamic Jihad* (Bloomington: Indiana University Press, 1994), 118.

CHAPTER 32

184 **an operation he had planned in Beit Lid:** The Beit Lid Junction operation targeted an Israeli bus and was carried out by Abedelfatah Rashed. See "Al-istish-hadi al-mujahed ʿabed al-fattah Muhammad Rashed: Munafeth ʿamaliat muftaraq beit lyd al-istish-hadiya," Saraya al-Quds website, September 9, 2015, https://tinyurl.com/pystrebs.

185 **assassinated a comrade, Iyad Hardan:** For an account of this assassination, see Reuters, "Palestinians Say Phone Bomb Killed Militant," *Gulf News*, April 6, 2001, http://gulfnews.com/news/uae/general/palestinians -say-israeli-phone-bomb-killed-militant-1.412428.

185 **worked as a technology of resistance:** Adapted from Nadera Shalhoub-Kevorkian, "E-Resistance and Technological In/Security in Everyday Life: The Palestinian Case," *British Journal of Criminology* 52, no. 1: 55–72, http: //www.jstor.org/stable/44173471.

185 **a slightly different version:** See Mohammed Fateh and Rahef Barakat, "Ikhtiraq al-shabak: Heena athalla al-shaheed hammad al-dabet ʿowshar'," *Quds News Network*, May 23, 2019, https://tinyurl.com/dme26ktf and "Al-shaheed al-qaʾed Muʿtasem Mahmud Makhluf: Hayat hafila bil-jihad seyran ʿala khata al-shuhadaʾ," Saraya al-Quds website, accessed June 8, 2021, https://tinyurl.com/5xbfzb3u.

CHAPTER 33

Details of the battle in this chapter, including the block quote, are adapted from Ramzi Baroud, ed., *Searching Jenin: Eyewitness Accounts of the Israeli Invasion 2002* (Seattle, WA: Cune Press, 2002).

188 **the Damaj and Hawashin neighborhoods:** A few years later, I would walk through these streets. They would be wider, the homes repaired and the camp pristine, like a Hollywood set. The Abu Dhabi government had funded the reconstruction, allowing the Israeli government to effectively outsource its responsibility for the carnage it had committed. The rebuilding was also done in such a way to facilitate future military maneuvers by widening the camp's roads. See Phillip Misselwitz and Eyal Weizman, "Military Operations as Urban Planning," *Mute*, August 28, 2003, http://www.metamute.org/editorial/articles/military-operations -urban-planning; and UNRWA, "Rebuilding Jenin," *Electronic Intifada*, October 2, 2003, https://electronicintifada.net/content/rebuilding-jenin/1372.

188 **Ultimately, there was a massacre:** On the battle as a massacre, see Tanya Reinhart, "Jenin: The Propaganda War," April 22, 2002, *Dissident Voice*, http://dissidentvoice.org/Articles/ReinhartJenin.htm.

190 **a meeting was held late at night:** See Mohamed Abu Tabeekh, *Darb al-Sadiqeen*, part 1 (Ramallah: Nomaan Tahayneh Press, 2018), 178.

CHAPTER 35

197 **The Druze leadership:** For some history on the Druze under Israeli rule, see Rhoda Kanaaneh, *Surrounded: Palestinian Soldiers in the Israeli Military* (Stanford, CA: Stanford University Press, 2009). In 2015, the Druze-only unit of the army was disbanded, and Druze were integrated into other divisions.

200 **They met over several weeks:** See Mohamed Abu Tabeekh, *Darb al-Sadiqeen*, part 1 (Ramallah: Nomaan Tahayneh Press, 2018) 181.

CHAPTER 36

201 **Hamza Samudi was born in al-Yamun:** For details about Hamza Samudi, see "'Amaliyat muftaraq Meggido al-istish-hadiya," Saraya al-Quds website, accessed June 12, 2021, https://tinyurl.com/588h4abu.

202 **a Renault with yellow license plates:** Yellow license plates are for Israeli vehicles and can be driven on both sides of the Green Line, whereas green-numbered license plates are for cars registered with the Palestinian Authority and can only be driven in the West Bank and the Gaza Strip. See Amahl

Bishara, "Driving while Palestinian in Israel and the West Bank: The Politics of Disorientation and the Routes of a Subaltern Knowledge," *American Ethnologist* 42 (2015): 33–54.

204 **At the Meggido Junction:** This account is adapted from "Israel Attack Kills 17," BBC, June 5, 2002, http://news.bbc.co.uk/2/hi/middle_east/20 26113.stm; and Associated Press, "Driver of Bombed Bus Survives Fourth Attack," *USA Today*, June 5, 2002, https://usatoday30.usatoday.com/news/ world/2002/06/05/bus-explosion-scene.htm.

204 **Inside Meggido Prison:** This account of the prisoners comes from both English and Arabic sources. For a fuller account, see "'Amaliyat Meggido: 'Indama yatahawal al-junud 'ila ashla'," Saraya al-Quds website, July 5, 2015, https://tinyurl.com/r695e9wx.

205 **The village of al-Lajjun:** For a description of al-Lajjun, see the village's entry on the Zochrot website: "Al-Lajjun," Zochrot, accessed June 12, 2021, https://www.zochrot.org/villages/village_details/53285/en.

206 **Hamza's mother recalls:** Details in this section provided by Hamza's mother come from an interview with her conducted by a research assistant in August 2019.

CHAPTER 38

212 **"*Tawakali 'alla-llah*":** In response to "*Dir ballak*," Iyad would also often say, "'*Umur al-shaqi baki*," or, "The naughty one lives long."

CHAPTER 42

Details for this chapter come from "Chronology," *Journal of Palestine Studies* 32, no. 2 (2003): 172–94; and Michele K Esposito, "The al-Aqsa Intifada: Military Operations, Suicide Attacks, Assassinations, and Losses in the First Four Years," *Journal of Palestine Studies* 34, no. 2 (2005): 85–122. For details on who volunteers for such operations, see Nasser Abufarha, *The Making of a Human Bomb: An Ethnography of Palestinian Resistance* (Durham, NC: Duke University Press, 2009), 138.

226 **Suad Jaber boarded Egged bus:** For details about Suad Jaber, see Vered Levy-Barzilai, "The Other Victims, part 2," *Haaretz*, June 27, 2003, http:/ /www.haaretz.com/cmlink/the-other-victims-2-of-2-1.92482. Suad's presence has been like an apparition over this project. I often wonder about her family and want to apologize to them for ultimately not giving more space to her in this story.

227 **Ashraf al-Asmar and Mohammed al-Hasnein:** For details on the two

martyrs, see "Al-shaheed Ashraf al-Asmar . . . 14 ʿaman wa-al-khudaira tash-had," *Palestine Today*, October 23, 2016, https://tinyurl.com/55b7tjeu.

232 **women in prison:** See the case of Rasmea Odeh for how women are treated in prison: Nehad Khader, "Rasmea Odeh: The Case of an Indomitable Woman," *Journal of Palestine Studies* 46, no. 4 (2017): 62–74.

CHAPTER 43

Many details in this chapter come from B'Tselem, *Human Shield: Use of Palestinian Civilians as Human Shields in Violation of High Court Justice Order*, information sheet, November 2002, 14–17; an article by Jonathan Cook, "Mariam as Human Shield," *Al-Ahram Weekly*, November 28, 2002, http://www.jonathan-cook.net/2002-11-28/miriam-as-human-shield/; and Justin Huggler, "Ceasefire Hopes Dashed as Israel Kills Militant," *Independent*, November 10, 2002, http://www.independent.co.uk/news/world/middle-east/ceasefire-hopes-dashed-as-israel-kills-militant-127171.html. I have also visited the site, listened to accounts from his friends and family, and read other accounts of that day that are largely similar, with varying degrees of detail.

238 **lose forever:** The words "lose forever" come from a quote in Ibrahim Nasrallah, *Time of White Horses: A Novel* (Cairo, Egypt: Hoopoe Press, 2016), 458.

238 **We all die alone:** This particular phrasing is inspired by Hans Fallada, *Every Man Dies Alone: A Novel* (New York: Melville House, 2010).

CHAPTER 45

247 **people were chanting resistance slogans:** These specific slogans are from Nasser Abufarha, *The Making of a Human Bomb: An Ethnography of Palestinian Resistance* (Durham, NC: Duke University Press, 2009), 123. They translate to, "O Iyad, rest, rest, we will carry on the struggle," and "O Sharon, O vile one, the blood of martyrs is very dear."

250 **"Sabbal ʿayouno wa mad eedo wa hanulo":** This translates to, "She winked at me and stretched out her arms for Henna." It is a common song sung at weddings for the groom. For an example, see Luai Ahmaro, "Palestinian Mashup – Luai Ahmaro & Natalie Saman (Official Music Video)" YouTube video, 6:54, December 30, 2019, https://youtu.be/NKxf7B2owV8.

250 **gave a eulogy:** For the text of the eulogy in Arabic, see "Kalimat al-doctur Ramadan Abdallah Shallah fi wadaʿ al-kaʾed Iyad Sawalha," Saraya al-Quds website, accessed April 11, 2023, https://tinyurl.com/mccuz7ex.

CHAPTER 46

253　**where the searching souls of dreamers meet the dead:** These words are taken from Diana Allan, *Refugees of the Revolution: Experiences of Palestinian Exile* (Stanford, CA: Stanford University Press, 2013), 147.

CHAPTER 47

256　**sixty-one checkpoint births:** For stories of these births, see the website of the Arab Documentary Photography Program (http://arabdocphotography .org/project/beyond-checkpoints) and "Checkpoints 101," *Occupied Palestine* (blog), accessed June 8, 2021, https://occupiedpalestine.wordpress .com/special-topics/checkpoints/.

RETURN

268　**a straightforward explanation:** For Mariam's father's thoughts, see Jonathan Cook, "Mariam as Human Shield," *Al-Ahram Weekly*, November 28, 2002, http://www.jonathan-cook.net/2002-11-28/miriam-as-human -shield/.

269　**it would have cost her nothing to be more loving:** Adapted quote from Jorge Luis Borges, "There Are More Things," in *The Book of Sand*, trans. Andrew Hurley (1975; repr., London, UK: Penguin Classics, 2007), 437.

269　**lessons from Algeria's liberation struggle:** Gillo Pontecorvo's words are adapted from an interview; see PierNico Solinas, ed., *Gillo Pontecorvo's The Battle of Algiers: A Film Written by Franco Solinas* (New York: Scribner, 1973), 165.

272　**the grave of Mohammed Bassam Abu Amshi:** For news of Mohammed Bassam Abu Amshi's death, see "Qowat al-ihtilal taqtahem manzel al-shaheed Abu ʿamshe fi Kufr Raʿi wa-tahtajez ʿaʾilatuhu," *Wattan*, April 15, 2015, https://www.wattan.net/ar/news/143868.html.

272　**fifteen other martyrs:** For this list, see the Kufr Raʿi municipality website at https://www.kufrrai.ps/page-345-ar.html, accessed October 24, 2022.

273　**Sireen is overcome with silence:** This sentiment is influenced by Alessandro Portelli, who writes, "The struggle over memory and meaning begins with the act of burial." See Alessandro Portelli, *The Order Has Been Carried Out: History, Memory, and Meaning of a Nazi Massacre in Rome* (New York: Palgrave Macmillan, 2003), 189.